LAFCADIO HEARN

Lafcadio Hearn and his Wife.

LAFCADIO HEARN

BY

NINA H. KENNARD

CONTAINING SOME LETTERS FROM LAFCADIO HEARN
TO HIS HALF-SISTER MRS. ATKINSON

KENNIKAT PRESS, INC./PORT WASHINGTON, N. Y.

REMEMBRANCE

No regret is vain.   It is sorrow that spins the
thread,—softer than moonshine, thinner than
fragrance, stronger than death,—the Gleipnir-
chain of the Greater Memory.

LAFCADIO HEARN

Originally published in 1912
Reissued in 1967 by Kennikat Press

Library of Congress Catalog Card No: 67-27613

Manufactured in the United States of America

CONTENTS

CHAP.		PAGE
I	EARLY YEARS	13
II	BOYHOOD	38
III	TRAMORE	49
IV	USHAW	56
V	LONDON	69
VI	CINCINNATI	83
VII	VAGABONDAGE	100
VIII	MEMPHIS	107
IX	NEW ORLEANS	113
X	WIDER HORIZONS	123
XI	LETTERS AND PERSONAL CHARACTERISTICS	133
XII	THE LADY OF A MYRIAD SOULS	147
XIII	RELIGION AND SCIENCE	161
XIV	WEST INDIES	173
XV	JAPAN	186
XVI	MATSUE	199
XVII	MARRIAGE	206
XVIII	THE KATCHIU-YASHIKI	215
XIX	KUMAMOTO	228
XX	OUT OF THE EAST	264
XXI	KOBE	271
XXII	TOKYO	295
XXIII	USHIGOME	311
XXIV	NISHI OKUBO	324
XXV	HIS DEATH	339
XXVI	HIS FUNERAL	351
XXVII	VISIT TO JAPAN	355
XXVIII	SECOND VISIT TO NISHI OKUBO	372
	CONCLUSION	384
	INDEX	399

LIST OF ILLUSTRATIONS

To face page

LAFCADIO HEARN AND HIS WIFE . . *Frontispiece*

MAJOR CHARLES BUSH HEARN (HEARN'S FATHER) . . 30

MRS. ATKINSON (HEARN'S HALF-SISTER) 234

KAZUO AND HIS NURSE 252

KAZUO, AGED ABOUT SEVEN 262

DOROTHY ATKINSON 271

KAZUO, AGED ABOUT SEVENTEEN 353

CARLTON ATKINSON 360

PREFACE

When Death has set his seal on an eminent man's career, there is a not unnatural curiosity to know something of his life, as revealed by himself, particularly in letters to intimate friends. "All biography ought, as much as possible, to be autobiography," says Stevenson, and of all autobiographical material, letters are the most satisfactory. Generally written on the impulse of the moment, with no idea of subsequent publication, they come, as it were, like butter fresh from the churning with the impress of the mind of the writer stamped distinctly upon them. One letter of George Sand's written to Flaubert, or one of Goethe's to Frau von Stein, or his friend Stilling, is worth pages of embellished reminiscences.

The circumstances surrounding Lafcadio Hearn's life and work impart a particular interest and charm to his correspondence. He was, as he himself imagined, unfitted by personal defects from being looked upon with favour in general society. This idea, combined with innate sensitive shyness, caused him, especially towards the latter years of his life, to become more or less of a recluse, and induced him to seek an outlet in intellectual commune with literary comrades on paper. Hence the wonderful series of letters, edited by Miss Elizabeth Bisland (Mrs. Wetmore), to Krehbiel, Ellwood Hendrik, and Chamberlain. Those to Professor Chamberlain, written during the most productive literary period of his life, from the vantage ground, as it were, of many years of intellectual work and experience, are particularly interesting, giving a unique and illuminating revelation of a cultured and passionately enthusiastic nature.

During his stay at Kumamoto, when the bulk of the letters to Chamberlain were written, he initiated a correspondence with his half-sister, Mrs. Atkinson, who had written to him from Ireland. His erratic nature, tamed and softened by the birth of his son, Kazuo, turned with yearning towards his kindred, forgotten for so many years, and these Atkinson letters, though not boasting the high intellectual level of those to Professor Chamberlain, show him, in their affectionate playfulness, and in the quaint memories recalled of his childhood, under a new and delightful aspect.

There has been a certain amount of friction with his American Editress, owing to the fact of my having been given the right to use these letters. It is as well, therefore, to explain that owing to criticisms and remarks made about people and relatives, in Hearn's usual outspoken fashion, it would have been impossible, in their original form, to allow them to pass into the hands of any one but a person intimately connected with the Hearn family; but I can assure Mrs. Wetmore and Captain Mitchell McDonald—those kind friends who have done so much for the sake of Hearn's children and widow—that Mrs. Koizumi, financially, suffers nothing from the fact of the letters not having crossed the Atlantic.

Besides being indebted to Mrs. Atkinson for having been allowed to make extracts from the letters written to her, my thanks are due to Miss Edith Hardy, her cousin, for the use of diaries and reminiscences; also to the Rev. Joseph Guinan, of Priests' House, Ferbane, for having put me in communication with the Ecclesiastical authorities at Ushaw; also to Mr. Achilles Daunt, of Kilcascan Castle, County Cork, who was apparently Lafcadio's most intimate comrade at Ushaw, and was therefore able to give me much information concerning his college career.

I must also express my indebtedness to friends in Japan, to Mr. W. B. Mason, who was so obliging and helpful, when Mrs. Atkinson, her daughter and I arrived as strangers at Yokohama; also to Mr. Robert Young, who gave me copies of all the leading articles written by Hearn during the period of his engagement as sub-editor to the *Kobe Chronicle and Japan Mail*.

But still more are my thanks due to the various American publishers of Hearn's works for permission to make quotations from them. To Messrs. Macmillan & Co., 64–66, Fifth Avenue, New York, for permission to quote from *Kotto* and *Japan, an Attempt at Interpretation*. To Messrs. Little, Brown & Co., Boston, for permission to quote from *Exotica and Retrospectives*, *In Ghostly Japan*, *Shadowings*, and *A Japanese Miscellany*. To Messrs. Gay & Hancock for permission to quote from *Kokoro;* to Messrs. Harper for permission to quote from *Two Years in the French West Indies;* and, above all, to Messrs. Houghton, Mifflin & Co. for permission to quote from *Glimpses of Unfamiliar Japan*, and *Hearn's Letters*, for without quoting from his letters it would be an almost futile task to attempt to write a biography of Lafcadio Hearn.

What a pathos there is in the thought, that only since Lafcadio Hearn became "a handful of dust in a little earthen pot" hidden away in a Buddhist grave in Japan, has real appreciation of his genius reached England. On the top of the hill at Nishi Okubo, isolated from the sound of English voices, cut off from the clasp of English hands, he was animated by an intense longing for appreciation and recognition in the Anglo-Saxon literary world. "At last," he writes to a friend, "you will be glad to hear that my books are receiving some little attention in England," and again, "Favourable criticism in England is worth a great deal more than favourable criticism elsewhere."

How overwhelmed he would have been to find his name now bracketed amongst the nineteenth century's best-known prose writers, to whom he looked up from the depths of his own imagined insignificance. Indeed, in that country where he longed for appreciation, the idea is gradually growing, that when many shining lights in the literary world of to-day stand unread on topmost library shelves, Lafcadio Hearn will still be studied by the scientist, and valued by the cultured, because of the subtle comprehension and sympathy with which he has presented, in exquisite language, a subject of ever-increasing importance and interest— the soul of the people destined, in the future, to hold undisputed sway in the Far East.

Southmead,
  Farnham Royal. 1911.

LAFCADIO HEARN

CHAPTER I

EARLY YEARS

" Buddhism finds in a dewdrop the symbol of that other microcosm which has been called the soul. . . . What more, indeed, is man, than just such a temporary orbing of viewless ultimates,—imaging sky, and land, and life—filled with perpetual mysterious shudderings—and responding in some wise to every stir of the ghostly forces that environ him? . . . In each of a trillion of dewdrops there must be differences infinitesimal of atom-thrilling and of reflection, and in every one of the countless pearls of ghostly vapour, updrawn from the sea of birth and death, there are like infinitesimal peculiarities. Personality, individuality, the ghosts of a dream in a dream! Life infinite only there is; and all that appears to be is but the thrilling of it,—sun, moon, and stars,—earth, sky, and sea,—and mind and man, and space and time, all of them are shadows, the shadows come and go; the Shadow-maker shapes for ever."

ON the fly-leaf of a small octavo Bible, given to Charles Hearn by his grandmother, the following entry may be read: "Patricio, Lafcadio, Tessima, Carlos Hearn. August 1850, at Santa Maura."

The characters are in cramped Romaic Greek, the paper is yellow, the ink faded with age. Whether the entry was made by Lafcadio's father or mother it is difficult to say; one fact is certain: it announces the appearance on this world's stage of one of the most picturesque and remarkable figures of the end of the last century.

13

Those who like to indulge in the fascinating task of tracing the origin of genius will find few instances offering more striking coincidences or curious ancestral inheritances than that afforded by Lafcadio Hearn.

On his father's side he came of the Anglo-Hibernian stock—mixture of Saxon and Celt—which has produced poets, orators, soldiers, signal lights in the political, literary, and military history of the United Kingdom for the last two centuries. We have no proof that Lafcadio's grandfather,—as has been stated,—came over with Lionel Sackville, Duke of Dorset, when he was appointed Lord Lieutenant of Ireland in 1731. The Rev. Daniel Hearn undoubtedly acted as Private Chaplain to his Grace, and about the same time—as recognition for services done, we conclude—became possessed of the property of Correagh in the County of Westmeath.

A Roman Catholic branch of the Hearn family is to be found in County Waterford—has been settled there for centuries. At Tramore, the seaside place near the city of Waterford, where Lafcadio spent several summers at the Molyneux's house with his great-aunt Mrs. Brenane, the Rev. Thomas Hearn is still remembered as a prominent figure in the Roman Catholic movement against Protestantism. He founded the present Cathedral, also the Catholic College in Waterford, and introduced one of the first of the Conventual Orders into the South of Ireland. It is through these Waterford Hearns that Henry Molyneux claimed relationship with the County Westmeath portion of the family.

As to the English origin of the family, the Irish Hearns have an impression that it was a West Country

(Somersetshire) stock. Records certainly of several Daniel Hearns—it is the Christian name that furnishes the clue—occur in ecclesiastical documents both in Wiltshire and Somersetshire.

In Burke's *Colonial Gentry* there is a pedigree given of a branch of Archdeacon Hearn's descendants, who migrated to Australia about fifty years ago. There it is stated that the Hearn stock was originally "cradled in Northumberland." Ford Castle in that county belonged to the Herons—pronounced Hearn—to which belonged Sir Hugh de Heron, a well-known North Country baronet, mentioned in Sir Walter Scott's *Marmion*. The crest, as with Lafcadio's Irish Protestant branch of Hearns, was a heron, with the motto, "The Heron Seeks the Heights."

Mrs. Koizumi, Hearn's widow, tells us that her husband pronounced his name "H*e*r'un," "and selected 'Sageha No Tsuru'—Heron with Wings down—for the design which he made to accompany his name and number at the Literary College, Tokyo University." There can be no doubt that the place-names and families, bearing the Hearn name in various countries, are of different, often entirely distinct origin. Nevertheless, the various modifications of the word—namely Erne, Horne, Hearn, Hern, Herne, Hearon, Hirn, etc., are derived from one root. In the Teutonic languages it is *irren*, to wander, stray, err or become outlaw. *Hirn*, the brain or organ of the wandering spirit or ghost, the Latin *errare* and Frankish *errant*, with the Celtic *err* names are related, though the derivation comes from ancient, Indo-Germanic languages. In the West Country in England the name Hearn is well-known as a Gipsy one, and in the

Provincilia Dictionary for Northumberland, amongst other worthies of note, a certain " Francis Heron " or " Hearn," King of the " Faws " or Gipsies, is referred to.

I give all these notes because they bear out the tradition stoutly maintained by some members of the family, that gipsy blood runs in their veins. An aunt of Lafcadio's tells a story, of having once met a band of gipsies in a country lane in Ireland; one of them, an old woman, offered to tell Miss Hearn's fortune. After examining her hand, she raised her head, looked at her meaningly, and tapping her palm with her finger said, " You are one of us, the proof is here." Needless to say that Lafcadio valued a possible gipsy ancestor more than all the Archdeacons and Lieutenant-Colonels that figured in his pedigree, and was wont to show with much pride the mark on his thumb supposed to be the infallible sign of Romany descent.

Some foreign exotic strain is undoubtedly very apparent in many members of the Hearn family. Lafcadio's marked physiognomy, dark complexion, and black hair could not have been an exclusive inheritance from his mother's side, for it can be traced in Charles Hearn's children by his second wife, and again in their children. This exotic element—quite distinct from the Japanese type—is so strong as to have impressed itself on Hearn's eldest son by his Japanese wife, creating a most remarkable likeness between him and his cousin, Mrs. Atkinson's son. The nearsighted eyes, the marked eyebrows, the dark brown hair, the soft voice and gentle manner, are characteristics owned by both Carleton Atkinson and Kazuo Koizumi. History says that the original birthplace of the gipsies was India. Even in Egypt, the country claimed by the gipsies themselves as the place where their race originated, the native gipsy is not Egyptian in appearance, but Hindoo. Curious to think that Lafcadio Hearn, the interpreter of Buddhism and Oriental legend to the West, may, on his father's side, have been descended from Avatars, whose souls were looked upon as gods, centuries ago, in India.

On his mother's side the skein of Lafcadio's lineage is still more full of knots and entanglements than on his father's. It is impossible to state with any amount of accuracy to what nationality Mrs. Charles Hearn belonged. It has been generally taken for granted that she was Greek; Lafcadio used to say so himself. Some of the Hearns, on the other hand, maintain that she was Maltese, which is quite probable. Owing to the agricultural richness of the Ionian Islands, Italians, Greeks, Levantine Jews, and Maltese had all taken up their abode in the Sept-Insula at various times and seasons. Lafcadio's third name, Tessima, was his mother's maiden-name, and is one that figures continually in Maltese Census- and Rent-rolls. When Mrs. Hearn separated from her husband to return to her own family she went to Malta, not to the Ionian Islands. The fact, as Lafcadio states, that he could only stammer half Italian, half Romaic when he first arrived in Dublin, rather points to a Maltese origin. What wild Arabic blood may he not, therefore, have inherited on his mother's side? For, as is well-known, in times gone by Arab tribes, migrating from the deserts of Asia and Africa, overran the shores of the Mediterranean and settled in Malta, intermarrying with the original Venetian Maltese.

"We are all compounds of innumerable lives, each a sum in an infinite addition—the dead are not dead, they live in all of us, and move us, stirring faintly in every heart beat." Certainly Lafcadio was an exemplification of his own theory. During the course of his strange life all the characteristics of his manifold outcome manifested themselves,—the nomadic instincts of the Romany and Arab, the revolutionary spirit of the Celt, the luxuriant imagination of the Oriental, with that unquenchable spark of industry and energy inherited from his Anglo-Saxon forbears.

From the time they settled in Ireland the Hearns served their country for the most part in Church and Army. Lafcadio's grandfather was Colonel of the 43rd Regiment, which he commanded at the battle of Vittoria in the Peninsular War. He married Elizabeth Holmes, member of a family distinguished in Irish legal and literary circles. To her children she bequeathed musical and artistic gifts of no mean order. From his father Lafcadio inherited a remarkable aptitude for drawing, and, as is easy to see from his letters to Krehbiel, an ardent love of music.

Elizabeth Holmes's second son, Richard Holmes Hearn, insisted while quite a boy on setting forth to study art in the studios in Paris. He never made money or a great name, but some of his pictures, inspired by the genius of Corot and Millet, are very suggestive and beautiful. He was quite as unconventional in his mode of thought, and quite as erratic and unbusinesslike as his famous nephew—"Veritable blunderers," as Lafcadio says, "in the ways of the world."

Writing from Japan to his half-sister, Mrs. Atkinson, about some photographs she had sent him of her children, he says : " They seem to represent new types; that makes no difference in one sense and a good deal of difference in another. I think, though I am not sure, as I have never known you or the other half-sister, that we Hearns all lacked something. The something is very much lacking in me, and in my brother. I mean ' force ' . . . I think we of father's blood are all a little soft of soul . . . very sweet in a woman, not so good in a man. What you call the ' strange mixture of weakness and firmness' is essentially me; my firmness takes the shape of an unconquerable resistance in particular directions—guided by feeling mostly, and not always in the directions most suited to my interests. There must have been very strong characteristics in father's inheritance to have made so strong a resemblance in his children by two different mothers—and I want so much to find out if the resemblance is also psychological."

Charles Bush Hearn, Lafcadio's father, elected to enter the Army, as his father and grandfather had done before him. According to Hart's *Army List* he joined the 45th Nottinghamshire Regiment of Foot as Assistant Surgeon on April 15th, 1842. In the year 1846 he was sent on the Medical Staff to Corfu. The revolutionary spirit which swept over Europe in 1849 infected the Ionian Islands as well as the mainland of Greece. At Cephalonia they nominated a Regent of their own nationality, and strenuous efforts were made to shake off the yoke of the English Government. At the request of Viscount Seaton, the then Governor, additional troops were sent from England to restore order. When they arrived, they, and the other regiments stationed at Corfu, were quartered on the inhabitants of the various islands.

Oriental ideas on the subject of women still existed in this half-Eastern region. Ladies hardly ever appeared at any of the entertainments. If a dinner was given none but men were present. Many stories were told of the expedients resorted to by English officers in their endeavours to institute a closer intercourse with the female portion of the population. Now that troops were quartered in their homes this state of things was speedily changed. Young ladies were induced to join their guests in riding, boating, and walking expeditions. Picnics were instituted at which people got lost in the woods, and did not return until the small hours of the morning, pleasure boats went ashore, necessitating the rescue of lovely ladies from the danger of the deep; the so-called " pleasure boats " being presumably some of the numerous ferry boats that plied to and fro between the islands.

But in telling the love story of Charles Hearn and Rosa Tessima, there is really no need to conjure up imaginary shipwrecks, or lost pathways. Good-looking, clever, a smart officer, handling sword or guitar with equal dexterity, singing an Irish or Italian love song with a melodious tenor voice, Charles Hearn was gifted with all the qualifications for the captivation of a young girl's fancy, and by all accounts he had never allowed these qualifications to deteriorate for want of use.

Only the other day, I was looking over some old papers in an Irish country house with a friend. Amongst them we came across a poem by Charles Bush Hearn, written from Correagh, the Hearns' place in

County Westmeath, to a lady who at that time was very beautiful and an heiress. A lock of hair was enclosed:—

> " Dearest and nearest to my heart,
>   Thou art fairer than the silver moon,
>   And I trust to see thee soon."

There are quite half-a-dozen verses of the same quality ending up with the following:—

> " Adieu, sweet maid! my heart still bleeds with love
>   And evermore will beat for thee!!"

" Alas, I am no poet!" Lafcadio exclaims, half a century later. The power of song was apparently not a gift his father had to bequeath.

Before going to Corfu the young officer had fallen in love with a countrywoman of his own; means, however, were lacking on both sides, and she was persuaded by relations to accept a richer suitor. While still smarting under the pangs of disappointed love, lonely, heartsore, Rosa Tessima crossed his path, and the fate of both was sealed. Where they met we know not. The Tessimas were inhabitants of the Island of Cerigo, but communication between the islands was frequent.

As to the stories, which subsequently drifted to relations in Ireland, of the girl's brothers having attacked and stabbed Charles Hearn in consequence of the injury done to their sister's reputation, it is more than likely they are entirely legendary. The Ionian male had no exalted opinion of women, and was not likely to resort to revenge for imaginary wrongs. There may have been some difficulty with regard to her dowry, as in those days the sons inherited the land and were obliged, when a daughter left her paternal home, to bestow upon her the settlement she was entitled to ; this was sometimes accompanied by a considerable amount of friction.

Lafcadio was born at Santa Maura, the modern name for the ancient Leucadia of the Greeks. Charles Hearn, presumably, was transferred there by some necessity in his profession as military surgeon. The island, excepting Corfu, is the largest in the Sept-Insula. On the southern extremity of the western portion of the coast is situated the rock whence Sappho is supposed to have sought " the end of all life's ends." Not far off stand the ruins of the Temple of Apollo. A few stones piled together still mark the spot where ceremonies were celebrated at the altar in honour of the sun-god. The groves of cypress and ilex that clothe the slope were in days gone by supposed to be peopled by the divinities of ancient Greece. A crystalline stream of water, bubbling down the hill-side by the temple wall, runs into a well, familiarly knows as the Fountain of Arethusa. Standing in the courtyard of the temple a glimpse can be caught of the Island of Ithaca quivering in the luminous haze, with the Gulf of Corinth and the Greek hills beyond.

Although he left the Ionian Islands in infancy, the idea of having been born surrounded by associations of the ancient Hellenic world—the world that represented for him the ideal of supreme artistic beauty—impressed itself upon Hearn's imagination. Often, later, amidst the god-haunted shrines and ancient groves and ceme- teries of Japan, vague ancestral dreams of the mystery of his birth-place in the distant Greek island with its classic memories, stirred dimly within him. After seeing, for instance, the ancient cemetery of Hamamura, in Izumo, he pictures a dream of a woman, sitting in a temple court—his mother, presumably—chanting a

Celtic dirge, and a vague vision of the celebrated Greek poetess who had wandered amidst the ilex-groves and temples of the ancient Leucadia. . . . Awakening, he heard, in the night, the moaning of the real sea—the muttering of the Tide of the Returning Ghosts.

Towards the end of 1851, England agreed to relinquish her military occupation of the greater portion of the Ionian Islands. The troops were withdrawn, and Charles Hearn received orders to proceed with his regiment from Corfu to the West Indies. With a want of foresight typically Hibernian, he arranged that his wife and two-year-old son should go to Dublin, to remain with his relations during the term of his service in the West Indies. The trio proceeded together as far as Malta. How long husband and wife stopped there, or if she remained after he had left with his regiment, it is impossible to say.

Years afterwards, Lafcadio declared that he was almost certain of having been in Malta as a child, and that he specially remembered the queer things told him about the Old Palace, the Knights and a story about a monk, who, on the coming of the French had the presence of mind to paint the gold chancel railings with green paint. Precocious the little boy may have been, but it is scarcely possible that his brain could have been retentive enough to bear all this in memory when but two years old. He must have been told it later by his father, or read a description of the Island in some book of history or travels. From Malta Mrs. Hearn proceeded to Paris, to stop with her husband's artist brother Richard. Charles Hearn had written to him beforehand, begging him to smooth the way for his wife's arrival in Dublin. His brother " Dick "—indeed, all his belongings—were devoted to good-looking, easy-going Charles, but it was with many qualms and much hesitation that Richard undertook the task entrusted to him.

Charles Hearn's mother, and an unmarried aunt, Susan, lived in Dublin at Gardner's Place. " Auntie Sue," as the spinster lady is always referred to by the present generation of Hearns, was the possessor of a ready pen. A novel of hers entitled *Felicia* is still extant in manuscript; the melodramatic imagination, lack of construction, grammar and punctuation, peculiar to the feminine amateur novelist of that day, are very much in evidence. She also kept a diary record-ing the monotonous routine, usual to the life of a middle-aged spinster in the backwater of social circles in Dublin; the arrival and departure of servants, the interchange of visits with relations and friends; each day marked by a text from the Gospels and Epistles.

Because of the political and religious animus exist-ing between Protestants and Papists in Ireland, ortho-dox circles were far more prejudiced and bigoted than the narrowest provincial society in England. All the Hearns belonging to the Westmeath branch of the family were members of the Irish Protestant squirearchy, leaders of religious movements, presiding with great vigour at Church meetings and Parochial functions; it is easy, therefore, to understand the trepidation with which they viewed the arrival of this foreign relation of theirs, a Roman Catholic, who would consort with priests, and indulge in religious observances hitherto anathema to thoroughgoing Protestants. Richard Hearn, thoroughly appreciating all the difficulties of the situation, thought it expedient, apparently, to leave his sister-in-law in Liverpool and go on in front, to propitiate prejudices and mitigate opinions.

On July 28th, 1852, we read in Susan Hearn's diary: "Dear Richard arrived at 10 o'clock from Liverpool, and was obliged to return at 7 o'clock on Friday evening. We trust to see him again in the course of a day or two, accompanied by Charles' wife and son. May Almighty God bless and prosper the whole arrangement." Kindly, warm-hearted maiden lady! Providence is not wont to prosper arrangements made in direct opposition to all providential possibilities. On July 29th she writes: "A letter from Charles, dated the 25th June from Grenada, West Indies! Dear, beloved fellow! in perfect health, but in great anxiety until he hears of his wife and son's arrival. I trust we shall have them soon with us." Then on August 1st: "Richard returned at 7 this morning accompanied by our beloved Charles' wife and child, and a nice young person as attendant. Rosa we are all inclined to love, and her little son is an interesting, darling, child." The "nice young person" who came with Mrs. Hearn as attendant and interpreter, was an important factor in the misunderstandings that arose between Rosa and her relations, and later, in the troubles between husband and wife. Mrs. Hearn, unable to speak a word of English, was influenced and prejudiced by meanings imparted to perfectly harmless actions and statements.

Probably sensitive to sunlight, colour, and climate, as was her son, having passed her life hitherto in a Southern land amidst orange-groves and vineyards, overlooking a sea blue as the sky overarching it, it is easy to imagine the depressing influences to Rosa Hearn of finding herself beneath an atmosphere heavy with smoke, and thick with fog, the murky, sunless world of sordid streets, such as constitutes the major portion of the capital of Ireland.

The description, given by those who are impartial judges, rather divests Rosa of the poetical romance that her son has cast around her memory. She was handsome, report says, with beautiful eyes, but ill-tempered and unrestrained, sometimes even violent. Musical, but too indolent to cultivate the gift, clever, but absolutely uneducated, she lived the life of an Oriental woman, lying all day long on a sofa, complaining of the dullness of her surroundings, of the climate of Ireland, of the impossibility of learning the language. To her children she was capricious and tyrannical, at times administering rather severe castigation.

When people fell short of the height to which he had raised them in imagination, when he discovered that they had not all the qualities he imagined them to possess, Lafcadio, as a rule, promptly cast them from their high estate, and nothing was too bitter to say or think of them. In his mother's case, before the search-light of reality had time to dissipate the illusion, she had passed from his ken for ever.

When his own life was transformed by the birth of his first child, the idea of maternal affection was deepened and expanded, and gradually became connected with a belief in ancestral influences and transmission of a "Karma" ruling human existence from generation to generation. He then imagines the beauty of a mother's smile surviving the universe, the sweetness of her voice echoing in worlds still uncreated, and the eloquence of her faith animating prayers made to the gods of another time, another heaven.

Years later he makes an eloquent appeal to his brother, asking him if he does not remember the dark and beautiful face that used to bend over his cradle, or the voice which told him each night to cross his fingers, after the old Greek orthodox fashion, and utter the words " In the name of the Father, and of the Son, and of the Holy Ghost."

When he saw his brother's photograph, his heart throbbed; for here, he felt, was the unknown being in whom his mother's life was perpetuated, with the same strange impulses, the same longings, the same resolves as his own.

" My mother's face only I remember," he says in a letter to his sister, Mrs. Atkinson, written from Kumamoto, " and I remember it for this reason. One day it bent over me caressingly. It was delicate and dark, with large black eyes—very large. A childish impulse came to me to slap it. I slapped it—simply to see the result, perhaps. The result was immediate severe castigation, and I remember both crying and feeling I deserved what I got. I felt no resentment, although the aggressor in such cases is usually the most indignant at consequences."

The only person with whom Mrs. Charles Hearn seems to have forgathered amongst her Irish relations was a Mrs. Justin Brenane,—" Sally Brenane," Charles Hearn's aunt, on the maternal side. She had married a Mr. Justin Brenane,—a Roman Catholic gentleman of considerable means,—and had adopted his religion with all the ardour of a convert. Poor weak, bigoted, kindly old soul! She and Mrs. Charles Hearn had the bond in common of belonging to a religion antagonistic to the prejudices of the people with whom their lot was cast; she also, at that time, was devoted to her nephew Charles. Never having had a child of her own, she longed for something young on which to lavish the warmth of her affection. The delicate, eerie little black-haired boy Patricio Lafcadio became prime favourite in the Brenane establishment at Rathmines, and the old lady was immediately fired with the idea of having him educated at a Roman Catholic School, and of making him heir to the ample fortune and property in the County of Wexford left to her by her husband.

In the comfort and luxury of Mrs. Brenane's house, Mrs. Charles Hearn found, for the first time since she had left the Ionian Islands, something she could call a home. She enjoyed too, in her indolent fashion, driving in Mrs. Brenane's carriage, a large barouche, in which the old lady "took an airing" every day, driving into Dublin when she was at her house at Rathmines for shopping, or to the Cathedral for Mass. A curious group, the foreign-looking lady with the flashing eyes, accompanied by her dark-haired, olive-complexioned small boy, garbed in strange garments, with earrings in his ears, as different in appearance as was possible to the rosy-cheeked, sturdy Irish "gossoons" who crowded round gaping and amused, to gaze at them.

Mrs. Brenane herself was a noteworthy figure, always dressed in marvellous, quaintly-shaped, black silk gowns. Not a speck of dust was allowed to touch these garments; a large holland sheet being invariably laid on the seat of the carriage, and wrapped round her by the footman, when she went for her daily drive.

In July and August, 1853, there are various entries in Susan Hearn's diary, relating to her brother, Charles Hearn, in the West Indies. Yellow fever had broken out and had appeared amongst the troops. Charles had been ill, " a severe bilious attack and intermittent fever." Then on August 19th: "Letters from dearest Charles, dated July 28th, in great hopes that he may be sent home with the invalids; so we may see him the latter end of September, or the beginning of October." Then comes an entry that he had "sailed with the other invalids for Southampton."

The prospect was all sunlight, not the veriest film of a cloud was apparent to onlookers; yet the air was charged with the elements of storm!

Charles Hearn was a man particularly susceptible to feminine grace and charm. He found on his return a wife whose beauty had vanished, the light washed out of her eyes by weeping, a figure grown fat and un- wieldy, lines furrowed on the beautiful face by discon- tent and ill-humour; but, above all other determining causes for bringing about the unhappiness of this ill- matched pair, Charles Hearn had heard by chance from a fellow-officer on the way home, that his first love, the only woman to whom his wandering fancy had been constant, was free again, and was living as a widow in Dublin.

What took place between husband and wife these fateful days can only be surmised, but these significant entries occur in Susan Hearn's diary. "October 8th, 1853. Beloved Charles arrived in perfect health,

looking well and happy; through the Great Mercy of
Almighty God, my eyes once more behold him."
"Sunday, October 9th. Charles, his wife, and little
boy, dined with us in Gardner's Place, all well and
happy. That night we were plunged into deep afflic-
tion by the sudden and dangerous illness of Rosa,
Charles' wife. She still continues ill, but hopes are
entertained of her recovery." After this entry the
diary breaks off abruptly, and we are left to fill in details
by family statements and hearsay.

An inherited predisposition to insanity probably ran
in Rosa's veins. We are told that during her husband's
absence in the West Indies, whilst stopping at
Rathmines with Mrs. Brenane, she had endeavoured
to throw herself out of the window when suffering
from an attack of mania. Now, whether in consequence of the passionate jealousy of her Southern
nature, which for months had been worked upon by
that "nice person," Miss Butcher, or whether the same
predisposition broke out again, we only know that the
restraining link of self-control, that keeps people on
the right side of the "thin partition," gave way.
Gloomy fits of silence and depression were succeeded
by scenes of such violence, that the poor creature had
ultimately to be put under restraint. The attack was
apparently temporary. Daniel James, her second son,
was born a year later in Dublin, after the departure of
her husband for the Crimea.

Charles Hearn was undoubtedly a most gallant soldier;
he fought at the battles of Alma and Inkermann,
through the siege of Sevastopol, and returned in
March, 1855. After this his regiment was stationed
for some little time at the Curragh. Years afterwards

MAJOR CHARLES BUSH HEARN (HEARN'S FATHER)

Lafcadio described the scarlet-coated, gold-laced officers who frequented the house at this time, and remembered creeping about as a child amongst their spurred feet under the dinner-table.

It is extremely difficult to make out how much the little fellow knew, or did not know, of the various tragic circumstances that darkened these years—the unhappiness that at last led to the separation of his father and mother; and the cloud that at various periods overshadowed his mother's brain.

In the series of letters written to his half-sister, Mrs. Atkinson, which, unfortunately, we are not permitted to give in their entirety, strange lights are cast on the course of events. "I only once," he says, "remember seeing my brother as a child. Father had brought me some tin soldiers, and cannon to fire peas. While I was arranging them in order for battle, and preparing to crush them with artillery, a little boy with big eyes was introduced to me as my brother. Concerning the fact of brotherhood, I was totally indifferent—especially for the reason that he seized some of my soldiers, and ran away with them immediately. I followed him; I wrenched the soldiers from him; I beat him and threw him downstairs; it was quite easy, because he was four years my junior. What afterwards happened I do not know. I have a confused idea that I was scolded and punished. But I never saw my brother again."

The following reminiscence requires little comment:—

"I was walking in Dublin with my father. He never laughed, so I was afraid of him. He bought me cakes. It was a day of sun, with rain clouds above the roofs, but no rain. I was in petticoats. We walked a long way. Father stopped at a flight of stone steps before a tall house, and knocked the knocker, I think. Inside, at the foot of a staircase a lady came to meet us. She seemed to me tall—but a child cannot judge stature well except by comparison. What I distinctly remember is that she seemed to me lovely beyond anything I had ever seen before. She stooped down and kissed me: I think I can feel the touch of her hand still. Then I found myself in possession of a toy gun and a picture book she had given me. On the way home, father bought me some plum cakes, and told me never to say anything to 'auntie' about our visit. I can't remember whether I told or not. But 'auntie' found it out. She was so angry that I was frightened. She confiscated the gun and the picture book, in which I remember there was a picture of David killing Goliath. Auntie did not tell me why she was angry for more than ten years after."

The tall lovely lady was Mrs. Crawford, destined later to be Lafcadio's stepmother. By her first husband she had two daughters. The Hearn and Crawford children used apparently to meet and play together at this time in Dublin.

Mrs. Weatherall, one of these daughters, tells me that a more uncanny, odd-looking little creature than Patricio Lafcadio it would be difficult to imagine. When first she saw him he was about five years of age. Long, lanky black hair hung on either side of his face, and his prominent, myopic eyes gave him a sort of dreamy, absent look. In his arms he tightly clasped a doll, as if terrified that some one might take it from him.

" Tell Mrs. Weatherall I cannot remember the pleasant things she tells of—the one day's happy play with a little girl," he writes from Japan to Mrs. Atkinson. " I remember a little girl, but it can't have been the same. I went into the garden. The little girl stood with one hand on her hips, and said: ' I think I am stronger than you. Can you run? ' I said angrily ' Yes.' ' Let us run a race,' she said. We ran. I was badly beaten. Then she laughed, and I was red with shame, for I felt my face hot. ' I am certainly stronger than you,' she said; ' now shall we wrestle.' I resisted rudely. But in spite of my anger she threw me down easily. ' Ah! ' she said :—' now you must do what I tell you.' She tied my hands behind me, and led me into the house to a cage where there was a large parrot. My hair was long. She made the parrot seize my hair. When I tried to get away from the cage, the parrot pulled savagely. Then I cried, and the little girl sat down on the ground in her silk dress, and rolled with laughter. Then she called her mother to see. I hoped her mother would scold her and free me. But the mother also laughed, and went away again, leaving me there. I never saw that little girl again. I think, though, that her name was Jukes. She seemed to me to feel like a grown-up person. I was afraid of her, and disliked her because she was cleverer than me, and treated me like a little dog. But *how* I would love to see her now. I suppose she is the mother of men to-day—great huge men, perhaps generals, certainly colonels.

" At all events, tell Mrs. W. that I wish, ever so much, she were a little girl again and I a little boy, and that we could play together like then, in the day

I can't remember. Ask her if the sun was not then much larger, and the sky much bluer, and the moon more wonderful than now. I rather think I should like to see her."

Poor Lafcadio! What pathos there is in the question " Ask her if the sun was not then much larger, and the sky much bluer, and the moon more wonderful than now." Those were the days before the loss of his eye at Ushaw College had maimed his visual powers, and transformed his life. In his delightful impressionist description of a journey made from Nagasaki to Kumamoto, along the shores of the Inland Sea, the same idea is repeated. As mile after mile he rolled along the shore in his kuruma, the elusive fragrance of a most dear memory returned to him, of a magical time and place " in which the sun and the moon were larger, and the sky much more blue and nearer to the world," and he recalls the love that he had cherished for one whom he does not name, but who I know to be his aunt, Mrs. Elwood, who " softly ruled his world and thought only of ways to make him happy." Mrs. Elwood was an elder sister of Charles Hearn, married to Frank Elwood, owner of a beautiful place, situated on Lough Corrib in the County Mayo. She was a most delightful and clever person, beloved by her children and all her family connections, especially by her aunt, Mrs. Brenane, who was often in the habit of stopping at the Elwoods' place with her adopted son. We can imagine her telling the little fellow stories, in the " great hush of the light before moonrise," and then crooning a weird little song to put him to sleep. " At last there came a parting day, and she wept and told me of a charm she had given which I must never, never lose, because it would

keep me young and give me power to return. But I
never returned. And the years went; and one day
I knew that I had lost the charm, and had become
ridiculously old." [1]

" The last time I saw father was at Tramore," he
tells his half-sister, when retailing further his childish
memories, " he had asked leave to see me. We took a
walk by the sea. It was a very hot day; and father had
become bald then; and when he took off his hat I saw
that the top of his head was all covered with little drops
of water. He said : ' She is very angry; she will never
forgive me.' ' She ' was Auntie. I never saw him
again.

" I have distinct remembrances of my uncle Richard;
I remember his big beard, and a boxwood top he gave
me. Auntie was prejudiced against him by some tale
told her about his life in Paris."

The year after his return from the Crimea, Charles
and Rosa Hearn's luckless union was dissolved by
mutual consent. Gossip says that after her departure
she married the lawyer (a Jew) who had protected her
interests when she severed her connection with Ireland;
but we have no proof of this, neither have we proof of
the statement made by some members of the Hearn
family, that she returned a year or so later to see her
children but was prevented from doing so. From
what we know of Rosa Hearn, it is far more probable
that, in the sunshine amidst the vineyards and orange-
groves of her own Southern land, the gloom and misery
of those five years in Dublin was sponged completely
from the tablets of her memory.

[1] *Out of the East :* Gay & Hancock.

After the closing of the chapter of his first unhappy marriage, Charles Hearn married the lady he had been attached to before he met Rosa Tessima. At the Registration Office in Stephen's Green, Dublin, the record may be seen entered of the marriage in 1857 of Surgeon-Major Charles Bush Hearn, to Alicia (Posy), widow of George John Crawford.

Immediately afterwards, accompanied by his wife, Charles Hearn proceeded with his regiment to India. His eldest boy he entrusted to the care of Mrs. Justin Brenane, who promised to leave him her money, on condition that she was allowed to bring him up in the Roman Catholic faith.

Neither Mrs. Brenane nor Charles Hearn reckoned with the spirit that was housed in the boy's frail body, nor the fiery independence of mind that made him cast off all ecclesiastical rule and declare himself, as a boy at College, a Pantheist and Free Thinker, thus playing into the hands of those who for purposes of their own sought to alienate him from his grand-aunt.

Daniel James, the second boy, was ultimately sent to his Uncle Richard in Paris.

Of his father Lafcadio retained but a faint memory. In an article written upon Lafcadio after his death, Mr. Tunison, his Cincinnati friend, says he used often to refer to a "blonde lady," who had wrecked his childhood, and been the means of separating him from his mother. His father used to write to him from India, he tells Mrs. Atkinson, "printing every letter with the pen, so that I could read it. I remember he told me something about a tiger getting into his room. I never wrote to him, I think Auntie used to say something like this: ' I do not forbid you to write to your father, child,' but she did not look as though she wished me to, and I was lazy."

Lafcadio and his father never met again, for on November 21st, 1866, on his return journey to England, Surgeon-Major Charles Bush Hearn died of Indian fever, on board the English steamship *Mula* at Suez, thus ending a distinguished career, and a military service of twenty-four years.

With the separation of his parents Lafcadio's childhood came to an end. We now have to follow the development of this strange, undisciplined nature, through boyhood into manhood, and ultimately to fame, remembering always that henceforth he was unprotected by a father's advice or care, unsoothed by a mother's tenderness—that tenderness generally most freely bestowed on those least likely to conquer in the arena of life.

CHAPTER II

BOYHOOD

" You speak about that feeling of fulness of the heart with which we look at a thing—half-angered by inability to analyse within ourselves the delight of the vision. I think the feeling is unanalysable, simply because, as Kipling says, 'the doors have been shut behind us.' The pleasure you felt in looking at that tree, was it only your pleasure, no,—many who would have loved you, were looking through you and remembering happier things. The different ways in which different places and things thus make appeal would be partly explained ;—the supreme charm referring to reminiscences reaching through the longest chain of life, and the highest. But no pleasure of this sort can have so ghostly a sweetness as that which belongs to the charm of an ancestral home. Then how much dead love lives again, how many ecstasies of the childhoods of a hundred years must revive ! "

MOST of Lafcadio's life while with Mrs. Brenane seems to have been passed in Dublin, at her house, 73, Upper Leeson Street; at Tramore, a seaside place on the coast of Waterford in Ireland; at Linkfield Place, Redhill, Surrey, a house belonging to Henry Molyneux, a Roman Catholic friend of Mrs. Brenane's— destined to play a considerable part in the boy's life— and in visiting about among Mrs. Brenane's relatives, whose name was legion.

Mrs. Brenane, when left a widow, lived occasionally in a small house, Kiltrea, situated on the Brenane property, near Enniscorthy. We have records of Charles Hearn, Mrs. Brenane's favourite nephew, and his sister, Miss Hearn, visiting her there, but can nowhere hear of Lafcadio stopping in Wexford. In 1866 the old lady lost her money, and Kiltrea was let to a Mr. Cookman, whose son lives there now.

Mrs. Wetmore, in her sketch of Hearn's life, states that he " seems to have been removed about his seventh year to Wales, and from thenceforward only to have visited Ireland occasionally." This erroneous idea—common to most of Hearn's biographers—has originated from Hearn himself. He later makes allusions to journeyings in England and Wales, but never mentions Ireland. This is typical of his sensitive, capricious genius. Ireland was connected with unpleasant memories; he therefore preferred to transplant his imaginings to a more congenial atmosphere. Besides which, in his later years, he was fascinated by the descriptions of Welsh scenery given in Borrow's *Wild Wales*, and De Quincey's *Wanderings in Wales*.

Interpolated between a story of grim Japanese goblinry, and a delightful dream of the fairyland of Horai, in *Kwaidan*,[1] one of Hearn's last books, there is a sketch called " Hi-Mawari " (Sunflower), the scene of this sketch is undoubtedly laid in Ireland, at the Elwoods' place, and " the dearest and fairest being in his little world," alluded to here, and in his *Dream of a Summer's Day*, is his aunt, Mrs. Elwood. Beautiful as any Welsh hills are the Connemara Peaks, faintly limned against the forget-me-not Irish sky. But Lafcadio eliminates Ireland from his memory, and calls them " Welsh hills."

The " Robert " mentioned in the sketch was his cousin, Robert Elwood, who ultimately entered the navy, and was drowned off the coast of China, when endeavouring to save a comrade, who had fallen over-

[1] The publishers of *Kwaidan* are Messrs. Houghton, Mifflin & Co.

board.   Hence the allusion at the end of the essay . . .
" all that existed of the real Robert must long ago have
suffered a sea change into something rich and strange."
" Greater love hath no man than this, that a man lay
down his life for a friend."

The old harper, " the swarthy, unkempt vagabond,
with bold black eyes, under scowling brows," was Dan
Fitzpatrick of Cong, a well-known character in the
County Mayo.   One of his stock songs was " Believe
me, if all those endearing young charms."   A daughter
of his, who accompanied her father on his tramps
and collected the money contributed by the audience,
was, a few years ago, still living in the village of
Cong.

Forty-six years later, noticing a sunflower near the
Japanese village of Takata, memories of the Irish
August day came back to him, the pungent resinous
scent of the fir-trees, the lawn sloping down to Lough
Corrib, his cousin Robert standing beside him while
they watched the harper place his harp upon the doorstep, and troll forth—

> " Believe me, if all those endearing young charms,
>   Which I gaze on so fondly to-day . . ."

The only person he had ever heard sing these words
before, was she who was enshrined in the inmost sanctuary of his childish heart.   All Charles Hearn's sisters
were musical; but above all Mrs. Elwood was famous
for her singing of Moore's melodies.   The little fellow
was indignant, that a coarse man should dare to sing
the same words; but, with the utterance of the syllables
" to-day," the corduroy-clad harper's voice broke suddenly into pathetic tenderness, and the house, and lawn,

and everything surrounding the boy, trembled and swam in the tears that rose to his eyes.

In a letter to his half-sister, written probably in November, 1891, he thus alludes to the Elwoods: "I remember a cousin, Frank Elwood, Ensign in the Army. I disliked him, because he used to pinch me when I was a child. He was a handsome fellow, I liked to see him in his uniform. I forget when I saw my cousin, Robert Elwood, last. I might have been eight or nine years old—I might have been twelve. And that's all."

It was customary, in the middle of last century, for Irish people, who could afford it, to cross St. George's Channel for their summer holiday.

Mrs. Brenane, his grand-aunt, passed several summers at Bangor. These visits seemed to have been some of the happiest periods in Lafcadio's life. He was then the adopted child of a rich old lady, pampered, spoilt, and made much of by all the members of her circle. Carnarvon Castle was a favourite resort; there Lafcadio had his first experience of the artistic productions of the Far East.

One season he was sent with his nurse to reside in the cottage of a sea-captain, whose usual "run" had been to China and Japan. Piled up in every corner of the little house were Eastern grotesqueries, ancient gods, bronze images, china animals. We can imagine the ghostly influence these weird curiosities would exercise over the sensitive brain of a lonely little boy. Years after, writing to Krehbiel, he gives a vivid description of a Chinese gong that hung on an old-fashioned stand in the midst of the heterogeneous collection. When tapped with a leather beater, it sobbed, like waves upon a low beach . . . and with each tap the roar grew deeper and deeper, till it seemed like an abyss in the Cordillera, or a crashing of Thor's chariot wheels.

By his own showing, Lafcadio must have been a most difficult boy to manage. He tells his half-sister, should any thought come to her that it would have been better that they could have grown up together, she ought to dismiss it at once as mere vexation of spirit. "We were too much alike as little ones to have loved each other properly; and I was, moreover, what you were not, wilful beyond all reason, and an incarnation of the spirit of contrariness. We should have had the same feelings in other respects; but they would have made us fall out, except when we would have united against a common oppressor. Character is finally shaped only by struggle, I fancy; and assuredly one can only learn the worth of love and goodness by a large experience of their opposites. I think I have been tolerably well ripened by the frosts of life, and that I should be a good brother now. I should not have been so as a child; I was a perfect imp."

Hearn's widow, Mrs. Koizumi, told us that often when watching his children at play he would amuse them with anecdotes of what he himself was as a child. Apparently from his earliest days, he was given to taking violent likes and dislikes, always full of whims and wild imaginings, up to any kind of prank, with a genius for mischief—traps arranged with ink-bottles above doors so that when the door was opened, the ink-bottle would fall. One lady apparently, was the object he selected for playing off most of his practical jokes. "She was a hypocrite and I could not bear her.

When she tapped my head gently, and said 'Oh, you dear little fellow,' I used to call out at her, 'Osekimono' (flatterer) and run away and hide myself."

He hated meat, but his grand-aunt would insist on his eating it; when she wasn't looking he would hide it away in the cupboard, where, days after, she would discover it half-rotten.

Surely it was the irony of fate that gave such a creature of fire and touchwood, with quivering nerves and abnormal imagination, into the charge of an injudicious, narrow-minded, bigoted person, such as Sally Brenane; and yet she was very fond of him, and he of her. At Tramore, an old family servant said that he used to "follow her about like a lap-dog."

But it was Mrs. Brenane's maid, his nurse as well, Kate Mythen, who was one of the principal influences in his life, in these days at Tramore, and Redhill, before he went to Ushaw. To Kate's care he was, to a great extent, committed. As Robert Louis Stevenson, used to make Allison Cunningham, or "Cummie," the confidante of his childish woes, and joys, and imaginings, so Lafcadio Hearn communicated to Kate Mythen all that was in his strange little heart and imaginative brain. But "Cummie" was staunch, with the old Scotch Covenanter staunchness. The last book Stevenson wrote was sent to her with "the love of her boy." After he left Ushaw, Lafcadio Hearn never saw Kate Mythen and held no communion with her of any kind. She must have known of the banishment of the boy, of the alienation of his adopted mother's affections, of the transference of his inheritance to others, yet she died in Mrs. Molyneux's house at Tramore in 1903, only a year before her nursling, whose name then had become so famous; to her it was tainted and defiled, for had he not cast off the rule of Holy Mother Church, and declared himself a Buddhist and a Pagan? Such is the power of priest and religion over the Celtic mind.

Hearn's references to the nameless terror of dreams, to which he was a prey in his childhood, especially as set forth in a sketch entitled *Nightmare Touch*, reveals the sufferings of a creature highly strung and sensitive to the point almost of lunacy.

He was condemned, when about five years of age, it seems, to sleep by himself in a lonely room. His foolish old grand-aunt, who had never had children of her own and could not therefore enter into his sufferings, ordained that no light should be left in his room at night. If he cried with terror he was whipped. But in spite of the whippings, he could not forbear to talk about what he heard on creaking stairways and saw behind the folds of curtains. Though harshly treated at school, he was happier there than at home, because he was not condemned to sleep alone, and the greater part of his day was spent with " living human beings " and not " ghosts."

The most interesting portion of Dr. Gould's book, *Concerning Lafcadio Hearn*, is that which treats of Hearn's eyesight. As an oculist, he maintains that Hearn must have suffered from congenital eyestrain, brought on by pronounced myopia from his earliest childhood, long before the accident at Ushaw.

The description that Hearn gives somewhere of the " sombre yellowish glow, suffusing the dark, making objects dimly visible, while the ceiling remained pitch black, as if the air were changing colour from beneath," is a phenomenon familiar to all who have suffered from eyestrain.

After Hearn's death, in a drawer of his library at Tokyo half-a-dozen envelopes were found, each containing a sketch neatly written in his small legible handwriting. He apparently had intended to construct a book of childish reminiscences after the manner of Pierre Loti's *Livre de la Pitié et a de la Mort*. These sketches throw many sidelights on his early years, but, except the one named "Idolatry" they are not up to the level of his usual work. The material is too scanty, events seen through the haze of memory are thrown out of focus, unimportant incidents made too important.

"Only with much effort," he writes to Mrs. Atkinson, "can I recall scattered memories of my boyhood. It seems as if a much more artificial self were constantly trying to speak instead of the self that is in me—thus producing obvious incongruities."

My Guardian Angel relates the sufferings inflicted on his childish mind, by a certain cousin Jane— apparently one of the Molyneux clan, a convert to the Roman Catholic Church, who made the little fellow intensely unhappy by telling him that he would burn for ever in Hell fire if he did not believe in God.

When she left in the spring he hoped she might die. He was haunted by fears of her vengeance during her absence, and when she returned later, dying of consumption, he could not bear to be near her. She left him a bequest of books, of which he hardly appreciated the value then. It included a full set of the "Waverley Novels," the works of Miss Edgworth, Martin's *Milton*, Pope's *Iliad and Odyssey*, some quaint translations of the *Arabian Nights*, and Locke's essay on *The Human Understanding*. Curiously enough, there was not a single theological book in the collection. His cousin Jane's literary tastes were apparently uninfluenced by her religious views.

In 1859 Henry Molyneux was living at Linkfield Lodge, Linkfield Lane, Redhill. The Redhill of to-day, with its acres of bricks and mortar, its smart shops, its imposing Town Hall, and Protestant and Roman Catholic Churches, is a very different place from the straggling village that it was in those days. The few gentlemen's houses were occupied by business men, the London, Brighton and South Coast Railway being the first in England to run fast morning and evening trains for the convenience of those who wanted to come and go daily to London.

Mrs. Brenane seems to have been in the habit of going over periodically to Redhill from Ireland to stop with Molyneux and his wife. She had, at various times, invested most of the fortune left to her by her husband in Molyneux's business, a depot for Oriental goods in Watling Street.

When Henry Molyneux became bankrupt—we see his name assigned by the Court in the London List of Bankrupts for 1866—the house at Redhill was given up, and he and his wife, accompanied by Mrs. Brenane, settled permanently at Tramore, and there, apparently, when he was allowed to leave college, Lafcadio spent his vacations. His grand-aunt by that time had become a permanent inmate of the Molyneux establishment.

Before I had seen the Atkinson letters, I wondered how much Hearn knew of the influences brought to bear on his life at this time. In the second Atkinson letter he openly reveals his entire knowledge of the incidents that appear to have deprived him of his inheritance.

Jesuits, he thought, managed the Molyneux introduction—but was not sure. "It was brought about by
the Molyneuxs claiming to be relatives of Aunty's dead
husband." (Here, Lafcadio was mistaken, for Molyneux, on the contrary, declared himself to be connected
with the Hearns and called himself Henry Hearn
Molyneux.) "Aunty adored that husband," he goes
on, "she was all her life troubled about one thing.
When he was dying he had said to her: 'Sally, you
know what to do with the property?' She tried to
question him more, but he was already beyond the
reach of questions. Now the worry of her whole life
was to know just what those words meant. The priests
persuaded her they meant that she was to take care the
property remained in Catholic hands, in the hands of
the relatives of her husband. She hesitated a long
time; was suspicious. Then the Molyneux people
fascinated her. Henry had been brought up by the
Jesuits. He had been educated for commerce, spoke
four or five languages fluently. He soon became om-
nipotent in the house. Aunty told me she was going
to help him for her husband's sake. The help was soon
given in a very substantial way, by settling five hundred
a year on the young lady he was engaged to marry.
. . . Mr. Henry next succeeded in having himself
declared heir in Aunty's will; I to be provided for by
an annuity of (I think, but am not sure) £500.
'Henry,' who had 'made himself the darling,' was not
satisfied. He desired to get the property into his hands
during Aunty's life. This he was able to do to his
own, as well as Aunty's, ruin. He failed in London.
The estate was put into the hands of receivers. I was
withdrawn from college, and afterwards sent to America,

to some of Henry's friends. I had some help from them in the shape of five dollars per week for a few months. Then I was told to go to the devil and take care of myself. I did both. Aunty died soon after. Henry Molyneux wrote me a letter, saying that there were many things to be sent me, etc., he also said he had been made sole Executor, but told me nothing about the Will. (If you ever have a chance to find out about it, please do.) I wrote him a letter which probably troubled his digestion, as he never was heard of more by me. . . . There was a daughter, however, quite attractive. ' My first love '—at fourteen. I used to write her foolish letters, and wore a lock of her hair for a year or two. . . .

" Well,—there is enough reminiscences for once. If you wish for any more, little sister mine, I'll chatter another time. To-day, under pressure of work, I have to say good-bye.

" Lovingly ever,

" LAFCADIO HEARN."

In another letter, he says, " I know Aunt Brenane made a Will; for she told me so in Dublin, when living at 73, Upper Leeson Street; and I used to go to an aged Lawyer with her, but I can't remember his name. I don't think the matter is very important after all; but it might, if accurately known, give revelation about some other matters."

CHAPTER III

TRAMORE

" If you, O reader, chance to be a child of the sea ; if in early childhood, you listened each morning and evening to that most ancient
and mystic hymn-chant of the waves, . . . if you have ever watched
wonderingly, the far sails of the fishing vessels turn rosy in the blush
of sunset, or once breathed as your native air the divine breath of the
ocean, and learned the swimmer's art from the hoary breakers. . . .
When the long, burning summer comes, and the city roars dustily
around you, and your ears are filled with the droning hum of machinery,
and your heart full of the bitterness of the struggle for life, does not
there visit you at long intervals in the dingy office or the crowded
street some memory of white breakers and vast stretches of wrinkled
sand and far-fluttering breezes that seem to whisper, 'Come ! ' ?

" So that when the silent night descends, you find yourself re-
visiting in dreams those ocean shores thousands of miles away. The
wrinkled sand, ever shifting yet ever the same, has the same old
familiar patches of vari-coloured weeds and shining rocks along its
level expanse : and the thunder-chant of the sea which echoes round
the world, eternal yet ever new, is rolling up to heaven. The glad
waves leap up to embrace you ; the free winds shout welcome in your
ears ; white sails are shining in the west ; white sea-birds are flying
over the gleaming swells. And from the infinite expanse of eternal
sky and everlasting sea, there comes to you, with the heavenly ocean-
breeze, a thrilling sense of unbounded freedom, a delicious feeling as
of life renewed, and ecstasy as of life restored. And so you start into
wakefulness with the thunder of that sea-dream in your ears and tears
of regret in your eyes, to find about you only heat and dust and toil ;
the awakening rumble of traffic, and 'the city sickening on its own
thick breath.' "

TRAMORE is situated six miles south of the city of
Waterford, at the end of a bay three miles wide. The

facilities for sea-bathing and the picturesqueness of the surrounding scenery have made it a favourite resort for the inhabitants of Waterford. On summer mornings when a light wind ripples the water, or on calm dewy nights when the stars rule supreme in a vault of purple ether, or on stormy days when the waves come rolling in, driven by the back-wash of an Atlantic storm, to break with thunderous clamour on the long stretch of beach, Tramore Bay presents scenes striking and grand enough to stamp themselves for ever on a mind such as Lafcadio Hearn's.

There are periods, only to be measured by days, hours, seconds, when impressions are garnered for a lifetime. Amidst work that is stereotyped, artificial, the recollection, stirring in the artist's brain—perhaps after the lapse of years—of a day spent by the sea listening to the murmur of the waves, or sometimes even of only a ray of sunlight falling through a network of leaves on a pathway, or the scent of flowers under a garden wall, will infuse a fragrance, a freshness, something elemental and simple, into a few lines of prose or verse, raising them at once out of dull common-place into the region of pathos, sometimes of inspiration.

Not seldom was Hearn inspired when he took pen in hand, but never so bewitchingly, as when he described the sea, or set down, sometimes unconsciously, memories of these childish days.

At the fishing village of Yaidzu on the coast of Suruga, twenty years later, while watching the wild sea roaring over its beach of sand, there came to him the sensation of seeing something unreal, looking at something that had no more tangible existence than a memory! Whether suggested by the first white vision of the surf over the bamboo hedge—or by those old green tide-lines in the desolation of the black beach—or by some tone of the speaking sea, or by something indefinable in the touch of the wind,—or by all of these —he could not say; but slowly there became defined within him the thought of having beheld just such a coast very long ago, he could not tell where, in those childish years of which the recollections were hardly distinguishable from dreams. . . .

Then he found himself thinking of the vague terror with which he had listened years before as a child to the voice of the sea; and he remembered that on different coasts, in different parts of the world, the sound of surf had always revived the feeling. Certainly this emotion was older than he was himself by thousands and thousands of centuries, the inherited sum of numberless terrors ancestral.

The quotation set at the beginning of this chapter, taken from a fragment entitled *Gulf Winds*,[1] shows his inspiration at its best. Freeing himself from the trammels of journalistic work on the *Commercial* newspaper, while cooped up in the streets of New Orleans, he recalls the delights of the sea in connection with the Levantine sailors in the market-place, and breaks into a piece of poetic prose which I maintain has not been surpassed by any English prose. writer during the course of last century.

Chita, Hearn's first work of fiction, is in no way an artistic production; it lacks construction and the delicate

---

[1] *Gulf Winds* is in print, but it is not known when and where it was published. Dr. Gould quotes it in his book, *Concerning Lafcadio Hearn*, published by Messrs. Fisher Unwin.

touches that constitute the skilful delineation of character; but every now and then memories of his childhood fall across its pages, illumining them as with
sudden light. Chita, at the Viosca Chénière, conquering her terror of the sea, and learning to swim, watching
the quivering pinkness of waters curled by the breath
of the morning under the deepening of the dawn—like
a far-fluttering and scattering of rose leaves; Chita
learning the secrets of the air, many of those signs of
heaven, which the dwellers in cities cannot comprehend,
the scudding of clouds, darkening of the sea-line, and
the shriek of gulls flashing to land in level flight, fore-
telling wild weather, are but reminiscences of his own
childish existence at Tramore.

For him as for Chita there was no factitious life
those days, no obligations to remain still with every
nimble nerve quivering in dumb revolt; no being sent
early to bed for the comfort of her elders; no cruel
necessity of straining eyes for long hours over grimy
desks in gloomy school-rooms, though birds might
twitter and bright winds flutter in the trees without.

When Lafcadio returned to Tramore from Ushaw for
his vacations, long days were spent boating or swim-
ming. One old Wexford boatman was his especial companion. The boy would sit listening with unabated
interest for hours to stories of shipwreck or legendary
adventure, which every Irish fisherman can spin inter-
minably; legends of Celtic and Cromwellian warfare,
of which the vestiges, in ruined castles and watch-
towers are to be seen on the cliffs surrounding the
Bay.

Kate Mythen, his nurse, was wont to say, that the
small Patrick, as he was always called in those days,

would recount these yarns with many additions and embellishments inspired by his vivid imagination. Often too vivid indeed, for not infrequent punishment had to be administered for his habit of "drawing the long bow."

Accuracy is seldom united with strong imaginative power, and certainly during the course of his life, as well as in his childhood, Hearn was not distinguished by accuracy of statement.

The real companions of the boy's heart at that time were not those surrounding him—not his grand-aunt, or Kate Mythen, or the Wexford fishermen. Ideas, images, romantic imaginings caught from books, or from wanderings over hill and dale, separated him from the outside world. While other children were building castles of sand on the beach, he was building castles with towers reaching to the sky, touched by the light of dawn and deepening fire of evening; impregnable ramparts over which none could pass and behind which, for the rest of his days his soul entrenched itself.

Lying on the sea strand, rocked in the old fisherman's boat, his ears filled with the echo of voices whispering incomprehensible things, he saw, and heard, and felt much of that which, though old as the heavens and the earth, ever remains eternally new, eternally mystical and divine—the delicious shock that follows upon youth's first vision of beauty supreme. The strange perception, or, as Hearn calls it, *recognition*, of that sudden power moving upon the mystery of thought and existence, was not to Hearn an attribute of this life, but the shadowing of what had been, the phantom of rapture forgotten, an inheritance from countless generations of people that had preceded him, a surging up from the "ancestral sea of life from whence he came."

It was probably here at Tramore that occurred the incidents recorded in the sketch called "Idolatry." It is one of the half-dozen referred to as having been found amongst his papers after his death.

His grand-aunt apparently, though a bigoted Roman Catholic convert, with a want of logic that was characteristic, had never given him any religious instruction. His boyish yearning for beauty found no spiritual sustenance except from an old Greek icon of the Virgin Mary, or ugly, stiff drawings of saints and patriarchs. One memorable day, however, exploring in the library, he found several great folio books, containing figures of gods and of demi-gods, athletes and heroes, nereids and all the charming monsters, half man, half animal of Greek mythology. Figure after figure dazzled and bewitched him, but filled him with fear. Something invisible seemed thrilling out of the pictured pages; he remembered stories of magic that informed the work of the Pagan statuaries; then a conviction, or rather intuition, came to him that the gods had been belied *because* they were beautiful. The mediæval creed seemed to him at that moment the very religion of ugliness and hate.

The delight he felt in these volumes was soon made a source of sorrow; the boy's reading was subjected to severe examination. One day the books disappeared. After many weeks they were returned to their former places, but all unmercifully revised. The religious tutelage under which he was placed had been offended by the nakedness of the gods, parts of many figures had been erased with a penknife, and, in some cases, drawers had been put on the gods—large, baggy bathing drawers, woven with cross strokes of a quill pen, so designed as to conceal all curves of beauty. . . . The barbarism, however, he says, proved of some educational value. It furnished him with many problems of restoration; for he tried persistently to reproduce in pencil drawing the obliterated lines. By this patient study Greek artistic ideas were made familiar. . . .

After the world of Hellenic beauty had thus been revealed all things began to glow with unaccustomed light. . . . In the sunshine, in the green of the fields, in the blue of the sky he found a gladness before unknown. Within himself new thoughts, new imaginings, dim longings for he knew not what, were quickening and thrilling. He looked for beauty and found it in attitudes and motions, in the poise of plants and trees, in long white clouds, in the faint blue lines of the far-off hills. At moments the simple pleasures of life would quicken to a joy so large, so deep, that it frightened him. But at other times there would come to him a new, strange sadness, a shadowy and inexplicable pain.

A new day had dawned for this impressionable, ardent young spirit, he had crossed the threshold between childhood and youth; henceforth the " Eternal Haunter " abode with him; never might he even kiss the hem of her garment, but hers the shining presence that, however steep and difficult the pathway, led him at last into the "great and guarded" city of artistic appreciation and accomplishment.

CHAPTER IV

USHAW

" Really there is nothing quite so holy as a College friendship. Two lads, absolutely innocent of everything in the world or in life, living in ideals of duty and dreams of future miracles, and telling each other all their troubles, and bracing each other up. I had such a friend once. We were both about fifteen when separated. Our friendship began with a fight, of which I got the worst; then my friend became for me a sort of ideal which still lives. I should be almost afraid to ask where he is now (men grow away from each other so): but your letter brought his voice and face back—just as if his ghost had come in to lay a hand on my shoulder."

St. Cuthbert's College, Ushaw, is situated on a slope of the Yorkshire Hills, near Durham. In the estimation of English Roman Catholics, it stands next to Stonyhurst as an educational establishment. Since Patrick Lafcadio Hearn's days it has counted amongst its pupils Francis Thomson, the Poet, and Cardinal Wiseman, the Archbishop, both of whom ever retained an affectionate and respectful memory of their Alma Mater.

Lafcadio Hearn was sent there from Redhill in Surrey, arriving on September 9th, 1863, at the age of thirteen. Mrs. Brenane is not likely to have been a determining influence in sending him to College. For all her narrow-minded piety, the old lady was warm-hearted and intensely attached to Lafcadio, and must have known how unfitted he was for collegiate life in

56

consequence of constitutional delicacy and defective eyesight.

We have seen also that she had little to do with his religious education. In a letter written from Japan to his half-sister, Mrs. Atkinson, Lafcadio declares that he was sent to a school " kept by a hateful, venomous-hearted old maid," but this idea must either have been prompted by a sort of crazy fear of the far-reaching power of the Jesuits, or by the inaccuracy of his memory with regard to many early impressions.

That he was sent to Ushaw with a view to entering the Priesthood is incorrect. The education at Ushaw is by no means exclusively devoted to preparing boys for the Priesthood. In a letter to his brother, he says: " You are misinformed as to Grand-Aunt educating your brother for the Priesthood. He had the misfortune to spend some years in Catholic Colleges, where the educational system chiefly consists in keeping the pupils as ignorant as possible. I was not even a Catholic."

Monsignor Corbishly, the late Ecclesiastical Head of Ushaw College and a school-fellow of Lafcadio's stated that if there were any ideas on the part of Hearn's relatives that he should enter the Priesthood, the authorities of Ushaw College, as soon as they had become aware of the " mental and moral tendencies " of the boy, would have decided that he was quite unfit to become a member of the Roman Catholic Priesthood. This disposes of one of the many Hearn myths.

That non-success should have attended the endeavours of the authorities of Ushaw and that most of his contemporaries, now shining lights in the Church of Rome, should refer to Lafcadio Hearn as a " painful subject " was a foregone conclusion. The same fanciful, vagrant, original spirit that had characterised his childhood, characterised him apparently in his college career. Besides an emphatic antagonism to laws and conventions, a distinguishing characteristic of his was a horror of forms and ceremonies; one of the manifestations that fascinated him in Shintoism and Buddhism later was their worship of nature and entire absence of ceremonial or doctrinal teaching.

All the aims and thoughts of his boyish heart were directed against prescribed studies and ordinary grooves of thought. A rebellion against restraint, a something explosive and incalculable, places Hearn amongst those whom the French term *deséquilibrés,* one of those ill-poised and erratic spirits, whose freaks and eccentricities are so nearly allied to madness.

Besides his rebellion against restraint, his dislike to ecclesiasticism was artistic and æsthetic.

Before he came to College his mind, as we have seen, was kindled and informed with enthusiasm for natural beauty and the grace of the ancient Hellenic idea. And from nature and Hellenic ideas, Christianity, as exemplified by the Roman Catholic Church, has always stood aloof.

"I remember," he relates in one of his essays, "when a boy, lying on my back in the grass, gazing into the summer blue above me, and wishing I could melt into it, become a part of it. For these fancies I believe that a religious tutor was innocently responsible; he had tried to explain to me, because of certain dreamy questions, what he termed 'the folly and the wickedness of Pantheism,' with the result that I immediately became a Pantheist, at the tender age of fifteen. And my imaginings presently led me not only to want the sky for a playground, but also to become the sky!"

That there were faults and misunderstandings and mistaken ideas of discipline on the part of his preceptors is perhaps possible. Those were the days of " stripes innumerable," and what was a right-minded ecclesiastic to do with a boy, but thrash him, when, in the very stronghold of Catholicism, he declared himself a Pantheist?

If Monsignor Corbishly with his tactful and unprejudiced mind had been at that time head of Ushaw, as he ultimately became, instead of a contemporary of Hearn's, it is open to conjecture that the life of the little genius might have taken an entirely different course. Like his prototype Flaubert there was a *fond d'ecclésiastique* in Hearn's nature, as was proved by his later life. Had his earnestness, industry, and ascetic self-denial been appealed to, with his warm heart and pliable nature, might he not have been tamed and brought into line?

It is the old story where genius is concerned. Because an exceptional youth happens to place himself in revolt against the system of a University, the authorities cannot remake their laws to fit into his eccentricity. Hearn, as he himself confesses, voluntarily handicapped himself all his life, and lost the race, run with stronger, better-conditioned competitors. But that he should have come away from Ushaw College, as he declares, knowing as little as when he entered, is plainly one of his customary exaggerations. The Reverend H. F. Berry, French Master during his residence there, was certainly not competent to instil a finished French style into the future translator of *Sylvestre Bonnard*. But it

is impossible that he could have left College entirely
ignorant of English literature of the 16th, 17th and
18th centuries, remaining, as he did, at the head of his
class in English composition for three years of his
residence at Ushaw.

He himself gives a valid explanation for the reasons
of his ignorance on many subjects. His memories, he
says, "of early Roman history were cloudy, because
the Republic did not interest him; but his conceptions
of the Augustan era remained extremely vivid; and
great was his delight in those writers who related
how Hadrian almost realised that impossible dream
of modern æsthetics, the 'Resurrection of Greek
Art.'

"Of modern Germany and Scandinavia he knew nothing; but the Eddas, and the Sagas, and the Chronicles
of the Heimskringla, and the age of the Vikings and
Berserks, he had at his finger ends, because they were
mighty and awesomely grand."

Ornamental education, he declared, when writing to
Mr. Watkin from Kobe in 1896, was a wicked, farcical
waste of time. "It left me incapacitated to do anything; and still I feel the sorrow and the sin of having
dissipated ten years in Latin and Greek stuff, when a
knowledge of some one practical thing, and of a modern
language or two, would have been of so much service.
As it is, I am only self taught; for everything I learned
at school I have since had to unlearn. You helped me
with some of the unlearning, dear old Dad! . . ."

In answer to a letter of inquiry Canon D——, one
of those in his class at the time, writes: "Poor Paddy
Hearn! I cannot tell you much about him, but what
little I can, I will now give you. I remember him as

a boy about 14 or 15 very well. I can see his face
now, beaming with delight at some of his many mischievous plots with which he disturbed the College and
usually was flogged for. He was some two or three
classes, or more, below my own, hence never on familiar
terms. But he was always considered 'wild as a March
hare,' full of escapades, and the terror of his masters,
but always most kind and good-natured, and I fancy
very popular with his school-mates. He never did
harm to anybody, but he loved to torment the authorities. He had one eye either gone or of glass. There
was a wildish boy called 'St. Ronite,'[1] who was one
of his companions in mischief. He laughed at his many
whippings, wrote poetry about them and the birch, etc.,
and was, in fact, quite irresponsible."

Monsignor Corbishly (during the latter years of his
life head of Ushaw College) gives the following information about Lafcadio :—

"He came here from Redhill, Surrey, a few months
after I did; no one could be in the College without
knowing him. He was always very much in evidence,
very popular among his school-fellows. He played
many pranks of a very peculiar and imaginative kind.
He was full of fun, wrote very respectable verses for a
boy, was an omnivorous reader, worshipped muscle, had
his note-book full of brawny arms, etc.

"As a student he shone only in English writing; he
was first in his class the first time he composed in
English, and kept first, or nearly first, all the time he
was here, and there were several in his class who were
considered very good English writers—for boys. In
other subjects, he was either quite middling or quite

---

[1] I give this name as it is written in Canon D——'s letter.

poor. I do not suppose he exerted himself except in English.

"I should say he was very happy here altogether, had any amount to say and was very original. He was not altogether a desirable boy, from the Superior's point of view, yet his playfulness of manner and brightness, disarmed any feeling of anger for his many escapades. . . . He was so very curious a boy, so wild in the tumult of his thoughts, that you felt he might do anything in different surroundings." Most of the accounts given by his school-fellows at the time repeat the same as to his wildness and his facility in writing English. In this subject he seems to have excelled all his school-fellows, invariably getting the prize for English composition. Later, at Cincinnati, Lafcadio told his friend Mr. Tunison that he remembered, as a boy, being given a prize for English Literature and feeling such a very little fellow, when he got up before the whole school to receive it.

His appearance seems to have been somewhat ungainly, and he was exceedingly shortsighted. When reading he had to bring the book very close to his eyes. He had a great taste for the strange and weird, and had a certain humour of a grim character. There was always something mysterious about him, a mystery which he delighted in increasing rather than dissipating. The confession which he is supposed to have made to Father William Wrennal that he hoped the devil would come to him in the form of a beautiful woman, as he had come to the Anchorites in the desert, was worthy of his fellow-countryman Sheridan, in its Celtic mischief and humour.

Mr. Achilles Daunt, of Kilcascan Castle, County

Cork, seems to have been Lafcadio's principal chum at Ushaw. Mr. Daunt has considerable literary talents himself, and has written one or two delightful books of travel. His reminiscences of Lafcadio Hearn at Ushaw are far the most detailed and interesting. He says that Lafcadio's descriptive talent was already noticeable in those days. The wild and ghostly in literature was what chiefly attracted him. "Naturally of a sceptical turn of mind, he once rather shocked some of us by demanding evidence of beliefs, which we had never dreamt of questioning. He loved nature in her exterior aspects, and his conversation, for a lad of his age, was highly picturesque. Knightly feats of arms, combats with gigantic foes in deep forests, low red moons throwing their dim light across desolate spaces, and glinting on the armour of great champions, storms howling over wastes and ghosts shrieking in the gale—these were favourite topics of conversation, and in describing these fancies his language was unusually rich.

"I believe he was regarded as slightly off his mental balance. He and I were at one time in the same class; but he was kept for two years in, I think, the class or 'school,' as we called it, of 'High Figures.'[1] This separated us a little, as the lads in the High Figures

---

[1] "High Figures" is the name of a class or "School" (as we call "classes" at Ushaw), e.g. Low Figures, High Figures, Grammar, Syntax, Poetry, Rhetoric, etc.

If a boy is kept in the same school or class for two years, e.g. High Figures, it is owing to his not being fit to be moved up into the next class, Grammar.

Each class has its own library, so that a boy in the class of High Figures would not be allowed to intrude into the Library of the school or class above him, Grammar.

were not permitted to use the same library as we used in the 'Grammar Class.' A note was handed to me one evening from him as I sat reading in this library, inviting me to take a stroll. The style of this epistle was eminently characteristic of his tastes and style, and although it is now more than forty years ago, I think the following is very nearly a correct copy of it :—

'Meet me at twelve at the Gothic door,
Massive and quaint, of the days of yore ;
When the spectral forms of the mighty dead
Glide by in the moonlight with silent tread ;
When the owl from the branch of the blasted oak
  Shrieks forth his note so wild,
And the toad from the marsh echoes with croak
  In the moonlight soft and mild.
When the dead in the lonely vaults below
  Rise up in grim array
And glide past with footsteps hushed and slow,
  Weird forms, unknown in day ;
When the dismal death-bells clang so near,
  Sounding o'er wold and lea,
And the wail of the spirits strikes the ear
  Like the moan of the sobbing sea.'

" He was always at school called Paddy. He would never tell what the initial 'L' stood for; probably fearing that his companions would make sport of a name which to them would seem outlandish, or at least odd. His face usually bore an expression of sadness, although he now and then romped as gaily as any of his comrades. But the sadness returned when the passing excitement was over. He cared little, or not at all, for school games, cricket, football, etc., and this not merely because of his want of sight, but because they failed to interest him. I and he were in the habit of walking round the shrubberies in the front of the

College, indulging our tastes in fanciful conversation until the bell summoned us again to study.

"A companion one day alluded to the length of his home address. Lafcadio said his address was longer— 'P. L. Hearn, Esq., Ushaw College, near Durham, England, Europe, Eastern Hemisphere, The Earth, Universe, Space, God.' His companion allowed that his address was more modest.

"You ask if Hearn ever spent his holidays with relatives in Ireland or Wales. As far as I can remember, he latterly never left Ushaw during the vacations. He was reticent regarding his family, and although I believe I was his most intimate friend I cannot recall his ever having told me anything of his relations with his family, or of his childhood."

It is presumably to Mr. Achilles Daunt that Hearn alludes in a letter written thirty years after he had left Ushaw, which has been placed as a heading to this chapter.

At this time occurred an incident that influenced the whole of Hearn's subsequent life. While playing a game known as the "Giant's Stride" one of his companions allowed the knotted end of the rope to slip from his hand. It struck Lafcadio, and in consequence of the inflammation supervening he lost the sight of an eye. "I am horribly disfigured by the loss of my left eye," he tells Mrs. Atkinson, "punched out at school. They are gentle in English Schools, particularly in Jesuitical schools!" He elsewhere mentions an operation undergone in Dublin in the hope of saving the eye. Of this statement we have no confirmation.

Lafcadio seems to have been born with prominent near-sighted eyes. They must have been a Hearn inheritance, for Mrs. Atkinson's son, Carleton, has prominent myopic eyes, and Lafcadio's eldest son has been disqualified, by his near-sight, from entering the Japanese army.

There is something intensely pathetic in Hearn's perception of the idea of beauty, and of the reality manifested in his own person. Something of the ghostliness in his present shell must have belonged, he imagined, to the vanished world of beauty, must have mingled freely with the best of youth and grace and force, must have known the worth of long, lithe limbs on the course of glory, and of the pride of a winner in contests, and the praise of maidens, stately as the young sapling of a palm which Odysseus beheld springing by the altar in Delos.

Little of beauty, or grace, or lithe limbs belonged to Paddy Hearn. He never was more than five feet three inches in height and was much disfigured by his injured eye. The idea that he was repulsive in appearance, especially to women, always pursued him.

Adversity sows the seed. With his extraordinary recuperative power, Lafcadio all his life made ill-luck an effective germinating power.

Twenty years later, in one of his editorials in the *Times Democrat*, he alludes to the artistic value of myopia for an impressionist artist, declaring that the inability to see detail in a landscape, makes it more mystical and impressive. Certainly, in imaginative work his defective sight seems, if one can say so, a help, rather than a drawback in the conjuring up of ghostly scenes and wraiths and imaginings, glimpses, as it were, enlarging and extending the world around him and insight into others far removed from ordinary

comprehension or practical insight. The quality of
double perception became at last a cultivated habit of
mind. "I have the double sensation of being myself
a ghost, and of being haunted—haunted by the prodigious, luminous spectre of the world," he says, in his
essay on "Dust."

The fact remains, however, that no pursuits requir-
ing quickness and accuracy of sight were henceforth
possible for him; the cultivation of his quite remarkable talent for drawing was out of the question. No
doubt his sight had been defective from birth, but the
entire loss of the sight of one eye intensified it to a
considerable extent, and kept him in continual terror
of complete loss of visual power.

It has been stated that Lafcadio Hearn was expelled
from Ushaw. Ecclesiastics are not prone to state their
reasons for any line of action they may choose to take.
No inquiries were made and no reasons were given.
His departure is easily accounted for without any question of expulsion. In fact, it was a matter of necessity,
for in consequence of the loss of the money, invested
in the Molyneux business, his grand-aunt was no longer
able to pay his school fees.

Towards the end of his residence at College he
generally spent his holidays (or a portion of them) at
Ushaw, going home less and less as time went on.

Mrs. Brenane's mind, weakened by age and misfortune, was incapable any longer of forming a sound
opinion. Those surrounding her persuaded her that
the boy whom she had hitherto loved as her own
son and declared her heir, was a "scapegrace and
infidel, no fit inmate for a Christian household."
Besides which the lamentable fact remained that she,

who only a few years before had lived in affluence, no longer owned a home of her own, and Lafcadio was hardly likely to care to avail himself of Molyneux's hospitality.

At the time of Henry Molyneux's marriage to Miss Agnes Keogh, a marriage which took place a year before his failure in 1866, Mrs. Brenane bestowed the whole of the landed property her husband Justin Brenane had left her in the form of a marriage settlement on the young lady. The rest of her life, therefore, was spent as a dependent in the Molyneux's house, Sweetbriars, Tramore.

Thus did Lafcadio Hearn lose his inheritance, but if he had inherited it would he ever have been the artist he ultimately became? He was wont to say that hard knocks and intellectual starvation were, with him, a necessary stimulus to creative work, and pain of exceeding value betimes. "Everybody who does me a wrong, indirectly does me a right, I am forced to detach myself from things of the world, and devote myself to things of the imagination and spirit."

Amidst luxurious surroundings with a liberal competency to live upon might he not perhaps have spent his life in reading or formulating vague philosophical theories, seeking the "unknown reality," instead of being driven by the pressing reality of having to support a wife and children?

CHAPTER V

LONDON

"In Art-study one must devote one's whole life to self-culture, and can only hope at last to have climbed a little higher and advanced a little farther than anybody else. You should feel the determination of those Neophytes of Egypt who were led into subterranean vaults and suddenly abandoned in darkness and rising water whence there was no escape, save by an iron ladder.

As the fugitive mounted through heights of darkness, each rung of the quivering stairway gave way immediately he had quitted it, and fell back into the abyss, echoing; but the least exhibition of fear or weariness was fatal to the climber."[1]

A PARLOUR-MAID of Mrs. Brenane's, Catherine by name, who had accompanied her from Ireland when the old lady came over to the Molyneux's house at Redhill, had married a man of the name of Delaney, and had settled in London, near the Docks, where her husband was employed as a labourer. To them Hearn went when he left Ushaw. The Delaneys were in fairly comfortable circumstances, and Hearn's account in the letters—the only ones we have of his at this time—written to his school-friend, Mr. Achilles Daunt, of the grimness of the surroundings in which his lot was cast, of the nightly sounds of horror, of windows thrown violently open, or shattered into pieces, of shrieks of agony, cries of murder, and plunges in the river, are to be ascribed to his supersensitive and excitable imagination.

[1] *Life and Letters of Lafcadio Hearn*: Houghton, Mifflin & Co.

The artist cannot always be tied down to the strict letter of the law. It inspires a much deeper human interest to picture genius struggling against overwhelming odds—poverty-stricken, starving—than lazily and luxuriously floating down the current of life with unlimited champagne and chicken mayonnaise on board.

Stevenson was at this time supposed to be living like a "weevil in a biscuit," when his father was only too anxious to give him an allowance. Jimmy Whistler, only a little way up the river from Hearn, at Wapping, was said to be living on "cat's meat and cheese parings," when, if he had chosen to conform to the most elementary principles of business, he might have been in easy circumstances by the sale of his work.

As to direct penury, and Hearn's statement that he "was obliged to take refuge in the workhouse," if accurate it must have been brought about by his own improvident and intractable nature and invariable refusal to submit to discipline or restraint of any kind.

Hearn's memories of his youth were extremely vague. Referring to this period of his life later, in Japan, he tells a pupil, that though some of his relations were rich, none of them offered to pay to enable him to finish his education; and though brought up in a luxurious home, surrounded by Western civilisation, he was obliged to educate himself in spite of overwhelming difficulties, and in consequence of the neglect of his relations, partly lost his sight, spent two years in bed, and was forced to become a servant.

This is a remarkable case of Celtic rebellion against the despotism of fact. He never was called upon to fill the duties of a servant until he arrived in America. He never could have spent two years in bed, for there are no two years unaccounted for, either at this time or later in Cincinnati. It would not have suited the policy of those ruling his destiny to leave him in a state of destitution. A certain allowance was probably sent to Catherine Delaney, as later in Cincinnati to Mr. Cullinane, sufficient for his keep and every-day expenses.

With a knowledge of Lafcadio's methods we can imagine that any sum given to him would probably have run through his fingers within the first hour—his last farthing spent on the purchase of a book or curio that fascinated him in a shop window. Thus he might find himself miles away from home, obliged to obtain haphazard the means of supplying himself with food and shelter. Absence of mind was characteristic of all the Hearns, and unpunctuality, until he was drilled and disciplined by official life in Japan, one of Lafcadio's conspicuous failings. We can imagine the practical ex-parlourmaid keeping his meals waiting, during the first period of his stay, and gradually when she found that no dependence could be placed on his movements, taking no further heed or trouble, and paying no attention to his coming and going.

At various periods during the course of his life, Hearn indulged in the experiment of working his brain at the expense of his body—sometimes to the extent of seriously undermining his health, and having to submit to the necessity of knocking off work until lost ground had been made up. He held the opinion that the owner of pure " horse health " never possessed the power of discerning " half lights." In its separation of the spiritual from the physical portion of existence, severe sickness was often invaluable to the sufferer by the revelation it bestows of the psychological under-currents of human existence. From the intuitive recognition of the terrible, but at the same time glorious fact, that the highest life can only be reached by subordinating physical to spiritual influences, separating the immaterial from the material self, lies all the history of asceticism and self-suppression as the most efficacious means of developing religious and intellectual power.

Fantastic were the experiments and vagaries he indulged in now and then, as when he tried to stay the pangs of hunger at Cincinnati by opium, or when, on his first arrival in Japan, he insisted on adopting a diet of rice and lotus roots, until he discovered that endeavouring to make the body but a vesture for the soul, means irritated nerves, weak eyesight and acute dyspepsia.

Now, even as a lad, began Hearn's life of loneliness and withdrawal from communion with his fellows. Buoyed up by an undefined instinct that he possessed power of some sort, biding his time, possessing his soul in silence, and wrapping a cloak of reserve about his internal hopes and aims, he gradually turned all his thoughts into one channel.

Youth has a marvellous fashion of accepting injustice and misrepresentation, if allowed to keep its inner life untouched. Now he showed that strange mixture of weakness and strength, stoicism and sensibility, ignorance of the world, and stubborn resistance to external influence that distinguished him all through the course of his life. If those amongst whom his lines had hitherto been cast chose to cast him forth, and look upon him as a pariah, he would not even deign to excuse himself, or seek to be reinstated in their affections.

After all, what signify the nettles and brambles by the wayside, when in front lies the road leading to a shining goal of hope, of work, of achievement? What matter a heavy heart and an empty stomach, when you are stuffing your brain to repletion with new impressions and artistic material?

Slowly and surely even now he was coming to the conviction that literature was his vocation, and he began preparing himself, struggling, as he expresses it, with that dumbness, that imperfection of utterance, that beset the literary beginner arising generally from the fact that the latent thought or emotion has not yet defined itself with sufficient sharpness. "Analyse it, make the effort of trying to understand exactly the emotion that moves us, and the necessary utterance will come, until at last the emotional idea develops itself unconsciously. Analysing the feeling that remains dim, and making the effort of trying to understand exactly the emotion that moves us, prompt at last the necessary utterance. Every feeling is expressible. . . . You may work at a page for months before the idea clearly develops, the result is often surprising; for our best work is often out of the unconscious."

Already in the small frail body, with half the eyesight given to other men, dwelt that quality of perseverance, that indomitable determination which, with all Hearn's deviations from the straight path, with all his blunderings, guided him at last out of the perplexities and weariness of life into calm and sunlight, to the enjoyment of that happiness which was possible to a man of his temperament.

"All roads lead to Rome," but it is well for the artist if he find the right one early in his career. Hearn set forth on his pilgrimage within hearing of the tolling of the bell of St. Paul's, ending it within hearing of the "Bronze beat" of the Temple bell of Yokohama, carrying through all his romantic journeyings that most wonderful romance of all, his own genius.

"Well, you too have had your revelations,—which means deep pains. One must pay a price to see and to know," he writes to Mrs. Atkinson, recalling these days. "Still, the purchase is worth making."

Great as the deprivation must have been, not to return to the meadows and flowery lanes of Tramore, to the wind-swept bay, and the sound of the undulating tide, what a chance was now offered him! A free charter of the streets of London. If, as he says, he had received no education at Ushaw, he received it here, the best of all, in these grimy, sordid surroundings, noting the pathos of every-day things, fascinated by the sight of the human stream pouring through the streets of the great metropolis, its currents and counter-currents and eddyings, strengthening or weakening, as the tide rose or ebbed, of the city sea of toil. This was what gave his genius that breadth of vision and range of emotion, which half a century later enabled him to interpret the ceremony and discipline, the sympathy or repulsion, the "race ghost" of the most mysterious people on the face of the globe. We can see in imagination the odd-looking lad, creeping in his gentle, near-sighted fashion, through the vast necropolis of dead gods in the British Museum, where later, in an

eloquent passage at the end of one of his essays, he
pictures a Japanese Buddha, "chambered with forgotten
divinities of Egypt or Babylon under the gloom of a
pea soup fog," trembling faintly at the roar of London.
"All to what end?" he asks indignantly. "To aid
another Alma Tadema to paint the beauty of another
vanished civilisation or to illustrate an English dictionary of Buddhism; perhaps to inspire some future
Laureate with a metaphor startling as Tennyson's
figure of the 'Oiled and curled Assyrian Bull'? Will
they be preserved in vain? Each idol shaped by human
faith remains the shell of truth eternally divine, and
even the shell itself may hold a ghostly power. The
soft serenity, the passionless tenderness of those Buddha
faces might yet give peace of soul to a West weary of
creeds, transformed into conventions, eager for the
coming of another teacher to proclaim, 'I have the
same feeling for the High as the Low, for the moral
as the immoral, for the depraved as for the virtuous,
for those holding sectarian views and false opinions as
for those whose beliefs are good and true.'"

We can see him sitting on the parapet of the Dock
wall, watching the white-winged ships, "swift Hermæ
of traffic—ghosts of the infinite ocean," put out to
sea, some of them bound for those tropical lands of
which he dreamed. Others coming in, landing sphinx-
like, oblique-eyed little men from that country in the
Far East, of which he was one day destined to become
the interpreter.

We know of nothing that he wrote at this time, but
no doubt many were the sheets—destroyed then and
there as dangerous and heretical stuff—that fell into
Catherine Delaney's hands. What she could not

destroy, were the indelible visions and impressions, bitten deep by the aquafortis of memory on the surface of his sensitive brain.

"One summer evening, twenty-five years ago, in a London park, I heard a girl say ' good-night ' to somebody passing by. Nothing but those two little words —' good-night.' Who she was I do not know. I never even saw her face, and I never heard that voice again. But still after the passing of one hundred seasons, the memory of her ' Good-night ' brings a double thrill incomprehensible of pleasure and pain— pain and pleasure, doubtless, not of me, not of my own existence, but of pre-existence and dead suns.

"For that which makes the charm of a voice thus heard but once cannot be of this life. It is of lives innumerable and forgotten. Certainly there never have been two voices having precisely the same quality. But in the utterance of affection there is a tenderness of timbre common to the myriad million voices of all humanity. Inherited memory makes familiar even to the newly-born the meaning of this tone of caress. Inherited, no doubt, likewise our knowledge of the tones of sympathy, of grief, of pity. And so the chant of a blind woman in this city of the Far East may revive in even a Western mind emotion deeper than individual being—vague dumb pathos of forgotten sorrows, dim loving impulses of generations unremembered. The dead die never utterly. They sleep in the darkest cells of tired hearts and busy brains, to be startled at rarest moments only by the echo of some voices that recalls their past." [1]

It is interesting to feel the throb of the intellectual

[1] From *A Street Singer*, Kokoro : Messrs. Gay & Hancock.

pulse of England in the late sixties when Lafcadio Hearn was wandering about the wilderness of London, absorbing thoughts and storing ideas for the future.

Tennyson had done his best work. *Maud* and *Locksley Hall* were in every one's heart and on every one's lips, illustrating the trend and the expression of men's thoughts. Walter Pater and Matthew Arnold at Oxford, were forming the modern school of English prose; Ruskin in his fourth-floor room at Maida Vale, with "the lights of heaven for his candles," was opening the mind of middle-class England to a new set of Art theories. The Brownings were in Bryanston Square, she occupied in writing *Aurora Leigh*, he in completing *Sordello*. William Morris, "in dismal Queen's Square, in black, filthy old London, in dull end of October, was making a wondrous happy poem, with four sets of lovers, called ' Love is Enough.' " The Pre-Raphaelite Brotherhood were trying to lead Englishmen out of the " sloshy " bread-and-butter school of sentimentalism to what they called " truth " in subject and execution. The *Germ* was running its short and erratic career; Rossetti had published in its pages the " Blessed Damozel," had finished " The Burden of Nineveh," and had begun the " House of Life." Jimmy Whistler, during the intervals of painting " Nocturnes " at Cherry Tree Inn, was flying over to Paris, returning laden with " Japaneseries," exhibiting for the first time to the public, at his house in Chelsea, a flutter of purple fans, and *kakemonos* embroidered at the foot of Fuji-no-yama, which, in his whimsical way, he declared to be " as beautiful as the Parthenon Marbles."

Darwin had fulminated his scientific principles of

Natural Selection and Evolution, fanning into a flame the conflict between religious orthodoxy and natural science. Theologians were up in arms. To doubt a single theological tenet, or the literal accuracy of an ancient Hebraic text, seemed to them to place the whole reality of religious life and nature in question. Ten years before, Herbert Spencer had been introduced by Huxley to Tyndall as "Ein Kerl der speculirt," and well had he maintained the character; *Principles of Ethics* had already been written and he was at work at the "Synthetic Philosophy."

Science, however, in those days seems to have been a closed book to Lafcadio. The wrangles and discussions over Eastern legend and the creation of the world as set forth in Genesis never seem to have reached his mind, until years afterwards in New Orleans. He appears to have wandered rather in the byways of fiction, devouring any rubbish that came his way in the free libraries he frequented. It is surprising to think of the writer of *Japan, an Interpretation*, having been fascinated by Wilkie Collins's *Armadale*. The name "Ozias Midwinter," indeed, he used afterwards as a pseudonym for the series of letters contributed to the *Commercial* from New Orleans. There is a certain pathos in the appeal that the description of the personality and character of Midwinter made to his imagination. "What had I known of strangers' hands all through my childhood? I had only known them as hands raised to threaten. What had I known of other men's voices? I had known them as voices that jeered, voices that whispered against me in corners. . . . I beg your pardon, sir, I have been used to be hunted and cheated and starved."

Lafcadio's stay in London lasted a year; an imagination such as his lives an eternity in a year. A veil of mystery overhangs the period intervening between this and his arrival in America which I have in vain endeavoured to penetrate.

Mr. Milton Bronner, in his preface to the *Letters from the Raven*, alludes to the " travel-stained, poverty-burdened lad of nineteen, who had ' run away from a Monastery *in Wales*,' and who still had part of his monk's garb for clothing."

In writing Hearn's biography, it is always well to remember his tendency to embroider upon the drab background of fact. Mrs. Koizumi, his widow, told us in Japan that when applying for an appointment, as Professor at the Waseda University, her husband informed the officials that he had been educated in England and Ireland, " also some time in France." His brother, Daniel James, at present a farmer at St. Louis, Michigan, says that he knows Lafcadio to have been for some time at college in France, and Mr. Joseph Tunison his intimate friend at Cincinnati states that Lafcadio when talking of his later childhood and youth referred to Ireland, England, and " some time at school in France." Hitherto it has been a task of no difficulty to trace the inmates of Roman Catholic colleges abroad, it having been customary to keep records of the name of every inmate and student of each college, but since the breaking up of the religious houses in France, many of these records have been lost or destroyed.

Strong internal evidence, which it is unnecessary to quote here, leads to the conclusion that he was delivered, as a scapegrace and good-for-nothing, into the charge of the ecclesiastics at the Roman Catholic Institution of the *Petits Précepteurs* at Yvetot, near Rouen. Finding their methods of calling sinners to repentance unendurable, he took the key of the fields, and made a bolt of it. If, as we imagine, he went to Paris, he most certainly did not reveal himself to his Uncle Richard, who was living there at the time.

Though henceforward the ecclesiastical element, as an active factor, disappeared out of Hearn's life, he seems to have been pursued by a sort of half-insane fear of the possibility of Jesuitical revenge. The Church, he declared, was inexorable and cruel; he preferred, therefore, not to place himself within the domain of her sway, holding aloof, as far as possible, from Roman Catholic circles in New Orleans, and renouncing the idea of a visit to the Spanish island of Manila.

It is easy to imagine the intellectual eagerness and curiosity—appanage of his artistic nature—with which Hearn must have entered Paris. Paris, where, as he says, "talent is mediocrity; art, a frenzied endeavour to express the Inexpressible; human endeavour, a spasmodic straining to clutch the Unattainable."

A few weeks would have sufficed to enable him to collect vital memories—memories to be used so often afterwards in his literary work.

It was the period just before the outbreak of the Franco-Prussian war, when Paris, under the Empire, had reached her zenith of talent and luxury. A strange mixture of frivolity and earnestness characterised the world of art. Theophile Gautier was writing his *Mdlle. de Maupin*, while Victor Hugo was thundering forth his arraignment of Napoleon Buonaparte, and writing epics to Liberty. Hearn tells of French artists

who made what they called " coffee pictures " by empty-
ing the dregs of their coffee upon a sheet of soft paper
after dinner at the Chat Noir, and by the suggestions
of the shapes of the stains pictures were inspired and
developed, according to the artistic capacity of the
painter. Meanwhile, in his humble home in Brittany,
François Millet, in poverty and solitude, was living
face to face with Nature and producing the *Sowers and
the Angelus.*

Yet, even amongst the most dissipated members of
this Parisian world of Bohemia, one principle was established and followed, and this principle it was that made
it so invaluable a school for a nature such as Hearn's.
Never was the artistic vocation to be abandoned for any
other, however lucrative, not even when Art remained
blind and deaf to her worshippers. However forlorn
the hope of ultimate success, it was the artist's duty to
offer up burnt sacrifices on the altar of the divinity.

It is not to be wondered at that the boy was infected
by the theory that ruled supreme of " Art for Art's
sake." Art, not for the sake of the moral it might
preach or the call on higher spiritual sentiments but
for itself. This axiom it was that permeated the
sinister perfection of Baudelaire, the verbal beauty of
Flaubert and the picturesqueness of Gautier. For a
young craftsman still struggling with the manipulation
of his material the " Impressionist " School, as it was
called, presented exceptional fascinations; and no doubt
in that very slender outfit, which he tells us he carried
in the emigrant train between New York and Cincinnati, some volumes of these French Romantics were
packed away. He could hardly have obtained them
in the America of that day. The shelves of the Cin-

cinnati Free Library might hold Henry James's *Essays* in praise of the modern French literary school, but the circulation of the originals would certainly not have been countenanced by the directors.

It is not impossible that when in Paris Lafcadio came across Robert Louis Stevenson. The year that he was born in the Ionian Islands, Stevenson was born amidst the fogs and mists of Edinburgh. He was the same age, therefore, as the little Irishman, and was in Paris at about the same time. Whistler, " the Laird " and Du Maurier were both also frequenting the Quartier, the latter collecting those impressions which he afterwards recounted in *Trilby*,—*Trilby* of which Lafcadio writes later with the delight and appreciation of things experienced and felt.

In 1869 Lafcadio Hearn received a sum of money from those in Ireland who had taken the control of his life into their hands, and he was directed to leave Europe for Cincinnati in the United States of America. There he was consigned to the care of Mr. Cullinane, Henry Molyneux's brother-in-law.

It was characteristic that Hearn apparently did not attempt to propitiate or approach his grand-aunt, Mrs. Brenane, though he must have well known that by not doing so he forfeited all chance of any inheritance she might still have left to bestow upon him.

CHAPTER VI

CINCINNATI

"... I think there was one mistake in the story of Œdipus and the Sphinx. It was the sweeping statement about the Sphinx's alternative. It isn't true that she devoured every one who couldn't answer her riddles. Everybody meets the Sphinx in life;—so I can speak from authority. She doesn't kill people like me,—she only bites and scratches them; and I've got the marks of her teeth in a number of places on my soul. She meets me every few years and asks the same tiresome question,—and I have latterly contented myself with simply telling her, 'I don't know.'"[1]

In a letter to his sister, written from Kumamoto, in Japan, years later, Hearn tells her that he found his way to the office of an old English printer, named Watkin, some months after his arrival in Cincinnati. "I asked him to help me. He took a fancy to me, and said, 'You do not know anything; but I will teach you. You can sleep in my office. I cannot pay you, because you are of no use to me, except as a companion, but I can feed you.' He made me a paper-bed (paper-shavings from the book-trimming department); it was nice and warm. I did errand boy in the intervals of tidying the papers, sweeping the floor of the shop, and sharing Mr. Watkin's frugal meals."

In Henry Watkin's Reminiscences the purport is given of the conversation that passed between the future

[1] *Lafcadio Hearn's Life and Letters*, published by Houghton, Mifflin & Co.

author of *Kokoro* and himself at his shop in the city of Cincinnati, when Hearn first found his way there in the year 1859.

" Well, young man, what ambition do you nourish ? "

" To write, sir."

" Mercy on us. Learn something that will put bread in your mouth first, try your hand at writing later on."

Henry Watkin was a person apparently of elastic views and varied reading; self-educated, but shrewd and gifted with a natural knowledge of mankind. He was nearly thirty years older than the boy he spoke to, but he remembered the days when his ideal of life had been far other than working a printing-press in a back street in Cincinnati. At one time he had steeped himself in the French school of philosophy, Fourierism and St. Simonism; then for a time followed Hegel and Kant, regaling himself in lighter moments with Edgar Allan Poe and Hoffmann's weird tales.

The lad who had come to solicit his aid was undersized, extremely near-sighted—one of his eyes, in consequence of the accident that had befallen him at Ushaw, was prominent and white—he was intensely shy, and had a certain caution and stealthiness of movement that in itself was apt to influence people against him. But the intellectual brow, a something dignified and reserved in voice and manner, an intangible air of breeding, arrested Mr. Watkin's attention. As Hearn somewhere says, hearts are the supreme mysteries in life, people meet, touch each other's inner being with a shock and a feeling as if they had seen a ghost. This strange waif, who had drifted to the door of his printing-office, touched Henry Watkin's sympathetic nature; he discerned at once, behind the unprepossessing exterior, a specific individuality, and conceived an immediate affection for the boy.

Many were the shifts that Lafcadio had been put to from the time he left France until he cast anchor in the haven of Mr. Watkin's printing-shop in a retired back street in the city of Cincinnati.

Filling up the gaps in his own recital, we can see the sequence of events that invariably distinguished Hearn's progress through life. In his improvident manner he had apparently squandered the money that had been contributed by Mrs. Brenane for his journey, and thus found himself in considerable difficulties.

Amongst the papers found after his death was a sketch, inspired, he tells Professor Yrjo Hirn, writing from Tokyo in January 1902, by the names of the Scandinavian publishers, Wahlstrom and Weilstrand. It is sufficiently reminiscent of Stevenson to make one think that the reading of *Across the Plains*, rather than the names of Scandinavian publishers, was responsible for its inception. It relates very much the same experiences as Stevenson's on his journey from New York to Chicago in an American emigrant train. Absolutely destitute of money and food, he must have presented a forlorn appearance. Moved to pity, a Norwegian peasant girl, seated opposite him in the car, offered him a slice of brown bread and yellow cheese. Thirty-five years later he recalled the vision of this kind-hearted girl, no doubt endowing her memory with a beauty and charm that never were hers—and under the title of *My First Romance* left it for publication amongst his papers.

After his arrival in Cincinnati the lad seems very nearly to have touched the confines of despair; and for some months lived a life of misery such as seems incredible for a person of intellect and refinement in a civilised city. Sometimes when quite at the end of his tether he had, it appears, to sleep in dry-goods boxes in grocers' sheds, even to seek shelter in a disused boiler in a vacant "lot."

"My dear little sister," he writes years afterwards to Mrs. Atkinson, when recounting his adventures at this period, "has been very, very lucky, she has not seen the wolf's side of life, the ravening side, the apish side; the ugly facets of the monkey puzzle.

"I found myself dropped into the enormous machinery of life I knew nothing about, friends tried to get me work after I had been turned out of my first boarding-house through inability to pay. I lost father's photograph at that time by seizure of all my earthly possessions. I had to sleep for nights in the street, for which the police scolded me; then I found refuge in a mews, where some English coachmen allowed me to sleep in a hay-loft at night, and fed me by stealth with victuals stolen from the house."

This incident Mrs. Wetmore, in her biography, refers to as having taken place during his stay in London. His letter to his sister and his use of the word "dollars" in estimating the value of the horses, unmistakably connects the scene of it with the United States, where at that time it was the custom to employ English stablemen.

His sketch, written years after, recalling this night in a hay-loft, delightfully simple and suggestive, tells of the delights of his hay-bed, the first bed of any sort for many a long month! The pleasure of the sense of rest! whilst overhead the stars were shining in the frosty air. Beneath, he could hear the horses stirring heavily, and he thought of the sense of force and life that issued from them. They were of use in the world, but of what use was he? . . . And the sharp shining stars, they were suns, enormous suns, inhabited perhaps by creatures like horses, with small things like rats and mice hiding in the hay. The horses did not know that there were a hundred million of suns, yet they were superior beings worth a great deal of money, much more than he was, yet he knew that there were hundreds of millions of suns and they did not.

"I endeavoured later," he tells Mrs. Atkinson, "to go as accountant in a business office, but it was soon found that I was incapable of filling the situation, defective in mathematical capacity, and even in ordinary calculation power. I was entered into a Telegraph Office as Telegraph Messenger Boy, but I was nineteen and the other boys were young; I looked ridiculously out of place and was laughed at. I was touchy—went off without asking for my wages. Enraged friends refused to do anything further for me. Boarding-houses warned me out of doors. At last I became a Boarding-house servant, lighted fires, shovelled coals, etc., in exchange for food and privilege of sleeping on the floor of the smoking-room. I worked thus for about one and a half years, finding time to read and write stories. The stories were published in cheap Weeky Papers, long extinct; but I was never paid for them. I tried other occupations also—canvassing, show-card writing, etc. These brought me enough to buy smoking tobacco and second-hand clothes— nothing more."

It is typical of Hearn, that though driven to such straits he never applied to Mr. Cullinane, to whose charge he had been committed. We are not surprised that the little room at the back of Mr. Watkin's shop, with the bed of paper shavings, and Mr. Watkin's frugal meals, yes, even sleeping in dry-goods boxes in a grocer's shed, or the shelter of a disused boiler in a vacant " lot," was preferable to the acceptance of money sent through the intervention of Henry Molyneux to Henry Molyneux's brother-in-law.

In his book, *Concerning Lafcadio Hearn*,[1] Dr. George Milbury Gould alludes to this gentleman in the following terms:—

" There is still living, an Irishman, to whom Lafcadio was sent from Ireland, and in whose care, at least to a limited extent, the boy was placed. He was living in Cincinnati, Ohio, in 1870."

" He was not sure," says Gould in his account of an interview with Mr. Cullinane, " whether Mrs. Brenane was really Hearn's grand-aunt; the fact is, he declared that he knew nothing, and no one knew anything true of Hearn's life. Asked why the lad was shipped to him, he replied, ' I do not know—I do not even know whether he was related to my brother-in-law Molyneux or not.' "

From these statements Gould infers that the boy couldn't stop in any school to which he was sent, that he was apparently an unwelcome charge upon his father's Irish relations. Every one, indeed, who had anything to do with him made haste to rid themselves of the obligation.

The friendship with Mr. Watkin, the old English

[1] Messrs. Fisher Unwin.

printer, was destined to last for the term of Hearn's life.

Many of Hearn's friends in America have insinuated that Mr. Watkin exaggerated the strength of the tie that bound him to Lafcadio Hearn; but Hearn's letters to his sister bear out all the statements made in the introduction to the volume entitled *Letters from the Raven*. Even when Hearn succeeded in obtaining occupation elsewhere, he would return to Mr. Watkin's office during leisure hours, either for a talk with his friend, or, if Mr. Watkin was out, for a desultory reading of the books in the " library," the appellation by which the two or three shelves containing Mr. Watkin's heterogeneous collection was dignified. He was of no use in Mr. Watkin's business owing to defective eyesight, but when he returned after his day's work elsewhere, literary, political and religious subjects were discussed and quarrelled over.

As was now and afterwards his custom with his friends, in spite of daily intercourse Hearn kept up a frequent correspondence with Mr. Watkin. This correspondence has been edited and published by Mr. Milton Bronner under the title of *Letters from the Raven*. Edgar Allan Poe had died in 1849, but the influence of his weird and strange genius was still pre-eminent in America. Early in their acquaintance Hearn established the habit of addressing Mr. Watkin as " old man " or " Dad," while on the other hand the boy, in consequence of his sallow complexion, black hair, and admiration for Poe's works, was known as the " Raven." During the long years of their correspondence a drawing of a raven was generally placed in lieu of signature when Lafcadio wrote to Mr. Watkin.

Many of these pen-and-ink sketches interspersed with other illustrations here and there through the letters show considerable talent for drawing, of a fantastic sort, that might have been developed, had Hearn's eyesight permitted, and had he not nourished other ambitions.

Some of the letters are simply short statements left on the table for Mr. Watkin's perusal when he returned home, or a few lines of nonsense scribbled on a bit of paper and pinned on a door of the office.

Often when Hearn was offended by some observation, or a reprimand administered by the older man he would "run away in a huff." Mr. Watkin, who was genuinely attached to the erratic little genius and understood how to deal with him, would simply follow him, tell him not to be a fool, and bring him back again.

In the fourth autobiographical fragment, found amongst Hearn's papers after his death, is one entitled "Intuition." He there alludes to Watkin "as the one countryman he knew in Cincinnati—a man who had preceded him into exile by nearly forty years."

In a glass case at the entrance to a photographer's shop, Hearn had come across the photograph of a face, the first sight of which had left him breathless with wonder and delight. . . . The gaze of the large dark eyes, the aquiline curve of the nose, the mouth firm but fine—made him think of a falcon, in spite of the delicacy of the face. . . . He stood looking at it, and the more he looked, the more the splendid wonder of it seemed to grow like a fascination. But who was she? He dared not ask the owner of the gallery. To his old friend Watkin, therefore, he went and at once proposed a visit to the photographer's. The picture was as much a puzzle to him as to Hearn.

For long years the incident of the photograph passed from Hearn's memory until, in a Southern city hundreds of miles away, he suddenly perceived in a glass case in a druggist's shop, the same photograph.

"Please tell me whose face that is," he asked.

"Is it possible you do not know?" responded the druggist. "Surely you are joking?"

Hearn answered in the negative. Then the man told him—it was that of the great tragedienne Rachel.

Cincinnati is separated from Kentucky by the Ohio. It is there but a narrow river, and the Cincinnati folk were wont to migrate into Kentucky when there were lectures on spiritualism, revivalist meetings, or political haranguings going on. Hearn and his old "Dad" used often to make the journey when the day's work was done.

Hearn was ever fascinated by strange and unorthodox methods of thought. We can imagine him poring over Fourier's "Harmonie Universelle" as well as the strange theories set forth in Esoteric Buddhism with its astral visions and silent voices, even accepting the materialisation of tea-cups and portraits and the transportation of material objects through space.

These were not the only expeditions they made together. When, later, Hearn was on the staff of the *Enquirer* newspaper as night reporter, his "Dad" often accompanied him on his night prowls along the "levee," as the water edge is called on the river towns of the Mississippi valley.

At the time of Hearn's death in 1904 a member of the *Enquirer* staff visited Mr. Henry Watkin who was then living in the "Old Men's Home" (he died

a few months ago), a well-known Institution in Cincinnati where business people of small means spent
their declining years. An account of this visit was
printed in the newspaper on October 2nd. The writer
described the old bureau in Watkin's room with its
many pigeon-holes, holding gems more dear to the old
man than all " the jewels of Tual "—the letters of
Lafcadio Hearn. To it the old gentleman tottered
when the reporter asked for a glimpse of the precious
writings, and as he balanced two packages, yellow with
age, in his hand, he told, in a voice heavy with emotion,
how he first met Hearn accidentally, and how their
friendship ripened day after day and grew into full
fruition with the years.

" I always called him ' The Raven,' " said Watkin,
" because his gloomy views; his morbid thoughts
and his love for the weird and uncanny reminded
me of Poe at his best—or worst, as you might call
it; only, in my opinion, Hearn's was the greater
mind. Sometimes he came to my place when I
was out and then he left a card with the picture
of a raven varied according to his whim, and I
could tell from it the humour he was in when he
sketched it."

Mr. Watkin was then eighty-six years of age, and
dependence can hardly be placed on his memories of
nearly fifty years before. One of his statements that
Hearn had come, in company with a Mr. McDermott,
to see him twenty-four hours after he had been in
Cincinnati cannot be quite accurate, because of Hearn's
own account to his sister of having spent nights in the
streets of Cincinnati, of his various adventures after
his arrival, of his having worked as type-setter and

proof-reader for the Robert Clarke Co., before seeking employment at Mr. Watkin's office.

It was while he was sleeping on the bed of paper shavings behind Mr. Watkin's shop that he acted as private secretary to Thomas Vickers, librarian in the public library at Cincinnati. He mentions Thomas Vickers at various times in his letters to Krehbiel, and refers to rare books on music and copies of classical works to be found at the library.

During all this period, wandering from place to place, endeavouring to find employment of any kind, the boy's underlying ambition was to obtain a position on the staff of one of the large daily newspapers, and thus work his way to a competency that would enable him to devote himself to literary work of his own.

"I believe he would have signed his soul away to the devil," one of his colleagues says, "to get on terms of recognition with either Colonel John Cockerill, then Managing Editor of the Cincinnati *Enquirer*, or Mr. Henderson, the City Editor of the *Commercial*." Though Hearn may not have signed his soul to the devil, he certainly sold his genius to ignoble uses when he wrote his well-known description of the Tan-yard Murder. His ambition however was gratified. A reporter who could thus cater to the public greed for horrors was an asset to the Cincinnati press.

We have an account, given by John Cockerill, twenty years later, of Hearn's first visit to the *Enquirer*:—

"One day there came to the office a quaint, dark-skinned little fellow, strangely diffident, wearing glasses of great magnifying power and bearing with him evidence that Fortune and he were scarce on nodding terms.

"When admitted, in a soft, shrinking voice he asked if I ever paid for outside contributions. I informed him that I was somewhat restricted in the matter of expenditure, but that I would give consideration to what he had to offer. He drew from under his coat a manuscript, and tremblingly laid it upon my table. Then he stole away like a distorted brownie, leaving behind him an impression that was uncanny and indescribable.

"Later in the day I looked over the contribution which he had left. I was astonished to find it charmingly written. . . .

"From that time forward he sat in the corner of my room and wrote special articles for the Sunday Edition as thoroughly excellent as anything that appeared in the magazines of those days. I have known him to have twelve and fifteen columns of this matter in a single issue of the paper. He was delighted to work, and I was pleased to have his work, for his style was beautiful and the tone he imparted to the newspaper was considerable. Hour after hour he would sit at his table, his prominent eyes resting as close to the paper as his nose would permit, scratching away with beaver-like diligence and giving me no more annoyance than a bronze ornament. His eyes troubled him greatly in those days, one was bulbous, and protruded farther than the other. He was as sensitive as a flower. An unkind word from anybody was as serious to him as a cut from a whiplash, but I do not believe he was in any sense resentful. . . . He was poetic, and his whole nature seemed attuned to the beautiful, and he wrote beautifully of things which were neither wholesome nor inspiring. He came to be in time a member of the

City Staff at a fair compensation, and it was then that his descriptive powers developed. He loved to write of things in humble life. He prowled about the dark corners of the city, and from gruesome places he dug out charming idyllic stories. The negro stevedores on the steamboat-landings fascinated him. He wrote of their songs, their imitations, their uncouth ways, and he found picturesqueness in their rags, poetry in their juba dances."

A journalistic feat still remembered in Cincinnati for its daring was Hearn's ascent of the spire of the Cathedral on the back of a famous steeplejack, for the purpose of writing an account of the view of the city from that exalted position.

Mr. Edmund Henderson gives an account of the accomplishment of the performance. Hearn was told of the peril of the thing but he would not listen. Despite his physique he was as courageous as a lion, and there was no assignment of peril that he would not bid for avidly. " Before the climb began the Editor handed him a field glass with the suggestion that he might find it useful. Hearn however quietly handed it back with the remark ' perhaps I had better not take it; something might happen.' Amidst the cheers of the crowd beneath the foolhardy pair accomplished their climb. Hearn came back to the office and wrote two columns describing his sensations, and the wonders of the view he had obtained from the steeple top, though he was so near-sighted he could not have seen five feet beyond the tip of his nose."

Henceforth Hearn accepted the " Night Stations " on the staff of the paper. Amongst the policemen of Cincinnati, who accompanied him in his wanderings, he was a prime favourite, known as "O'Hearn" both to them and to his fellow-reporters.

After hours of exposure, weary and hungry, he might be seen sitting in the deserted newspaper office until the small hours of the morning, under a miserable gas-jet burning like a "mere tooth of flame in its wire muzzle," his nose close to paper and book, working at translations from Theophile Gautier, Gustave Flaubert, and Baudelaire.

Being a Meridional, he said, he felt rather with the Latin race than the Anglo-Saxon, and he hoped with time and study to be able to create something different from the stone-grey and somewhat chilly style of the latter-day English and American romance. Although later he modified considerably his opinion with regard to the moral tendency of their art, he ever retained the same admiration for the artistic completeness and finish of the French Impressionist School; their instinct for the right phrase, their deftness in setting it precisely in the right position, the strength that comes from reserve, and the ease due to vividly-realised themes and objects, all these elements combined conferred a particular charm on their method of expression to a stylist of Hearn's quality.

Not being able to find a publisher for Gautier's *Avatar*, his first translation from the French, he subjected it "to the holy purification of fire." He next attempted a portion of some of Gautier's tales, included under the title of *One of Cleopatra's Nights;* then he undertook the arduous task of translating Flaubert's *La Tentation de Saint Antoine.* "It is astonishing what system will accomplish. If a man cannot spare an hour a day he can certainly spare a half-hour. I translated

La Tentation by this method, never allowing a day to pass without translating a page or two. The work is audacious in parts; but I think nothing ought to be suppressed."

As well attempt, however, to gain a hearing for a free-thinking speech at Exeter Hall as to obtain readers for Gautier's or Flaubert's productions amidst a society nourished on Emerson, Longfellow, and Thoreau! Unorthodox in religious opinion some of the American prophets and poets might be, but rigid and narrow as a company of Puritans in the matter of social morality.

When we know that about this time Bret Harte's *Luck of Roaring Camp* was refused admittance to the pages of a San Francisco magazine as likely to shock the sentiments of its readers and injure the circulation of the periodical in consequence of the morals of the mother of the "Luck," we are not surprised that Hearn's attempt to introduce the American public to the masterpieces of the French Impressionist School was foredoomed to failure. There is a certain naïve, determined defiance of convention in his insistence on gaining admiration both from his friends and the public for productions that were really quite unsuited to general circulation at that time in America. We find him, for instance, recommending the perusal of *Mdlle. de Maupin* to a clergyman of the Established Church and sending a copy of Gautier's poems to Miss Bisland in New Orleans.

" I shall stick," he says, " to my pedestal of faith in literary possibilities like an Egyptian Colossus with a broken nose, seated solemnly in the gloom of my own originality, seeking no reward save the satisfaction of creating something beautiful; but this is worth working for."

It is a noteworthy fact and one that may be mentioned here that, in spite of his extraordinary mastery of the subtleties of the French language, he always spoke French with an atrociously bad accent. "He had a very bad ear," his friend Henry Krehbiel tells us in his article on "Hearn and Folk Music," "organically incapable of humming the simplest tune; he could not even sing the scale, a thing that most people do naturally."

From these Cincinnati days dates Hearn's hatred of the drudgery of journalism, "a really nefarious trade," he declared later; "it dwarfs, stifles and emasculates thought and style. . . . The journalist of to-day is obliged to hold himself in readiness to serve any cause. . . . If he can enrich himself quickly and acquire comparative independence, then, indeed, he is able to utter his heart's sentiments and indulge his tastes. . . ."

Amongst his colleagues on the staff of the *Enquirer* Hearn was not popular. He was looked upon as what Eton boys call a "sap"; his fussiness about punctuation and style soon earned for him the sobriquet of "Old Semi-Colon." This meticulous precision on the subject of punctuation and the value of words remained a passion with him all his life. He used to declare he felt about it as a painter would feel about the painting of his picture. He told his friend Tunison that the word "gray" if spelt "grey" gave him quite a different colour sensation.

We remember his delightful outburst in a letter to Chamberlain, that has been so often quoted. "For me words have colour, form, character: they have faces, ports, manners, gesticulations;—they have moods, humours, eccentricities:—they have tints, tones, personalities," etc., etc.

Though Hearn did not get on with others of the newspaper staff, he formed ties of intimacy with several choice spirits then moving in the best literary circles of Cincinnati and now well known in the literary life of the United States.

Henry Krehbiel, recognised in England and America as an eminent music lecturer and critic, was one of his most intimate friends. Joseph Tunison was another; he afterwards became editor of the *Dayton Journal*, and as well as Krehbiel wrote sympathetically of the little Irishman after his death, expressing indignation at the scurrilous attacks made upon his reputation by several papers in the United States. " He was a wonderfully attractive personality, full of quaint learning, and a certain unworldly wisdom. He had a fashion of dropping his friends one by one; or of letting them drop him, which comes to the same thing; whether indifference or suspicion was at the bottom of this habit it would be hard to say. But he never spoke ill of them afterwards. It was not his way to tell much about himself; and what he did say was let out as if by accident in the course of conversation on other topics. . . . It was impossible to be long in his company without learning that his early years had been years of bitterness. His reminiscences of childhood included not only his dark-haired, dark-eyed mother, but also a beautiful blonde lady, who had somehow turned his happiness to misery."

CHAPTER VII

VAGABONDAGE

" Now for jet black, the smooth, velvety, black skin that remains cold as a lizard under the tropical sun. It seems to me extremely beautiful ! If it is beautiful in art, why should it not be beautiful in nature ? As a matter of fact, it is, and has been so acknowledged, even by the most prejudiced slave-owning races. Either Stanley, or Livingstone perhaps, told the world that after long living in Africa, the sight of white faces produced something like fear (and the evil spirits of Africa are white). . . . You remember the Romans lost their first battles with the North through sheer fear . . . the fairer, the weirder . . . the more terrible. Beauty there is in the North, of its kind. But it is not, surely, comparable with the wonderful beauty of colour in other races." [1]

As to Hearn's more intimate life at this time there are many contradictory accounts. Published facts and the notoriety of legal proceedings, however, are stubborn things, and generally manage to work their way through any deposit of inaccurate scandal or imaginative rumour. At all hazards the truth must be set forth; otherwise how emphasise the redemption of this hapless genius by discipline and self-control out of the depths into which at this time he fell?

The episode in Hearn's life in Cincinnati, with the coloured woman, " Althea Foley," remains one of those obscure psychological mysteries, which, however distasteful, has to be accepted as a component part of his unbalanced mental equipment.

[1] *Life and Letters*, published by Messrs. Houghton, Mifflin & Co

On sifting all available evidence there is no doubt that while doing reporter's work for the *Enquirer* he fell under the "Shadow of the Ethiopian."

In treating of Hearn's vagaries it is well to remember that his brain was abnormal by inheritance, and at this time was still further thrown off its balance by privation, injustice, and unhappiness. All through the course of his life there was failure of straight vision and mental vigour when he was going through a period of difficulty and struggle.

"He may have been a genius in his line," his brother writes to Mrs. Atkinson, referring to Lafcadio, "but genius is akin to madness, and I do really think that dark, passionate Greek mother's blood had a taint in it. For me, instead of nobler aspirations and thoughts, it begat extremes of hate and love—a shrinking and sensitive morbid nature. Whatever of the man I have in me comes from our common father. If I had been as you were, a child of father's second wife, I could have told a different story of my life. . . . It was the Eastern taint in the blood that took Lafcadio to Japan and kept him there. His low vitality and lack of nerve force hampered him in the battle of life, as it has me. If we had the good old Celtic and Saxon blood in us, it would have been better for those dependent on us."

The girl was servant in the cheap boarding-house where he lodged. Hearn, then a struggling almost destitute newspaper writer, used to return from work in the dead of winter in the small hours of the morning. She was a handsome, kind-hearted mulatto girl, who kept his meals warm and allowed him to sit by her fire when wet and chilled. There was much in the circumstances surrounding her to set alight that spark of pity and compassion, one of Hearn's notable qualities. Born a slave near Marysville, Kentucky, about sixty miles from Cincinnati, in 1863 President Lincoln's Proclamation gave her her freedom, and she drifted into the city, a waif, like Hearn himself.

In consequence of hard work and exposure he fell seriously ill. She saved him almost from death, and while nursing him back to health they talked much of her early days and years of slavery.

His quixotic idea of legalising his connection with her surprised no one so much as the girl herself. It completely turned her head; she gave herself airs, became overbearing, quarrelsome, and Hearn found himself obliged to leave Cincinnati to escape from an impossible position.

After his death the woman made a claim upon his estate, and tried to assert her right in the American Courts to the royalties on his books. The *Enquirer* had articles running through several issues in 1906 on the claim of Althea Foley, "who sued to secure Hearn's estate after his death." The Courts decided against her on the ground that the laws of Ohio, in which State they both resided, did not recognise marriage between races. But, the Court added, "there was no doubt he had gone through the ceremony of marriage with the woman Althea Foley, a mulatto, or, as she preferred to call herself, a Creole."

It made Hearn very indignant, later, when some one criticising his work called him a "Decadent." Certainly at this time in Cincinnati it would have been impossible to defend him from the charge. The school of French writers who have been dubbed "Decadents" and who exercised so great an influence on him were infected with a strange partiality for alien races and coloured women. Exotic oddness and strangeness, primitive impulses, as displayed in the quest of strange tongues and admiration of strange people, were a vital part of the Impressionist creed, constituted, indeed, one of the most displeasing manifestations of their unwholesome opinions and fancies. Baudelaire boldly declared his preference for the women of black races. Most of Pierre Loti's earlier novels were but the histories of love affairs with women of "dusky races," either Eastern or Polynesian.

Hearn, as we have said before, was an exemplification of the theory of heredity. The fancy for mulattos, Creoles and Orientals, which he displayed all his life, is most likely to be accounted for as an inheritance from his Arabian and Oriental ancestors on his mother's side. He but took up the dropped threads of his barbaric ancestry.

All his life he preferred to mix in the outer confines of society; the "Levee" at Cincinnati; the lower Creoles and mixed races at New Orleans; fishermen, gardeners, peasants, were chosen by preference as companions in Japan. He railed against civilisation. "The so-called improvements in civilisation have apparently resulted in making it impossible to see, hear, or find anything out. You are improving yourself out of the natural world. I want to get back amongst the monkeys and the parrots, under a violet sky, among green peaks, and an eternally lilac and luke-warm sea —where clothing is superfluous and reading too much of an exertion. . . . Civilisation is a hideous thing. Blessed is savagery! Surely a palm two hundred feet high is a finer thing in the natural order than seventy times seven New Yorks." [1]

Hearn was a born rebel, and every incident of his life hitherto had goaded him into further rebellion against all constituted authority. That a race should be trampled upon by one regarding itself as superior was a state of things that he could not contemplate without a protest, and by his action, he protested in the most emphatic manner possible. He never took into consideration whether it was wise to do so or not. Later, when the turbulent spirit of youth had settled down to accept the discipline of social laws and conventions, he took a very different view of the racial question in the United States and confessed the want of comprehension he had displayed on the subject. Writing years afterwards to a pupil in Japan, he alludes to the unfortunate incident in Cincinnati. He resolved to take the part of some people who were looked down upon in the place where he lived. He thought that those who looked down upon them were morally wrong, so he went over to their side. Then the rest of the people stopped speaking to him, and he hated them. But he was then too young to understand. The trouble was really caused by moral questions far larger than those he had been arguing about.

Hearn was certainly correct in thinking that, from the point of view of the people amongst whom he was living, an attempt to legalise a union with a coloured woman was an unpardonable lapse from social law. Not only then, but for years afterwards public opinion was strongly influenced against him in consequence of this lamentable incident. Even at the time of his death

[1] *Life and Letters of Lafcadio Hearn :* Houghton, Mifflin & Co.

in 1904, a perfect host of statements and distorted legends exaggerating all his lapses from conventional standards were raked up. Amongst other accusations they declared that when in New Orleans he was the favoured admirer of Marie Levaux, known as "The Voodoo Queen."

Page Baker, the editor of the *Times Democrat*, immediately came forward to defend Hearn from the charge. Referring to the Voodoo Queen, the article says: "All this wonderful tale is based upon the fact that Hearn, like every other newspaper man in New Orleans who thought there might be a story in it, entered into communication with a negro woman, who called herself 'Marie Levaux,' and pretended, falsely as was afterwards shown, to know something of the mysteries of Voodooism.

"Whether as reporter, editor, or author, Hearn insisted on investigating for himself what he wrote about; but what the *Sun* states is not only untrue, but would have been impossible in a Southern city like New Orleans, where the colour line is so strictly drawn. If Hearn had been the man the *Sun* says he was, he could not have held the position he did a week, much less the long years he remained in this city. . . . He certainly was not conventional in the order of his life any more than he was in the product of his brain. For this, the man being now dead and silent, the conventional takes the familiar revenge upon him."

In 1875, as far as we can make out, Hearn left the *Enquirer* newspaper, and in the latter part of 1876 was on the staff of the *Commercial*, but he had too seriously wounded the susceptibilities of society in Cincinnati to make existence any longer comfortable, or, indeed, possible. The uncongenial climate also of Ohio did not suit his delicate constitution. He longed to get away.

Dreams had come to him of the strange Franco-Spanish city, the Great South Gate, lying at the mouth of the Mississippi. These dreams were evoked by reading one of Cable's stories. When he first viewed New Orleans from the deck of the steamboat that had carried him from grey north-western mists into the tepid and orange-scented air of the South, his impression of the city, drowsing under the violet and gold of a November morning, were oddly connected with *Jean ah-Poquelin*. Even before he had left the steamboat his imagination had flown beyond the wilderness of cotton bales, the sierra-shaped roofs of the sugar sheds, to wander in search of the old slave-trader's mansion.

A letter to his half-sister, Mrs. Atkinson, effectually disposes of the statement that he left Cincinnati in consequence of any difference of opinion with the editor of the *Commercial*. In fact, money for the journey was given to him as well as a roving commission for letters from Louisiana to be contributed to the columns of the newspaper.

CHAPTER VIII

MEMPHIS

" So I wait for the poet's Pentecost—the inspiration of Nature—the descent of the Tongues of Fire. And I think they will come when the wild skies brighten, and the sun of the Mexican Gulf reappears for his worshippers—with hymns of wind and sea, and the prayers of birds. When one becomes bathed in this azure and gold air—saturated with the perfume of the sea, he can't help writing something. And he cannot help feeling a new sense of being. The Soul of the Sea mingles with his own, is breathed into him : the Spirit that moveth over the deep is the Creator indeed—vivifying, illuminating, strengthening. I really feel his Religion—the sense of awe that comes to one in some great silent temple. You would feel it too under this eternal vault of blue, when the weird old Sea is touching the keys of his mighty organ . . ." [1]

It was in the autumn of 1877 that Lafcadio Hearn, with forty dollars in his pocket and a head full of dreams, started for Memphis on his way to New Orleans. Mr. Halstead and Mr. Edward Henderson, editors of the *Commercial*, and his old friend, Mr. Watkin, were at the little Miami Depot to bid him God speed.

Memphis is situated at the confluence of the Mississippi and Ohio rivers. Hearn had to await the steamboat there on its return journey from New Orleans. In those days punctuality was not rigidly enforced, and very often the arrival of the steamer necessitated a wait of several days at Memphis. The only person with whom Hearn kept up communication in the Northern

[1] Letter to Dr. Matas in Dr. Gould's book, *Concerning Lafcadio Hearn*, published by Messrs. Fisher Unwin.

city he had left was Henry Watkin. Hieroglyphs of ravens, tombstones, and crescent moons illustrate the text. It is in moments of loneliness and depression, such as these days at Memphis, that the real Hearn shows himself. He becomes now and then almost defiantly frank in his self-revelations and confessions.

On October 28 he dispatched a card bearing two drawings of a raven; "In a dilemma at Memphis" was the inscription under a raven scratching its head with a claw. The other is merely labelled "Remorseful." His finances had, apparently, run out, and in spite of paying two dollars a day for his accommodation, he, according to his own account, had to lodge in a tumble-down, dirty, poverty-stricken hotel.

I have already referred to Hearn's choice of the name of "Ozias Midwinter," as signature to his series of letters contributed at this time to the *Commercial*. These letters, his first professional work, except "The Tanyard Murder" and "The Ascent of the Spire of St. Peters," rescued from destruction, show how long hours of unflagging industry spent on achieving a finished style were at last to bear fruit, giving them that extraordinary variety, ease, and picturesqueness which, combined with originality of thought and keenness of judgment, placed him ultimately in the forefront of the writers of the day.

A postcard, written to Mr. Watkin on November 15, 1877, enabled the identification in the files of the *Commercial* of these "Midwinter" letters.

He approached the Memphis of the Mississippi, he said, dreaming of the Memphis of the Nile, and found but tenantless warehouses with shattered windows, poverty-stricken hotels vainly striving to keep up appearances. . . . The city's life, he said, seemed to have contracted about its heart, leaving the greater portion of its body paralysed. It gave him the impression of a place that had been stricken by some great misfortune beyond the hope of recovery. When rain and white fogs came, the melancholy of Memphis became absolutely Stygian; all things wooden uttered strange groans and crackling sounds; all things of stone or of stucco sweated as if in the agony of dissolution, and beyond the cloudy brow of the bluffs the Mississippi flowed a Styx flood, with pale mists lingering like shades upon its banks.

" Elagabalus, wishing to obtain some idea of the vastness of Imperial Rome, ordered all the cobwebs in the city to be collected together and heaped before him. Estimated by such a method, the size of Memphis would appear vast enough to astonish even Elagabalus."

Of Forrest, the great Confederate leader, whose funeral took place at Memphis while Hearn was there, he gives a vivid description. " Rough, rugged, desperate, uncultured. His character fitted him rather for the life of the borderer and the planter. He was by nature a typical pioneer—one of those fierce and terrible men who form in themselves a kind of protecting fringe to the borders of white civilisation."

Then comes a typical paragraph : " The night they buried him, there came a storm. . . . From the same room whence I had watched the funeral, I saw the Northern mists crossing the Mississippi into Arkansas like an invading army; then came grey rain, and at last a fierce wind, making wild charges through it all. Somehow or other the queer fancy came to me that the dead Confederate cavalrymen, rejoined by their desperate leader, were fighting ghostly battles with the men who died for the Union."

To Mr. Watkin he wrote describing his big, dreary hotel room overlooking the Mississippi whence he could hear the panting and puffing of the cotton boats and the deep calls of the river traffic, but of the *Thompson Dean* there was not a sign to be seen or heard. In every corner between the banisters of the old stairway spiders were busy spinning their dusty tapestries, and when he walked over the floors at night they creaked and groaned as if something or somebody was following him in the dark.

It was, he declared, a lonely sensation, that of finding yourself alone in a strange city. He felt inclined to cry during the solitary hours of the night, as he used to do when a college boy returned from vacation. . . . "I suppose," he adds, "you are beginning to think I am writing quite often. I suppose I am, and you know the reason why; and perhaps you are thinking to yourself, 'He feels lonely, and is accordingly affectionate, but by and by he will forget.' Well, I suppose you are right." By and by, when he was less lonely, he said, he would write perhaps only by weeks, or perhaps by months, or perhaps, again, only by years—until the times and places of old friendships were forgotten and old faces had become dim as dreams.

At last the New Orleans steamer, the *Thompson Dean*, arrived, and Hearn floated off on board into the current of the mighty river, and also, inspired by the enchantment of his surroundings, into the flood-tide of his genius. A letter contributed to the *Commercial*, describing the "Fair Paradise of the South," the great sugar country, in which he now found himself, shows how he was gaining in the manipulation of his material, also gaining in the power of appreciating the splendour of the vision, the inmost ultimate secret Nature ever reveals to those who can comprehend and decipher it.

As the little half-blind genius sat on the cotton bales on the deck of the *Thompson Dean* those autumn days, peering forth one moment, the next with nose close to the paper, his pen scratching rapidly, describing the marvellous pictures, setting down the impressions that slipped by on either hand, all the joy of an imprisoned tumultuous soul set free, mentally and morally free, must have come to him. It breathes in every line, in every paragraph of his work. And not only was this passionate joy his, but also the exhilarating assurance of knowing that by self-denial, industry and the determination to succeed he had achieved and perfected the power to describe and expound the marvellous pageant to others. From the horizon widening in front of him, through the " Great South Gate," from " The Gulf " and the Tropics, from Martinique and Florida came the health-giving breeze, carrying on its wings courage, regeneration, and the promise of future recognition and fame.

Many were his backslidings, even to the extent of meditating suicide during the first years of his sojourn in New Orleans, but never did he fall so morally low as at Cincinnati. That life of sordidness and ignominy was left behind, the unclean spirit exorcised and cast forth! He had made his body a house of shame, but that very shame had set throbbing subtle, infinite vibrations, a spiritual resonance and response to higher endeavour and hope. He knew himself to be a man again, sane, clear-brained, his deep appreciation of beauty able to rise on the heights of the music of utterance as he poured forth the delight of his soul.

Surely some light from the Louisiana sun must have flashed from the page athwart the gloom of the dusty office of the *Commercial;* some magic, bewitching the senses of the practical, hard-headed editor, inducing him to offer the piece of poetic prose contributed by his " Ozias Midwinter " correspondent, describing a Louisiana sunrise, to the ordinary reading public of a Cincinnati daily newspaper.

CHAPTER IX

NEW ORLEANS

" The infinite gulf of blue above seems a shoreless sea, whose foam is stars, a myriad million lights are throbbing and flickering and palpitating, a vast stillness filled with perfume prevails over the land,— made only more impressive by the voices of the night-birds and crickets ; and all the busy voices of business are dead. The boats are laid up, cotton presses closed, and the city is half empty. So that the time is really inspiring. But I must wait to record the inspiration in some more energetic climate."

It is by Hearn's letters to Mr. Watkin that we are able to follow his more intimate feelings and mode of life at this period of his career. He was at first extravagantly enthusiastic about the quaint beauty and novelty of his surroundings, the luxuriant vegetation, the warmth of the climate, the charm of the Creole population of the older portion of the city. The wealth of a world, unworked gold in the ore, he declared, was to be found in this half-ruined Southern Paradise; in spite of her pitiful decay it still was an enchanting city. This rose-coloured view of New Orleans was soon dissipated by pressing financial anxiety.

He had been visiting his uncle, he wrote, and was on the verge of beggary. It was possible, however, to live on fish and vegetables for twenty cents a day. Not long after, we find him begging his old Dad to sell all his books, " except the French ones," and send him the proceeds, as he was in a state of desperation with no friend to help him. The need of money, indeed, so cramped and hindered his movements that he was un-able any longer to get material for the " copy " of his newspaper correspondence.

Want of money seems also to have necessitated frequent change of residence. His first card is written from 228 Baronne Street, care of Mrs. Bustellos. In the left-hand corner is the drawing of a raven sitting disconsolate beside a door. Shortly afterwards he describes himself as living in an old house with dove-cot-shaped windows shadowed with creeping plants, where we have a picture of him sitting close to the fire, smoking his pipe of " terre Gambièse," conjuring up fancies of palm-trees and humming-birds, and per-fume-laden winds, while a " voice from the far tropics called to him across the darkness."

It is easy with our knowledge of Hearn to imagine how the money he started with in his pocket from Cincinnati melted away during his sojourn at Memphis, his journey down the Mississippi, and two or three days spent amidst the attractions of the curio shops and restaurants of the Crescent City. Gould mentions indignantly Hearn's "intolerable and brutalising im-providence." Without using language quite so intem-perate, it must be acknowledged that he had a most irritating incapacity for mastering the ignoble neces-sity for making expenditure tally with revenue. The editor of the *Commercial*, being accustomed to deal with the ordinary American journalist to whom forty dollars was as a fortune, did not reckon apparently with Hearn's Celtic recklessness in the matter of ways and means.

Seven months later, he declared that he hadn't made seven cents by his literary work in New Orleans. His books and clothes were all gone, his shirt was sticking through the seat of his pants, and he could only enjoy a five-cent meal once every two days. At last he hadn't even a penny to buy stamps to mail his letters, and still the *Commercial* hadn't sent him any supplies. Mr. Watkin's means did not admit of his helping the woebegone " raven." He was also prevented by business affairs from sending a reply for some weeks.

His silence elicited another post-card, a tombstone this time, surmounted by a crescent moon, with a dishevelled-looking raven perched close by.

" I dream of old, ugly things," Hearn writes years later from Japan, when referring to the possibility of his son being subjected to the poverty and suffering he had experienced himself. " I am alone in an American city; and I've only ten cents in my pocket— and to send off a letter that I must send will take three cents. That leaves me seven cents for the day's food. . . . The horror of being without employ in an American city appals me—because I remember."

The Hermes of Æschylus ventured the opinion, as an impartial observer of events, that adversity was no doubt salutary for Prometheus. The same might be said of most of those touched with Promethean fire. Not only does privation and struggle keep the spark alight, but often blows it into a flame. In spite of hunger and straitened means, Hearn was absorbing impressions on every hand. New Orleans in the seventies and eighties of last century, presented conditions for the nourishing and expanding of such a genius as his, that were most likely unattainable in any other city in the world.

From an article written by him, entitled " The Scenes of Cable's Romances," that appeared at this time in the

Century Magazine, we can conjure up this strange city rising out of the water like a dream, its multi-coloured dilapidated Franco-Spanish houses, with their eccentric façades and quaint shop-signs and names. We can see the Rue Royale, its picturesqueness almost unadulterated by innovation, its gables, eaves, dormers, projecting balconies or verandahs, over-topping or jutting out of houses of every imaginable tint; each window adorned with sap-green batten shutters, and balustraded with Arabesque work in wrought iron, framing some monogram of which the meaning is forgotten. We can imagine the little genius wandering along such a street, watching the Indians as they passed in coloured blankets, Mexicans in leather gaiters, negresses decked out in green and yellow ban-danas, planters in white flannels, American business men in broadcloth and straw hats—sauntering backwards and forwards beneath the quaint arcades, balconies and coloured awnings.

We picture the Savannahs and half-submerged cypress-groves on the river bank, the green and crimson sunsets, the star-lit dusks, the sound of the mighty current of the Mississippi as it slipped by under the shadow of willow-planted jungle and rustling orange-groves towards Barataria and the Gulf.

He describes a planter's house, an "antique vision," relic of the feudal splendours of the great cotton and sugar country, endeavouring to hide its ruin amidst overgrown gardens and neglected groves, oak-groves left untouched only because their French Creole owners, though ruined, refused to allow Yankee interlopers to cart them to the sawmill, or to allow them to be sent away to the cities up north.

We follow him as, in his near-sighted, observant way he wandered through the city, listening to the medley of strange tongues peculiar to the great Southern port; observing the Chinese in the fruit-market, yellow as bananas, the quadroons with skins like dead gold, swarthy sailors from the Mediterranean coasts and the Levant—from Sicily and Cyprus, Corsica and Malta, the Ionian Archipelago, and a hundred cities fringing the coasts of Southern Europe, wanderers who have wandered all over the face of the earth, sailors who have sailed all seas, sunned themselves at a hundred tropical ports, casting anchor at last by the Levee of New Orleans, under a sky as divinely blue, in a climate as sunny and warm as their own beloved sea. Amongst them all he was able, he imagined, to distinguish some on whose faces lay a shadow of the beauty of the Antique World—one, in particular, from Zante, first a sailor, then a vendor; some day, perhaps, a merchant. Hearn immediately purchased some of his oranges, a dozen at six cents.

From the market he made his way to the Spanish Cathedral, founded by the representation of His Most Catholic Majesty, Don Andre Alminaster, where plebeian feet were blotting out the escutcheons of the knights of the ancient régime, and the knees of worshippers obliterating their memory from the carven stone.

Side by side with him you find your way to the Cotton Landing of the Levee, thence watch the cotton presses with monstrous heads of living iron and brass, fifty feet high from their junction with the ground, with their mouths five feet wide, opening six feet from the mastodon teeth in the lower jaw, "the more I looked at the thing," he says, "the more I felt as though its prodigious anatomy had been studied after the anatomy of some extinct animal,—the way those jaws worked, the manner in which those muscles moved. Men rolled a cotton bale to the mouth of the monster. The jaws opened with a loud roar, and so remained. The lower jaw had descended to the level with the platform on which the bale was lying. It was an immense plantation bale. Two black men rolled it into the yawning mouth. The Titan muscles contracted, and the jaws closed silently, steadily, swiftly. The bale flattened, flattened, flattened down to sixteen inches, twelve inches, eight inches, five inches,—positively less than five inches! I thought it was going to disappear altogether. But after crushing it beyond five inches the jaw remained stationary and the monster growled like rumbling thunder. I thought the machine began to look as hideous as one of those horrible yawning heads which formed the gates of the Teocallis at Palenque, through whose awful jaws the sacrificed victims passed."

The romance that hung over the French colony of New Orleans appealed to Hearn's love of the picturesque. The small minority, obliged to submit to the rules and laws of the United States, but animated by a feeling of futile rebellion against their rulers, still remaining devoted to their country that had sold them for expediency.

With the sympathy of his Celtic nature he entered into the misery of those who had once been opulent. The princely misery that never doffed its smiling mask, though living in secret from week to week on bread and orange-leaf tea. The misery that affected condescension in accepting an invitation to dine, staring at the face of a watch (refused by the *mont de piété*) with eyes half-blinded by starvation; the pretty misery, young, brave, sweet, asking for "a treat" of cakes too jocosely to have its asking answered, laughing and coquetting with its well-fed wooers, and crying for hunger after they were gone.

Here for the first time since the France of his youthful days, Hearn mixed with Latins, seldom hearing the English tongue.

During this time, while he was loafing and dreaming, he at various intervals contributed letters to the *Commercial*. Now that his genius has become acknowledged, these "Ozias Midwinter" letters, written in the autumn and winter of 1877 and 1878, are appreciated at their just value; but it would be absurd to say that from the accepted signification of the word they come under the head of satisfactory newspaper reporting. The American public wanted a clear and dispassionate view of political affairs in the State of Louisiana, and how they were likely to affect trade in the State of Ohio.

We can imagine an honest Cincinnati citizen puzzling over the following, and wondering what in all creation the "Louisianny" correspondent meant by giving him such rubbish to digest with his morning's breakfast : —

"I think there is some true poetry in these allusions to the snake. Is not the serpent a symbol of grace? Is not the so-called 'line of beauty' serpentine? And is there not something of the serpent in the beauty of all graceful women? something of undulating shapeliness, something of silent fascination? something of Lilith and Lamia?"

In April 1878, apparently in response to a demand for news more suited to the exigencies of a daily Northern newspaper, came two letters on political questions, written in so biassed and half-hearted a fashion that it was not surprising to see the next letter from New Orleans signed by another name. So the little man lost his opportunity, an opportunity such as is given to few journalists, situated as he was, of earning a competency and achieving a literary position. He himself acknowledged that his own incompatibility of temper and will were to be credited with most of the adverse circumstances which beset him so frequently during the course of his life. A little yielding on his part was all that was necessary at this time to enable him to keep his head above water until regular work came his way.

Not long after this catastrophe Hearn attained his twenty-eighth birthday. Alluding to this fact, he says that, looking back to the file of his twenty-eight years he realised an alarming similarity of misery in each of them, ill-success in every aim, an inability to make headway by individual force against unforeseen and unexpected disappointments. Indeed, sometimes, when success seemed certain, it was upset by some unanticipated obstacle, generally proceeding from his own waywardness and unpractical nature; some loss of temper, impatience, which instead of being restrained and concealed was shown with stupid frankness, might be credited with a large majority of failures. All this he confessed in one of his characteristic letters addressed to Mr. Watkin about this time. He then recounts the sufferings he had been through, how he found it impossible to make ten dollars a month when twenty was

a necessity for comfortable living. He had been
cheated, he said, and swindled considerably, and had
cheated and swindled others in retaliation. Then he
damns New Orleans and its inhabitants, as later he
damned Japan and the Japanese. But the real fact was
that with that gipsy-like nature of his he loved wandering and change of scene; he disliked the monotony of
staying beyond a certain time in the same place. "My
heart always feels like a bird, fluttering impatiently for
the migrating season. I think I could be quite happy
if I were a swallow and could have a summer nest in
the ear of an Egyptian Colossus, or a broken capital of
the Parthenon."

About this time an epidemic of yellow fever swept
over the city, desolating the population. Hearn did
not fall a victim, but underwent a severe attack of
" Dengue " fever.

" I got hideously sick, and then well again," he writes
to Mrs. Atkinson. It killed nearly seven thousand
people. He describes the pest-stricken city, with its
heat motionless and ponderous. The steel-blue of the
sky bleached from the furnace circle of the horizon;
the slow-running river, its current yellow as a flood of
fluid wax, the air suffocating with vapour; and the
luminous city filled with a faint, sickly odour—a stale
smell as of dead leaves suddenly disinterred from wet
mould, and each day the terror-stricken population
offering its sacrifice to Death, the faces of the dead
yellow as flame! On door-posts, telegraph-poles, pillars
of verandahs, lamps over Government letter-boxes, glim-
mered the white enunciations of death. All the city
was spotted with them. And lime was poured into the
gutters, and huge purifying fires kindled after sunset.

After his attack of fever, unable to regain his strength owing to insufficient food and the unhealthiness of the part of the city where he had elected to live, Hearn's eyesight became affected.

"I went stone blind, had to be helped to a doctor's office—no money, no friends. My best friend was a revolver kept to use in case the doctor failed," he tells his sister.

In *Chita*, which, as we have said, is only a bundle of reminiscences, he refers to the suicide of a Spaniard, Ramirez. From his tomb a sinister voice seemed to say, " Go thou and do likewise! " . . . Then began within that man the ghostly struggle between courage and despair, between darkness and light, which all sensitive natures must wage in their own souls at least once in their lives. The suicide is not a coward, he is an egotist; as he struggled with his own worst self something of the deeper and nobler comprehension of human weakness and human suffering was revealed to him. He flung the lattice shutters apart and looked out. How sweet the morning, how well life seemed worth living, as the sunlight fell through the frost haze outside, lighting up the quaint and chequered street and fading away through faint bluish tints into transparent purples. Verily it is the sun that gladdeneth the infinite world.

CHAPTER X

WIDER HORIZONS

" There are no more mysteries—except what are called hearts, those points at which individuals rarely touch each other, only to feel as sudden a thrill of surprise as at meeting a ghost, and then to wonder in vain, for the rest of life, what lies out of soul-sight." [1]

THE doctor Hearn alludes to in his letter to his sister was Rudolf Matas, a Spaniard, now an eminent physician and a very important person in New Orleans. He did not fail the little man who was brought almost stone blind to his consulting-room that winter of 1876. In six months his eyes were comparatively well, and he was able to return to regular literary work.

Matas always remained Hearn's firm partisan, and was an enthusiastic admirer of his genius; Hearn seems to have reciprocated his affection, and years afterwards addressed some of his most interesting letters from Martinique to "his dear brother and friend Rudolfo Matas." By him he is said to have been told the incidents in the story of *Chita*, and to him the book was dedicated.

After the yellow fever had passed away " there were plenty of vacancies waiting to be filled," Hearn significantly tells his sister. . . .

A daily newspaper called the *Item* was at that time issued in New Orleans. A great deal of clipping and

<hr />

[1] *Life and Letters :* Houghton, Mifflin & Co.

paste-pot went to its production, " items " taken from European and American sources filling most of its columns. Hearn described it as a poor little sheet going no farther north than St. Louis.

He was offered the assistant-editorship; the leisure that he found for literary pursuits on his own account more than compensated for the smallness of the salary. He hoped now to be able to scribble as much as he liked, and to have an opportunity for reading, with a view to more consecutive and concentrated work than mere contributions to daily and weekly newspapers. He also had many opportunities, he said, for mixing with strange characters invaluable as literary material—Creoles, Spaniards, Mexicans—all that curious, heterogeneous society peculiar to New Orleans.

If in Cincinnati to mix with coloured folk was deemed sufficient to place yourself under the ban of decent society, it was ten times more so in New Orleans; but Lafcadio Hearn, Bohemian and rebel, took the keenest pleasure in outraging public opinion, and challenging scandalous tongues, breaking out of bounds whenever the spirit prompted, and throwing in his lot with people who were looked upon as pariahs and outcasts from the world of so-called respectability.

At one time he took up his abode in a ruined house, under the same roof as a Creole fortune-teller. He describes her room with its darkened windows, skulls and crossbones, and lamp lit in front of a mysterious shrine. This was quite sufficient to associate his name with hers, and many were the unfounded rumours—Nemesis of the unfortunate episode with Althea Foley at Cincinnati—which floated northwards regarding the manner of his life.

Some members of a Brahminical Society visited New Orleans about this time. Needless to say that Hearn immediately foregathered with them, and in leisure hours took to studying the theories of the East, the poetry of ancient India, the teachings of the wise concerning " absorption and emotion, the illusions of existence, and happiness as the equivalent of annihilation," maintaining that Buddhism was wiser than the wisest of Occidental faiths. He astonished the readers of the *Item* by weird and mystical articles on the subject of the Orient and Oriental creeds, considerably increasing the sale of the little paper, and drawing attention, amongst cultured circles in New Orleans, to his own genius.

The routine of his life at this time is given in letters written to his " old Dad " and his friend Krehbiel.

The same ascetic scorn for material comfort, heritage of his Oriental ancestry, seems to have distinguished him at this period in New Orleans, as later in Japan. The early cup of coffee, the morning's work at the office," concocting devilment " for the *Item*, his Spanish lessons with José de Jesus y Preciado, the " peripatetic blasphemy," as he named him afterwards, dinner at a Chinese restaurant for an infinitesimal sum, an hour or two spent at second-hand book-stalls, and home to bed. There is, I am told, an individual, Armand Hawkins by name, owner of an ancient book-store at New Orleans, still alive, who remembers the curious little genius, with his prominent eyes, wonderful knowledge on all sorts of out-of-the-way subjects recounted in a soft, musical voice, who used to come almost daily to visit his book-store. He it was who enabled Hearn to get together the library about which there has been so much discussion since his death. Next to his love of buying old books, Hearn's great indulgence seems to have been smoking, not cigars, but pipes of every make and description.

The glimpses we get of him from his own letters and from reminiscences collected from various people in New Orleans all give the same impression. A Bohemian love of vagabondage, picking up impressions here and there, some of which were set down in pencil, some in ink; as far as his eyesight would permit, many were the sketches made at this time. None of them have been preserved, except the very clever Mephistophelian one sent to Mr. Watkin and reproduced in the volume entitled *Letters from the Raven*. "He was a gifted creature," says a lady who knew him at this time. "He came fluttering in and out of our house like a shy moth, and was adored by my children."

He had no ambitions, no loves, no anxieties, sometimes a vague unrest without a motive, sometimes a feeling as if his heart were winged and trying to soar; sometimes a half-crazy passion for a great night with wine and women and music; but the wandering passion was strongest of all, and he felt no inclination to avail himself of the only anchor which keeps the ship of a man's life in port. . . . Nights were so liquid with tropic moonlight, days so splendid with green and gold, summer so languid with perfume and warmth, that he hardly knew whether he was dreaming or awake.

In 1881 Hearn succeeded in becoming a member of the staff of the leading New Orleans paper, the *Times Democrat*, "the largest paper," he tells his sister, "in the Southern States." He now seemed to have entered on a halcyon period of life. Congenial society, romantic and interesting surroundings. Penetrated with enthusiasm for the modern French literary school as he was, he here met intellects and temperaments akin to his own. Now he was enabled to get his translations from Gautier and Baudelaire printed, and read for the first time by an appreciative public. "Everybody was kind," he tells his sister; "I became well and strong, lived steadily, spent my salary on books. I was thus able to make up for my deficiencies of education. . . . I had only a few hours of work each day;—plenty of time to study. I wrote novels and other books which literary circles approved of."

With Page Baker, the owner and editor-in-chief of the *Times Democrat*, he formed a salutary and enduring friendship. The very difference in character between the two seems to have made the bond all the more enduring. Page Baker was a man of great business capacity, and at the same time keen discrimination in literary affairs. From the first he conceived the highest opinion of Hearn's literary ability. However fantastic or out-of-the-way his contributions to the columns of the *Times Democrat*, they were always inserted without elision. Years afterwards, writing to him from Japan, Hearn declares, in answer to a panegyric written by Page Baker on some of his Japanese books, that the most delightful criticisms he ever had were Page Baker's own readings aloud of his vagaries in the "T. D." office, after the proofs came down, just fresh from the composition room, with the wet, sharp, inky smell still on the paper. Baker, apparently, in 1893 sent him substantial help, and Hearn writes thanking him from the bottom of his much-scarified heart. Often amidst the cramped, austere conditions of his existence in Japan, he recalled these days of communion with congenial spirits at New Orleans, and work with his colleagues at the *Times Democrat* office. "Ghosts! After getting your letter last night I dreamed. Do you remember that splendid Creole who used to be your city editor—John——?—is it not a sin that I have forgotten his name? He sat in a big chair in the old office, and told me wonderful things, which I could not recall on waking."

In a letter dated July 7, 1882, Hearn tells Mr. Watkin that he had entered into an arrangement with Worthington, the publisher, for the issuing of his translation of Gautier's stories made at Cincinnati. It was to cost him one hundred and fifty dollars, but there was an understanding that this money was to be repaid by royalties on the sale of the book and any extra profits. He announced his intention of going north in a few months by way of Cincinnati, as he wished to see Worthington about his new publication. Though he was making, he said, the respectable wage of thirty dollars a week for five hours' work a day, he felt enervated by the climate, incapable of any long stretch of work, and thought change to a northern climate for a bit might stimulate his intellectual powers. He then touched on the changes that passing years had wrought in his outlook on life. "Less despondent, but less hopeful; wiser a little and more silent; less nervous, but less merry; . . . not strictly economical, but coming to it steadily." His horizons were widening, the accomplishment of a fixed purpose in life was really the only pleasurable experience, and the grasp of a friendly hand the only real satisfaction of an existence that wisdom declared a delusion and a snare.

Hearn at times indulged in exaggerated fits of economy, the one thought that animated him being the idea of freeing himself from the yoke of dependence on the whims of employers—from the harness of journalism. He made up his mind to keep house for himself, so hired a room in the northern end of the French quarter, and purchased a complete set of cooking utensils and kitchen ware. He succeeded in reducing his expenses to two dollars a week, and kept them at that (exclusive of rent), although his salary rose to thirty dollars a week. Having saved a respectable sum, he formed the fantastical idea of trying to keep a restaurant, run on the lines of the cheap Spanish and Chinese restaurants he had been wont to frequent. "Business—ye Antiquities"; hard, practical business! he told Krehbiel; honourable, respectable business, but devoid of dreamful illusions. "Alas, this is no world for dreaming."

The venture ended as might have been expected. Hearn had not inherited the commercial instincts of his ancestors who sold oil and wine in the Ionian islands; his partner robbed him of all the money he had invested, and decamped, leaving him saddled with the restaurant and a considerable number of debts. A swindling building society seems to have absorbed the rest of his savings.

After these two catastrophes the little man became almost comically terrified at financial enterprise of any kind, even the investment of money in dividend-paying concerns. When Captain Mitchell McDonald later, in Japan, endeavoured to induce him to put his money into various lucrative concerns, Hearn declared that he would prefer to lose everything he owned than submit to the worry of investing it. The mere idea of business was "a horror, a nightmare, a torture unspeakable."

Though apparently only journalising and translating, Hearn was piling up experiences and sensations, not making use of them except in letters, but laying down the concrete and setting the foundation for his work in the West Indies and Japan. "The days come and go like muffled and veiled figures sent from a friendly, distant party; but they say nothing, and if we do not use the gifts they bring, they carry them silently away." Emerson did not take into account those apparently infertile periods in an artist's life, when the days come and go, but though they pass silently away, all their gifts are not unused, nor is their passage unproductive. How invaluable, for instance, was Hearn's study of Creole proverbs for his *Two Years in the French West Indies*. How invaluable for his interpretation of the Orient were the studies he undertook for *Strange Leaves from Strange Literature*, and his six small adaptations entitled *Chinese Ghosts*.

After several refusals *Stray Leaves* was accepted for publication by Osgood. He thus announced the fact to his friend Krehbiel :—

"DEAR K. (Private),

"*Stray Leaves*, etc., have been accepted by James R. Osgood and Co. Congratulate your little Dreamer of Monstrous Dreams,

"Aschadnan na Mahomet Rasoul Allah,

"Bismillah,

"Allah-hu-akbar."

The book was dedicated to " Page M. Baker, Editor of the New Orleans *Times Democrat*."

This series of small sketches is typical of the clarity of language and purity of thought that invariably distinguish Hearn's work; but it lacks the realism, the keenness of *choses vues*, so characteristic of his Japanese sketches. There is none of the haunting, moving tragedy and ghostliness, the spiritual imagination and introspection of *Kokoro* or the *Exotics*. Though polished and scholarly, showing refinement in the use of words, the interest is remote and visionary, permeated here and there also with a certain amount of Celtic sentimentality, a "Tommy Moore" flavour, somewhat too saccharine in quality. The one, for instance, called *Boutimar* treats of a very hackneyed subject, the offering of the water of youth, and life without end, to Solomon, and the sage's refusal, because of the remembrance suggested by Boutimar that he would outlive children, friends and all whom he loved; therefore " Solomon, without reply, silently put out his arm and gave back the cup. . . . But upon the prophet-king's rich beard, besprinkled with powder of gold, there appeared another glitter as of clear dew,—the diamond dew of the heart, which is tears."

Chinese Ghosts, though distinguished also by that *soigneux* flavour that gives a slightly artificial impression, holds far more the distinctive flavour of Hearn's genius. His own soul is written into the legend of " Pu the potter." " Convinced that a soul cannot be divided, Pu entered the flame, and yielded up his ghost in the embrace of the Spirit of the Furnace, giving his life for the life of his work,—his soul for the soul of his Vase."

By the publication of the *Letters from the Raven*
we are enabled to push those to Krehbiel, published by
Miss Bisland, into place, and assign fairly accurate
dates to each of them. He tells Mr. Watkin that he
was six months before finding a fixed residence. In
August 1878, he writes inviting him to come in the
autumn to pay him a visit, and telling him of delightful
rooms with five large windows opening on piazzas,
shaded by banana-trees. This apparently is the house
in St. Louis Street, which he describes to Krehbiel.
Miss Bisland places it almost at the beginning of the
series, but it must have been written at a considerably
later period. How picturesque and vivid is his description! With the magic of his pen he conjures up the
huge archway, with its rolling echoes, the courtyard
surrounded by palm-trees, their dry leaves rustling in
the wind, the broad stairway guarded by a hoary dog,
his own sitting-room and study, "vast enough for a
carnival ball," with its five windows and glass doors
opening flush with the floor and rising to the ceiling.

Gautier, the artist to whom at one time Hearn pinned
his faith, is said to have observed once to an admirer
of his art : "I am only a man to whom the visible world
is visible." So Lafcadio Hearn, though gifted with
only half the eyesight of ordinary folk, was by the
prescience of his genius enabled to see not only the
visible world that the Frenchman saw, but an immaterial
and spiritual world as well.

CHAPTER XI

LETTERS AND PERSONAL CHARACTERISTICS

" Writing to you as a friend, I write of my thoughts and fancies, of my wishes and disappointments, of my frailties and follies and failures and successes,—even as I would write to a brother. So that sometimes what might not seem strange in words, appears very strange upon paper."

LAFCADIO HEARN'S thoughts, aspirations and mode of life are revealed with almost daily minuteness during this period at New Orleans,—indeed for the rest of his life, by his interchange of letters with various friends. Those contained in the three volumes published by Miss Bisland (Mrs. Wetmore) are now indisputably placed in the first rank amongst the many series from eminent people that have been given to the world during the last half-century. It is apparent in every line that no idea of publicity actuated the writing of his out-pourings; indeed, we imagine that nothing would have surprised Hearn more than the manner in which his letters have been discussed, quoted, criticised. They are simply the outcome of an impulse to unburden an extraordinarily imaginative and versatile brain of its cargo of opinions, views, prejudices, beliefs; to pour, as it were, into the listening ear of an intelligent and sympathetic friend the confessions of his own intellectual struggles, his doubts and despairs. Shy, reserved, oppressed in social daily intercourse by a sense of physical disabilities, with a pen in hand and a sheet of paper in front of him, he cast off all disquieting considerations and allowed the spiritual structure of emotion and thought to show itself in the nakedness of its humanity.

To most authors letter-writing is an unwelcome task. "Ask a carpenter to plane planks just for fun," as Hearn quotes from Gautier; but to him it was a relaxation from his daily task of journalism and literary work. Dr. Gould says that while stopping in his house at Philadelphia, Hearn would sometimes break off suddenly in the midst of a discussion, especially if he were afraid of losing his temper, and retire to his own room, where he would fill sheets of the yellow paper, which he habitually used, with theories and reasons for and against his argument; these he would leave later on Gould's study table.

To his literary brother Krehbiel he discourses, as if they were face to face, of artistic endeavour and the larger life of the intellect. In his "jeremiads" to Mr. Watkin he reveals his most intimate feelings and sufferings; the routine of his daily work is told hour by hour. Perpetually standing outside himself, as it were, he studies his nature, inclinations, habits, and yet never gives you the impression of being egotistical. His attitude is rather that of a scientist studying an odd specimen. The intellectual isolation of his latter years, passed amongst an alien race with alien views and beliefs, seems to have created a necessity for converse with those of his own race and mode of thought; his correspondence with Chamberlain reflects all his perturbations of spirit—perturbations that he dared not confide to those surrounding him—a record of illusion and disillusion with regard to his adopted country. The Japanese letters, therefore, above all, have the charm of temperament, the very essence of the man, recorded in a style of remarkable picturesqueness and reality.

The series of letters to Mrs. Atkinson, of which I have been given possession for use in this sketch of Hearn's life, have an entirely different signification to those already referred to. Unfortunately I am not permitted to give them in their entirety, as Hearn in his usual petulant, reckless fashion refers to family incidents, and speaks of relations in a manner which it would be impossible to publish to the world.

Many of the most characteristic passages have necessarily therefore been omitted; in spite of this there are many portions intensely interesting as a revelation of a side of his character not hitherto shown to the public. Pathetic recurrences to childish memories, incidents of his boyhood that reveal a certain tenderness for places and people which, hitherto, reserved as he was, he never had expressed to outsiders. The sudden awakening of brotherly romantic attachment for his half-sister, and the equally sudden break-off of all communications and intercourse, are so thoroughly characteristic of Hearn's wayward and unaccountable character. How, after such an incident, absolve him of the charge so frequently made, of caprice and inconstancy; in fact you would not attempt to defend him were it not for the unwavering friendship and affection displayed in one or two instances; above all, in the unselfish and generous manner in which he gave up all his private inclinations and ambitions for the sake of his wife and family, and his undeviating devotion to Miss Bisland (Mrs. Wetmore), the Lady of a Myriad Souls to whom his most beautiful and eloquent letters are addressed.

It seems really to have only been during the last decade of his life that he allowed irritability and sensitiveness to interfere between him and his best friends. Years after he had left Cincinnati, he recalled the memory of the comrades he had left there; never were their mutual struggles and aspirations forgotten. "It seemeth to me," he writes to Krehbiel, "that I behold overshadowing the paper the most Dantesque silhouette of one who walked with me the streets of the far-off Western city by night, and with whom I exchanged ghostly fancies and phantom hopes. . . . How the old forces have been scattered! But is it not pleasant to observe that the members of the broken circle have been mounting higher and higher to the Supreme Hope? Perhaps we may all meet some day in the East whence, the legendary word hath it, 'Lightning ever cometh.'"

He always remained generously sympathetic to the literary interests and ventures of the "Cincinnati Brotherhood." Tunison wrote a book on the Virgilian Legend, Hearn devotes paragraphs, suggesting titles, publishers, and the best place for publication. To Farney, the artist, he offers hospitality, if he will come to New Orleans to paint some of the quaint nooks and corners; and later, he recommends him to Miss Bisland as an artist whom she might employ to do illustrations for her magazine. "Lazy as a serpent, but immensely capable."

Hearn was a strange mixture of humility and conceit, but there was not a particle of literary jealousy in his composition.

To Krehbiel he writes, "Comparing yourself to me won't do . . . dear old fellow! I am in most things a botch. You say you envy me certain qualities; but you forget how those qualities are at variance with an Art whose beauties are geometrical and whose perfection is mathematical. You envy me my power of application, if you only knew the pain and labour I have to create a little good work! And there are months when I cannot write. It is not hard to write when the thought is there; but the thought will not always come; there are weeks when I cannot even think."

Though humble about his own, he was intolerant of amateur art. Comically averse to criticising his friends' work, he implores Mitchell McDonald not to send him his literary efforts, and is loath even to express an opinion on Miss Bisland's. Reading these letters containing a record of the manner in which he goes to work, writing and re-writing until the thought re-shaped itself and the style was polished and fixed, we can see how high he pitched his ideal and how unlikely it was that others would reach the same standard.

In one letter, written in the fifty-third year of his age, to Professor Chamberlain, after thirty years of literary work, he, one of the most finished masters of English prose, confesses to drudgery worthy of his boyish days, when plodding over an English composition at Ushaw College.

He recommended Roget's *Thesaurus* to a young author who asked his advice; Skeat's Dictionary, too, and Brachet for French, as books that give the subtle sense of words, to which much that arrests attention in prose and poetry are due. The consciousness of art gives a new faith, he says, after one of these passages of good advice. Putting jesting on one side, he believed that if he could create something he knew to be sublime he would feel that the Unknown Power had selected him for a medium of utterance, in the holy cycle of its eternal purpose.

In consequence of various opinions and criticisms expressed by Lafcadio Hearn in his letters, a charge has been brought against him of showing no appreciation for the greater intellectual luminaries. The little man's personal prejudices were certainly too pronounced to make his a trustworthy opinion, either upon political or literary affairs. The mood or whim of the moment influenced his judgment, causing him often to commit himself to statements that must not be accepted at the foot of the letter. He admitted that, being a creature of extremes, he did not see what existed where he loved or hated, and confessed to being an extremely crooked visioned judge of art. It is these whimsical and unexpected revelations of his own method of thought and artistic theories that constitute the charm of his letters. You feel as though you were passing through a varied and strongly accentuated landscape. You never know what will be revealed over the brow of the hill, or round the next bend of the road. In a delightfully humorous, whimsical passage, he declares that his mind to him "a kingdom was—not! " Rather was it a fantastical republic, daily troubled by more revolutions than ever occurred in South America; he then goes on to enumerate his possession of souls, some of them longing to live in tropical solitude, others in the bustle of great cities, others hating inaction, and others dwelling in meditative isolation. He gives us, in fact, in this passage the very essence of his personality, with all his whims, vagaries, freakishness and inconstancy set down by his own incomparable pen.

Things moved him artistically rather than critically,

carrying him hither and thither in the movement of every whispering breeze of romance and poetry, equally prejudiced and intolerant in likes and dislikes of people and places as in literary affairs. "I had a sensation the other day," he writes to Basil Hall Chamberlain. "I felt as if I hated Japan unspeakably, and the whole world seemed not worth living in, when there came to the house two women to sell ballads. One took her samisen and sang; never did I listen to anything sweeter. All the sorrow and beauty, all the pain and the sweetness of life thrilled and quivered in that voice; and the old first love of Japan and of things Japanese came back, and a great tenderness seemed to fill the place like a haunting." [1]

In a moment of petulance he committed himself to the statement that he could not endure any more of Wordsworth, Keats, or Shelley, having learnt the gems of them by heart. He really thought he preferred Dobson, Watson, and Lang. It is generally easy to trace the impulse dictating the criticism of the moment. While he was writing the sketch at Kumamoto entitled "The Stone Buddha," Chamberlain lent him a volume of Watson's poems—*The Dream of Man* he declared to be "high sublimity," because Watson happened to enunciate philosophical ideas akin to his own. Dobson had translated some poems of Gautier's, and therefore was worthy of all honour; Miss Deland was "one of the greatest novelists of the century," because the heroine of *Philip and His Wife* reminded him of Miss Bisland. He pronounced Matthew Arnold to be "one of the colossal humbugs of the century; a fifth-rate poet, and an unutterably dreary essayist," because at the

---

[1] *Life and Letters*, published by Houghton, Mifflin & Co.

moment he was animated by one of his intense enthusiasms for *Edwin* Arnold, whose acquaintance Hearn had made during one of Arnold's visits to Japan. "Far the nobler man and writer, permeated with the beauties of strong faiths and exotic creeds; the spirit that, in some happier era, may bless mankind with the universal religion in perfect harmony with the truths of science, and the better nature of humanity."

But in spite of all his whimsicality, and when uninfluenced by pique or partiality, his criticisms are not to be surpassed, here and there expanding into an inspired burst of enthusiasm. On cloudy nights, when passing through southern seas, the waste of water sometimes spreads like a dark metallic surface round you. A shoal of fish or band of porpoises suddenly comes along; the surface begins to ripple and move; flakes of phosphorescence shoot here and there; illumined streaks flash alongside the ship, and in a few seconds the undulations of the waves are shimmering, a mass of liquid light. So in Hearn's letters, treating the dullest subjects—writing to Chamberlain, for instance, on the subject of his health, and diet, and the storage of physical and brain force, he suddenly breaks off, and takes up the subject of Buddhism and Shintoism. "There is, however, a power, a mighty power, in tradition and race feeling. I can't remember now where I read a wonderful story about a Polish brigade under fire during the Franco-Prussian war." Then he tells the story in his own inimitable way: "The Polish brigade stood still under the infernal hail, cursed by its German officers for the least murmur,—'Silence! you Polish hogs!' while hundreds, thousands fell, but the iron order always was to wait. Men sobbed with rage. At last, old Steinmetz gave a signal—*the* signal. The bugles rang out with the force of Roland's last blast at Roncesvalles, the air forbidden ever to be sung or heard at other times— the national air (you know it)—' *No* ! *Poland is not dead!* ' And with that crash of brass all that lives of the brigade was hurled at the French batteries. Mechanical power, if absolutely irresistible, might fling back such a charge, but no human power. For old Steinmetz had made the mightiest appeal to those ' Polish brutes ' that man, God, or devil could make, the appeal to the ghost of the Race. The dead heard it; and they came back that day,—the dead of a thousand years."

Or again, in his description of a chance hearing of the singing of " Auld Lang Syne " by Adelina Patti. He is writing in an ordinary strain on some everyday subject, in the next paragraph an association of ideas, connected with ballad music, evokes the memory thus exquisitely recounted : —

" ' Patti is going to sing at the St. Charles,' said a friend to me years ago. ' I know you hate the theatre, but you *must* go.' (I had been surfeited with drama by old duty as a dramatic reporter, and had vowed not to enter a theatre again.) I went. There was a great dim pressure, a stifling heat, a whispering of silks, a weight of toilet-perfumes. Then came an awful hush; all the silks stopped whispering. And there suddenly sweetened out through that dead, hot air a clear, cool, tense thread-gush of melody unlike any sound I had ever heard before save, in tropical nights, from the throat of a mocking-bird. It was ' Auld Lang Syne ' only, but with never a *tremolo* or artifice; a marvellous, audacious simplicity of utterance. The silver of that singing rings in my heart still."

Amidst the numerous oscillations of his fancies and partialities, there were one or two writers to whom Hearn owned an unswerving allegiance. Pierre Loti, Herbert Spencer, and Rudyard Kipling were foremost among these. Even in spite of Loti's description of Japan and his treatment of Japanese ladies in *Madame Chrysanthème*, Hearn retained the same admiration for him to the end. "Oh! do read the divine Loti's *Roman d'un Spahi*. No mortal critic, not even Jules Lemaître or Anatole France, can explain that ineffable and superhuman charm. I hope you will have everything of Loti's. Some time ago, when I was afraid I might die, one of my prospective regrets was that I might not be able to read *L'Inde sans les Anglais*. . . ."

Hearn had a wonderful memory;—he could repeat pages of poetry even of the poets he declared he did not care for. In Japan, Mr. Mason told us that one evening at his house at Tokyo, when he was present, an argument was started on the subject of Browning. In reply to some one's criticisms on the "Ring and the Book," Hearn, to verify a statement, repeated passage after passage from various poems of Browning in his soft musical voice.

A member of the Maple Club also mentioned an occasion when the subject of Napoleon cropped up. A little man whom no one noticed at first, sat apart listening. At last some one made a statement that roused him; the insignificant figure with prominent eyes bent forward and poured forth a flood of information on the subject under discussion so fluent, so accurate that the assembled company listened in amazement.

Hearn's personal characteristics have often been described. In the biographies and collections of letters that have been given to the world, there are photographs of him from the time when he was a little boy in collegiate jacket and turned-down collar, to his last years in Japan, when he nationalised himself a Japanese and habitually wore the Japanese "kimono."

At New Orleans, past his thirtieth year, looked upon as a writer of promise by a cultured few, though not yet successful with the public, he was a much more responsible and important person than the little "brownie" who used to sit in the corner of John Cockerill's office, turning out page after page of "copy" for the *Cincinnati Enquirer*, or doing the "Night Stations" for the *Commercial*. In later years, in consequence of his sedentary habits, he became corpulent and of stooping gait; at this time he was about five feet three inches in height, his complexion clear olive, his hair straight and black, his salient features a long, sharp, aquiline nose and prominent near-sighted eyes, the left one, injured at Ushaw, considerably more prominent than the other. In his sensitive, morbid fashion he greatly over-exaggerated the disfiguring effect this had on his personal appearance. When engaged in conversation, he habitually held his hand over it, and was always photographed in profile looking down.

In some ways the Hearn type was very visible, the square brow and well-shaped head and finely-modelled mouth and chin. He also inherited the delicate, filbert-nailed hands (always exquisitely kept) and the musical voice of his Celtic forbears. One of his pupils at Tokyo University speaks of the "voice of the old Professor with one eye, and white hair, being as lovely as his words." Professor Foxwell, who made his acquaintance in Japan, gives the following account of his personal manner in his delightful "Reminiscences of Lafcadio Hearn," read before the Japan Society in London: "I had just recovered from small-pox when I first met Hearn, and must have been an extraordinary object. My face, to begin with, was the colour of beetroot. Hearn took not the least notice; seemed hardly to notice my appearance. This fact impressed me very much, and when I knew him better I found that the same wide tolerance of mind ran through all his thoughts and actions. It might have been tact, but nothing seemed to surprise him. It was as if he had lived too much to be surprised at anything. He seemed to me on that particular morning, and whenever I met him afterwards, to be the most natural, unaffected, companionable person I had ever come across. Secondly, I thought he was extraordinarily gentle, more gentle than a woman, since it was not a physical gentleness, but a gentleness of thought. You noticed it in his tone, in his voice, in his manner. He had a mind which worked with velvet or gossamer touch. Thirdly, in spite of that softness and gentleness, he looked intensely male. You could see that in his eye, and you would feel it in the quiet mastery of every sentence. And fourthly, he seemed to be, unlike most foreigners, altogether at home in Japan. He appeared to have come into smooth water, placid and unconcerned. Yet I found him essentially European, in spite of his being so at home in Japan. You could see that from his very great fairness of complexion, tense facial expression, and delicate susceptibility. That was obvious. Then his nose settled it. It struck me at the time as curious that a foreigner so eager to interpret Japan should be himself so Occidental in appearance. Another point with regard to this first meeting: our acquaintance lasted for three years, but I do not think I knew him any better or any more at the end than I did at that first meeting."

Hearn was as unconventional in his dress as in most things, deliberately protesting against social restrictions in his personal attire. Shy, diffident people, who above all things wish to avoid attracting attention, seem so often to forget that if they would only garb themselves like the rest of the world it would be the best disguise they could adopt. The jeers and laughter of the passers-by in the streets of Philadelphia, even the fact that a number of street gamins formed a queue, the leader holding by his coat-tails while they kept in step, singing, " Where, where did you get that hat?" had not any effect, Gould tells us, in inducing him to substitute conventional headgear for the enormous tropical straw hat, or the reefer coat and flannel shirt, that he habitually wore.

Mr. Mason, in Japan, told us, that Hearn boasted of not having worn a starched shirt for twenty years. In fact, he looked upon white shirts as a proof of the greater facility of life in the East, where they don't wear white shirts, to the ease of life in the West, where they do. " Think for a moment," he says in one of his essays, " how important an article of Occidental attire is the single costly item of white shirts! Yet even the linen shirt, the so-called ' badge of the gentleman,' is in itself a useless garment. It gives neither warmth nor comfort. It represents in our fashion the survival of something, once a luxurious class distinction, but to-day meaningless and useless as the buttons sewn on the outside of coat-sleeves."

In spite of the unconventionality of his garments, every one is unanimous as to Hearn's radiant physical cleanliness, constantly bathing winter and summer and changing his clothes two and three times a day. His wife, in her *Reminiscences*, mentions his fastidiousness on the subject of underclothing. Everything was ordered from America, except his Japanese kimonos and "fudos." He paid high prices, and would have nothing that was not of the best make and quality.

In later years he was described by an acquaintance in Japan as an odd, nondescript apparition, with nearsighted eyes, a soft, well-modulated voice, speaking several languages easily, particularly dainty and clean in his person, and of considerable personal influence and charm when you came in contact with him.

CHAPTER XII

THE LADY OF A MYRIAD SOULS

" The lady wore her souls as other women wear their dresses and change them several times a day; and the multitude of dresses in the wardrobe of Queen Elizabeth was as nothing to the multitude of this wonderful person's souls. Sometimes she was of the South, and her eyes were brown; and again she was of the North, and her eyes were grey. Sometimes she was of the thirteenth, and sometimes of the eighteenth century; and people doubted their own senses when they saw these things . . . and the men who most admired her could not presume to fall in love with her because that would have been absurd. She had altogether too many souls."

THE year 1882 was a memorable one for Lafcadio Hearn; during the course of that winter the purest and most beneficent feminine influence that he had hitherto known entered his life, an influence destined to last for close on a quarter of a century, from these New Orleans days until the month of September, 1904, when he died.

In all the annals of literary friendships between men and women it is difficult to recall one more delightful or more wholly satisfactory than this, between Miss Elizabeth Bisland (Mrs. Wetmore) and the strange little Irish genius.

Many beautiful things has Lafcadio Hearn written, but none more tender, none more beautiful, than the story of his devotion and friendship, as told in his letters.

The affection between Jean Jacques Ampère and
Madame Récamier is the one that perhaps most nearly
approaches it. Here, however, the position is reversed.
Madame Récamier was a decade older than her admirer;
Elizabeth Bisland was a decade younger. Yet there
always seems to have been something maternal, protecting, in her affection for this "veritable blunderer
in the ways of the world." Her comprehension, her
pity, shielded and guarded him; into his wounded
heart she poured the balm of affection and appreciation,
soothing and healing the bruises given him in the tussle
of life.

Link by link we follow the sentiment that Lafcadio
Hearn cherished for Miss Bisland, as it runs, an un-
tarnished chain of gold athwart his life. Through
separation, through distances of thousands of miles, the
unwavering understanding remained, a simple, definite,
and dependable thing, never at fault, except once or
twice, when the clear surface was disturbed, apparently
by the expression of too warm a sentiment on his side.

"There is one very terrible Elizabeth," he writes to
Ellwood Hendrik from Japan, in reference to Miss
Bisland's marriage to Mr. Wetmore, "whom I had a
momentary glimpse of once, and whom it will not be
well for Mr. W. or anybody else to summon from her
retirement."

Time and again he returned to his friend as to his
own purer, better self, though he seems to have had a
pathetic, sad-hearted, clear-eyed conviction that her love
—as love is understood in common parlance—could
never be his.

And she, doubtless, acknowledged there was something intangible and rare in the feeling she nourished

for him that raised it above that of mere friendship. Whatever he had been, whatever he had done, she cared not; she only knew that he had genius far above any of those amongst whom her lines had hitherto been cast, and with tremendous odds against him was offering up burnt-offerings on the altar of the shrine, where she, as a neophyte, also worshipped.

Miss Elizabeth Bisland was the daughter of a Louisiana landowner, ruined, like many others, in the war. With the idea of aiding her family by the proceeds of her pen, the young girl quitted the seclusion of her parents' house in the country and bravely entered the arena of journalistic work in New Orleans.

Hearn at that time was regularly working on the staff of the *Times Democrat*. The faithfulness of his translations from the French, and the beauty of the style of some of his contributions, had found an appreciative circle in the Crescent City, and a clique had been formed of what were known as " Hearn's admirers."

His translations from Gautier, Maupassant, *Stray Leaves from Strange Literature*, all appeared in the columns of Page Baker's newspaper. He also, under the title of " Fantastics," contributed every now and then slight sketches inspired by his French prototypes. Dreams, he called them, of a tropical city, with one twin idea running through them all,—love and death. They gave him the gratification of expressing a thought that cried out within his heart for utterance, and the pleasant fancy that a few kindred minds would dream over them as upon pellets of green hashisch.

One of these was inspired by Tennyson's verse—

"My heart would hear her and beat
Had I lain for a century dead;—
Would start and tremble under her feet,
And blossom in purple and red."

The sketch appeared apparently in the columns of the *Times Democrat.* There Miss Bisland saw it, and in the enthusiasm of her seventeen years, wrote an appreciative letter to the author. By chance the " Fantastic " was recovered from his later correspondence. Writing to Mitchell McDonald years afterwards in Japan, we find Hearn referring to the expression " Lentor Inexpressible." " I am going to change ' Lentor Inexpressible,' which you did not like. I send you a copy of the story in which I first used it—years and years ago. Don't return the thing—it has had its day. It belongs to the Period of Gush."

Mitchell McDonald, we imagine, obeyed his injunction, and did not return the " Fantastic," but laid it away amongst his papers, and so " A Dead Love " has been saved for re-publication. It certainly is crude enough to deserve the designation of belonging to the " Period of Gush," and is distinguished by all the weakness and none of the strength of the French Impressionist School.

The idea of the spirit conquering material obstacles, a longing for the unattainable, the exceptional in life and nature, to the extent even of continued sensibility after death, are phases of thought that permeate every line, and may be found in two of Gautier's stories translated by Hearn, and in several of Baudelaire's poems.

A young man weary of life because of the hopelessness of his love, yielded it up at last, dying with the name of the beloved on his lips. . . . Yet the repose of the dead was not for him; even in the tomb the phantom man dreamed of life, and strength, and joy, and the litheness of limbs to be loved : also of that which had been and of that which now could never be. . . . Years came and went with "Lentor Inexpressible," but for the dead there was no rest . . . the echoes of music and laughter, the chanting and chattering of children at play, and the liquid babble of the beautiful brown women floated to his ears. And at last it came to pass that the woman whose name had been murmured by his lips when the shadow of death fell upon him, visited the ancient place of sepulture, he recognised the sound of her footstep, the rustle of her garments, knew the sweetness of her presence, but she, unconscious, passed by, and the sound of her footsteps died away for ever.

Hearn, at the time he first met Elizabeth Bisland, was going through a period of depression about his work, and a hatred of New Orleans. The problem of existence, he said, stared him in the face with eyes of iron. Independence was so hard to obtain; there was no scope for a man who preserved freedom of thought and action—absolute quiet, silence, dreams, friends in the evening, a pipe, a little philosophy, was his idea of perfect bliss. As he was situated at the time, he could not obtain even a woman's society, he complained, unless he buried himself in the mediocrity to which she belonged.

Twenty years later, writing to Mrs. Wetmore (as Miss Elizabeth Bisland had become), he refers to those first years of friendship in the strange old city of New Orleans. He recalls to her memory her dangerous illness, and people's fear that she might die in the quaint little hotel where she was stopping. Impossible, he said, to think of that young girl as a grey-haired woman of forty. His memory was of a voice and a thought, *une jeune fille un peu farouche* (no English word could give the same sense of shyness and force), " who came into New Orleans from the country, and wrote nice things for a paper there, and was so kind to a particular variety of savage, that he could not understand—and was afraid." But all this was long ago, he concludes regretfully; " since then I have become grey and the father of three boys."

For the greater part of Lafcadio Hearn and Elizabeth Bisland's friendship they seem to have occupied towards one another the position of literary brother and sister. From the very beginning he tried to induce her to share his literary enthusiasms. With that odd social unconventionality that distinguished him, he endeavoured to make this young girl of eighteen sympathise with his admiration of the artistic beauties of Flaubert and Gautier. Sending a volume of Gautier's poems, he writes: " I won't presume to offer you this copy; it is too shabby, has travelled about with me in all sorts of places for eight years. But if you are charmed by this ' parfait magicien des lettres francaises' (as Beaudelaire called him) I hope to have the pleasure of offering you a nicer copy. . . ."

Years afterwards he refers to literary obligations that he owed her, mentioning evening chats in her New York flat, when the sound of her voice, low and clear, and at times like a flute, was in his ears. " The gods only know what I said; for my thoughts in those times were seldom in the room—but in the future, which was black without stars! "

In 1884 Hearn went to Grande Isle, in the Archipelago of the Gulf, for his summer holiday. Miss Bisland would appear to have been there at the same time, yet with that half-tamed, barbaric, incomprehensible nature of his, his fancy seems to have been turned rather towards the copper-coloured ladies of Barataria. "A beauty that existed in the Tertiary epoch—three hundred thousand years ago. The beauty of the most ancient branch of humanity."

It was during this visit to Grande Isle that the story of *Chita* was written and contributed to *Harper's Magazine* under the title of "Torn Letters."

We know not at what date Miss Bisland left New Orleans to go to New York. One thing only is certain, that so firm a spiritual hold had she taken of Lafcadio Hearn's genius, that no distance of space nor spite of circumstance could separate her intellect from his. Like a delicious and subtle perfume, wafted from some garden close, her presence meets you as you pass from letter to letter in his correspondence; from chapter to chapter of his books. Far or near, dear to her or indifferent, the memory of her smile and the light of her eyes was henceforth his best inspiration. Thousands of miles away in the Far East it stimulated his genius and quickened his pen.

I, who have had the privilege of meeting the "Lady of a Myriad Souls" when she visited England a short time ago, could not help marvelling, as I looked at her, and talked to her, dainty and beautiful as she was in lace and diamonds, at the irony of the dictates of fate, or *Karma* (as he, Buddhist-wise, would have called it), that had ordained that hers was to be the ascendant influence in the life of Lafcadio Hearn,—the Bohemian, who, by his own confession, had for a decade never dressed for dinner, or put on a starched collar or shirt-front.

In New York Miss Bisland became joint-editor of a magazine called the *Cosmopolitan*, and after Hearn's arrival in June, 1887, a frequent correspondence was kept up between them on literary matters.

She solicited contributions, apparently, and he answered: "I don't think I can write anything clever enough to be worth your using. But it is a pleasure you should think so. . . . My work, however weak, is so much better than myself that the less said about me the better. . . . Your own personality has charm enough to render the truth very palatable. . . . Does a portrait of an ugly man make one desirous to read his books?

". . . I will try to give you something for the Christmas number anyhow, but not very long." He then goes on to set forth a theory that seems at this time rather to have influenced his literary output. With the nineteenth century, he believed that the long novel would pass out of existence; three-quarters of what was written was unnecessary, evolved simply out of obedience to effete formulas and standards. The secret of the prose fiction " that lives through the centuries, like the old Greek romances, is condensation, the expression of feeling in a few laconic sentences. . . . No descriptions, no preliminaries, no explanation —nothing but the feeling itself at highest intensity." As is so often the case, this opinion expressed in a letter is a running commentary on the work he was doing at the moment. *Chita*, the longest work of fiction he ever attempted, had appeared serially in *Harper's*

Magazine, and he was occupied in reconstructing it in book form. It certainly has feeling at highest intensity and no diffuseness, but it lacks the delicate touches, the indications of character by small incidents, and realistic details, that render Pierre Loti's novels, for instance, so vividly actual and accurate. It is strung to the highest emotional pitch, and some of the descriptions are marvellous, but the book gives the impression of being fragmentary and unfinished.

After two years of exclusively intellectual communion and discussion of literary matters between Lafcadio Hearn and Miss Bisland, he suddenly, writing from Philadelphia, declares his intention of never addressing her as Miss Bisland again except upon an envelope.

" It is a formality—and you are you; you are not a formality—but a somewhat—and I am only I." [1]

'After this the personal note becomes predominant, and Miss Bisland ceases, even on paper, to be a formality in Lafcadio Hearn's emotional life.

During the course of the same summer, Hearn went to the West Indies for his three months' midsummer trip. From thence he wrote one or two delightful letters to the Lady of a Myriad Souls. In the same year he was again in New York, but almost immediately accepted an offer made to him by the Harpers to return to the West Indies for two years.

The following letter tells its own tale, and so daintily and pathetically that you do not feel as if you could change a word : —

" Your letter reached me when everything that had seemed solid was breaking up, and Substance had

[1] *The Life and Letters of Lafcadio Hearn :* Houghton, Mifflin & Co.

become Shadow. It made me very foolish—made me cry. Your rebuke for the trivial phrase in my letter was very beautiful as well as very richly deserved. But I don't think it is a question of volition. It is necessary to obey the impulses of the Unknown for Art's sake,—or rather, you *must* obey them. The Spahi's fascination by the invisible forces was purely physical. I think I am right in going; perhaps I am wrong in thinking of making the tropics a home. Probably it will be the same thing over again : impulse and chance compelling another change.

" The carriage—no, the New York hack and hackman (no romance or sentimentality about these!) is waiting to take me to Pier 49 East River. So I must end. But I have written such a ridiculous letter that I shan't put anybody's name to it." [1]

In 1889 he again returned to America, and went for his famous visit to George Milbury Gould at Philadelphia.

On November 14th of the same year Miss Bisland received a request to call at the office of the *Cosmopolitan Magazine.* On her arrival at eleven o'clock in the morning, she was asked if she would leave New York for San Francisco the same evening for a seventy-five days' journey round the world. The proposition was, that she should "run" in competition with another lady sent by a rival magazine for a wager. Miss Bisland consented.

After her return, under the title of " A Trip Around the World," she published her experiences in the *Cosmopolitan Magazine.* These contributions were afterwards incorporated in a small volume. They are charm-

<hr />

[1] *Life and Letters of Lafcadio Hearn :* Houghton, Mifflin & Co.

ingly and brightly written. She, however, did not win
her wager, as the other lady completed the task in a
slightly shorter period.

Before he knew of the projected journey, Lafcadio
wrote to tell her that he had had a queer dream. A
garden with high clipped hedges, in front of a sort of
country house with steps leading down and everywhere
hampers and baskets. Krehbiel was there, starting for
Europe never to return. He could not remember what
anybody said precisely, voices were never audible in
dreams.

In his next letter he alludes to his imaginings. " So
it was you and not I, that was to run away. . . . When
I saw the charming notice about you in the *Tribune*
there suddenly came back to me the same vague sense
of unhappiness, I had dreamed of feeling,—an absurd
sense of absolute loneliness. . . . I and my friends have
been wagering upon you hoping for you to win your
race—so that every one may admire you still more, and
your name flash round the world quicker than the sunshine, and your portrait—in spite of you—appear in
some French journal where they know how to engrave
portraits properly. I thought I might be able to coax
one from you; but as you are never the same person
two minutes in succession, I am partly consoled; it
would only be one small phase of you, Proteus, Circe,
Undine, Djineeyeh! . . ."

I do not think that amidst all the letters of poets or
writers there are any more original or passionately
poignant than the last two or three of the series in
Miss Bisland's first volume of Hearn's letters. It seems
almost like tearing one of Heine's Lyrics to pieces to
endeavour to give the substance of these fanciful and

exquisite outpourings in any words but his own. Again and again he recurs to his favourite idea of the multiplicity of souls. Turn by turn, he says, one or other of the "dead within her" floats up from the depth within, transfiguring her face.

"It seems to me that all those mysterious lives within you—all the Me's that were—keep asking the Me that is, for something always refused;—and that you keep saying to them: 'But you are dead and cannot see—you can only feel; and I can see,—and I will not open to you, because the world is all changed. You would not know it, and you would be angry with me were I to grant your wish. Go to your places, and sleep and wait, and leave me in peace with myself.' But they continue to wake up betimes, and quiver into momentary visibility to make you divine in spite of yourself, —and as suddenly flit away again. I wish one would come—and stay: the one I saw that night when we were looking at . . . what was it?

"Really, I can't remember what it was: the smile effaced the memory of it,—just as a sun-ray blots the image from a dry-plate suddenly exposed. . . . Will you ever be *like that always* for any one being?—I hope you will get my book before you go: it will be sent on Tuesday at latest, I think. I don't know whether you will like the paper; but you will only look for the 'gnat of a soul' that belongs to me between the leaves."

Soon after the return of the lady of his dreams from her "trip around the world," Hearn left for the Far East, where he lived for the rest of his days. He wrote to her once or twice after his arrival in Japan, and then a long, long interval intervened. He married a Japanese lady, and she married Mr. Wetmore.

Not until 1900 were all the long estranging years
that lay between the time when he had last seen her
in New York and the period of his professorship at a
Japanese College forgotten, and he fell back on the
simple human affection of their early intercourse. No
longer did he think of her as the rich, beautiful, fashionable woman, but as the *jeune fille un peu farouche*,
who in distant New Orleans days had understood
and expressed a belief in his genius with all a girl's
unsophisticated enthusiasm. She had written to him,
and he gives her a whimsically pathetic answer, touching
on memories, on thoughts, on aspirations, which had
been a closed book for so long a period of time, and
now when re-opened was seen to be printed as clearly
on mind and heart as if he had parted with her but an
hour before.

About a dozen letters succeed one another, and in
September, 1904—the month in which he died—comes
his last. He tells her that to see her handwriting again
upon the familiar blue envelope, was a great pleasure;
except that the praise she lavished upon him was un-
deserved. He then refers to the dedication of the
Japanese Miscellany which he had made to her. " The
book is not a bad book in its way, and perhaps you will
later on find no reason to be sorry for your good
opinions of the writer. I presume that you are far too
clever to believe more than truth, and I stand tolerably
well in the opinion of a few estimable people in spite of
adverse tongues and pens. . . ."

He then tells her that the " Rejected Addresses,"
the name in writing to her he had given to *Japan, an
Interpretation*, would shortly appear in book form. . . .
" I don't like the idea of writing a serious treatise on
sociology; I ought to keep to the study of birds and

cats and insects and flowers, and queer small things—
and leave the subject of the destiny of Empires to men
of brains. Unfortunately, the men of brains will not
state the truth as they see it. If you find any good in
the book, despite the conditions under which it was
written, you will recognise your share in the necessarily
ephemeral value thereof.

" May all good things ever come to you, and abide."

It is said by many, especially those who knew Hearn
in later years, that he was heartless, capricious, incapable
of constancy to any affection or sentiment, and yet, set
forth so that all " who run may read," is this record of
a devotion and friendship, cherished for a quarter of a
century, lasting intact through fair years and foul,
through absence and change of scene, even of nationality.

> " Fear not, I say again ; believe it true
> That not as men mete shall I measure you. . . ."

Time, besides his scythe and hour-glass, carries an
accurate gauge for the estimation of human character
and genius.

CHAPTER XIII

RELIGION AND SCIENCE

" For the Buddha of the deeper Buddhism is not Gautama, nor yet any one Tathagata, but simply the divine in man. Chrysalides of the infinite we all are : each contains a ghostly Buddha, and the millions are but one. All humanity is potentially the Buddha-to-come, dreaming through the ages in Illusion ; and the teacher's smile will make beautiful the world again when selfishness shall die. Every noble sacrifice brings the hour of his awakening ; and who may justly doubt—remembering the myriads of the centuries of man—that even now there does not remain one place on earth where life has not been freely given for love or duty ? "

THOUGH some years were yet to elapse before Hearn received his definite marching orders, each halt was but a bivouac nearer the field of operations where effective work and fame awaited him.

"Have wild theories about Japan," he writes prophetically to Mr. Watkin. "Splendid field in Japan—a climate just like England—perhaps a little milder. Plenty of European and English newspapers. . . ." And again, " I have half a mind to study medicine in practical earnest, for as a doctor I may do well in Japan."

When the New Orleans Exposition was opened in 1885, Harper's, the publishers—who had already sent Hearn on a tour in Florida with an artist of their staff —now made an arrangement with him, by which he was to supply descriptive articles, varied by sketches and drawings, copied from photographs, of the principal exhibits.

On January 3rd Hearn's first article appeared in *Harper's Weekly*. In it he described the fans, the *kakemonos*, the screens in the Japanese department. Long lines of cranes flying against a vermilion sky, a flight of gulls sweeping through the golden light of a summer morning; the heavy, eccentric, velvety flight of bats under the moon; the fairy hovering of moths, of splendid butterflies; the modelling and painting of animal forms, the bronzed tortoises, crabs, storks, frogs, not mere copies of nature, but exquisite idealisations stirred his artistic sense as did also the representations of the matchless mountain Fuji-no-yama—of which the artist Houkousai alone drew one hundred different views, on fans, behind rains of gold, athwart a furnace of sunset, or against an immaculate blue burnished by some wizard dawn; exhaling from its mimic crater a pillar of incense smoke, towering above stretches of vineyards and city-speckled plains, or perchance begirdled by a rich cloud of silky shifting tints, like some beauty of Yoshiwara.

It seems almost as if he already saw the light of the distant dreamy world and the fairy vapours of morning, and the marvellous wreathing of clouds, and heard the pilgrims' clapping of hands, saluting the mighty day in Shinto prayer, as a decade later he saw, and heard, when he ascended Fuji-no-yama. . . .

A year after the Exposition, Hearn made the acquaintance of a young Lieutenant Crosby. Young Crosby was a native of Louisiana, educated at West Point, stationed at the time with his regiment at New Orleans. He was a person, apparently, of considerable culture. He and Hearn frequented the same literary circles. Interest in science and philosophy was as widespread in America as in Europe during the course of last century.

One day Crosby lent his new acquaintance Herbert Spencer's *First Principles*. In his usual vehement impressionable way Hearn immediately accepted all the tenets, all the conclusions arrived at. And from that day began what only can be called an intellectual idolatry for the colourless analytic English philosopher that lasted till his death.

The terms in which he alludes to him are superexaggerated: " the greatest mind that this world has yet produced—the mind that systematised all human knowledge, that revolutionised modern science, that dissipated materialism for ever . . . the mind that could expound with equal lucidity, and by the same universal formula, the history of a gnat or the history of a sun."

Always excitable in argument, he would not be gainsaid, and indeed at various periods of his life, when people ventured to doubt the soundness of some of Spencer's conclusions, Hearn would not only refuse to discuss the subject, but henceforth abstained from holding communication with the offending individual.

" A memory of long ago . . . I am walking upon a granite pavement that rings like iron, between buildings of granite bathed in the light of a cloudless noon. . . . Suddenly, an odd feeling comes to me, with a sort of tingling shock,—a feeling, or suspicion, of universal illusion. The pavement, the bulks of hewn stone, the iron rails, and all things visible, are dreams! Light, colour, form, weight, solidity—all sensed existences—are but phantoms of being, manifestations only of one infinite ghostliness for which the language of man has not any word. . . ."

This experience had been produced, he says, by the study of the first volume of Spencer's *Synthetic Philosophy*, which an American friend had taught him how to read. Very cautious and slow his progress was, like that of a man mounting for the first time a long series of ladders in darkness. Reaching the light at last, he caught a sudden new view of things,—a momentary perception of the illusion of surfaces,— and from that time the world never again appeared to him quite the same as it had appeared before.

It is a noteworthy fact that, though the mid-Victorian scientists and philosophers were in the zenith of their influence when Hearn was in London, twenty years before these New Orleans days, he never seems to have taken an interest in their speculations or theories. We, of the present generation, can hardly realise the excitement created by the new survey of the Cosmos put forth by Darwin and his adherents. Old forms of thought crumbled; the continuity of life was declared to have been proved; lower forms were raised and their kinship with the higher demonstrated; man was deposed and put back into the sequence of nature. Hardly a decade elapsed before the enthusiasm began to wane. Some of Darwin's adherents endeavoured to initiate what they called a scientific philosophy, attempting to prove more than he did. Herbert Spencer, in his *Principles of Ethics*, when dealing with the inception of moral consciousness, appealed to the "Time Process," to the enormous passage of the years, to explain the generation of sentiency, and ultimately, moral consciousness. " Out of the units of single sensations, older than we by millions of years, have been built up all the emotions and faculties of man," echoes his disciple, Lafcadio Hearn. Spencer also put forward the view, from which he ultimately withdrew, that natural selection tended towards higher conditions, or, as he termed it, " Equilibration,"—a state in which all struggle had ceased, and from which all disturbing influences, passion, love, happiness and fear were eliminated.

These statements were contested by Darwin and Huxley, both declaring that evolution manifested a sublime indifference to the pains or pleasures of man; evil was as natural as good and had been as efficacious a factor in helping forward the progress of the world.

In his celebrated Romanes lecture of 1893 on the subject of " Nature and Evolution," Huxley turned the searchlight of his analytical intellect on Buddha's theories with regard to Karma and the ultimate progress of man towards the Perfect Life, and effectually, so far as his opinion was concerned, demolished any possible reconciliation between Buddhism and Science. " The end of life's dream is Nirvana. What Nirvana is, the learned do not agree, but since the best original authorities tell us there is neither desire, nor activity, nor any possibility of phenomenal reappearance, for the sage who has entered Nirvana, it may be safely said of this acme of Buddhist philosophy—' the rest is silence! ' "

It is plain, therefore, that the two points of contact upon which Hearn, in his attempted reconciliation between Buddhism and Modern Science laid most stress, were disproved by leading scientists even before he

had read Spencer's *First Principles* at New Orleans in
1886, and it is disconcerting to find him using his
deftness in the manipulation of words, to reconcile
statements of Huxley's and Darwin's, with his own
wishes. His statement, indeed, that the right of a
faith to live is only to be proved by its possible reconciliation with natural and scientific facts, proves how
little fitted he was to expound Natural Science.

Long before he went to Japan, he had been interested
in Oriental religion and ethics. But his Buddhism was
really only a vague, poetical theory, as was his Christianity. "When I write God, of course I mean only
the World-Soul, the mighty and sweetest life of Nature,
the great Blue Ghost, the Holy Ghost which fills planets
and hearts with beauty." The deeper Buddhism, he
affirmed, was only the divine in man.

Bruised and buffeted in the struggle for existence, it
is easy to imagine the attraction that the Buddhist ideal
of discipline and self-effacement would exercise over a
mind such as his. Shortly after his arrival in Japan,
standing opposite the great Dai Batsu with its picturesque surroundings in the garden at Kamakura, he was
carried away by the ideal of calm, of selflessness that
it embodied.

It has generally been taken for granted that he died a
Buddhist; he emphatically declared, during the last
year of his life, that he subscribed to no Buddhistical
tenets.

Invariably the best critic of his own nature—"Truly
we have no permanent opinions," he writes, "until our
mental growth is done. The opinions we have are
simply lent us for awhile by the Gods—at compound
interest!"

There is a characteristic anecdote told of him by a cousin who went to visit him when a boy at Ushaw. He asked her to bow to the figure of the Virgin Mary, which stood upon the stairway. She refused, upon which he earnestly repeated his request. Shortly after this incident he volunteered the statement to one of the college tutors, who found him lying on his back in the grass, looking up at the sky, that he was a Pantheist.

After he had been reading some of the Russian novelists, though he confessed to a world of romance in old Romanism, the Greek Church, he thought, had a better chance of life. Russia seemed the Coming Race, a Russian Mass would one day be sung in St. Peter's, and Cossack soldiers would wait at Stamboul in the reconsecrated Basilica of Justinian for the apparition of that phantom priest destined to finish the Mass, interrupted by the swords of the Janizaries of Mahomet II.

In spite of frequently declaring himself a Radical, the trend of Hearn's mind was distinctly Conservative. Old beliefs handed down from century to century, old temples sanctified for generations, old emotions that had moulded the life of the people, had for him supreme attraction. When he arrived at Matsue and found an Arcadian state of things, a happy, contented, industrious people, and an artistic development of a remarkable kind, the girl he married also, Setsu Koizumi, having been brought up in the tenets of the ancient faith, it was a foregone conclusion that he should endeavour to harmonise Shintoism and Buddhism with the philosophy propounded by his high-priest, Herbert Spencer. Following the lead of his master, he committed himself to the statement that "ancestor worship was the root of all religion." Cut off from communication with outside opinion, he did not know how hotly this idea had been contested, Frederic Harrison, amongst others, asserting that the worship of natural objects —not Spirit or ancestor worship—was the beginning of the religious sentiment in man.

It was of the nature of Hearn's mind that he should have taken up and clung to this Spencerian idea of ghost-cult, the religion of the dead. From his earliest childhood the "ghostly" had always haunted him. Even the name of the Holy Ghost as taught him in his childish catechism was invested with a vague reverential feeling of uncanny, ghostly influences. When therefore in the *Synthetic Philosophy* he found Spencer declaring that ancestor worship, the influence of spirits or ghosts, was the foundation of all religion, he subscribed to the same idea. "The real religion of Japan," he says in his essay on the ancient cult, "the religion still professed in one form or other by the entire nation, is that cult which has been the foundation of all civilised religion and of all civilised society, 'Ancestor worship.' Patriotism belongs to it, filial power depends upon it, family love is rooted in it, loyalty is based upon it. The soldier who, to make a path for his comrades through the battle, deliberately flings away his life with a shout of 'Teikoku manzai' (Empire, good-bye), obeys the will and fears the approval of ghostly witnesses."

Mr. Robert Young, editor of the *Japan Chronicle*, and Mr. W. B. Mason, who both of them have lived in Japan for many years, keen observers of Japanese characteristics and tendencies, in discussing the value of

Hearn's books as expositions of the country, were unanimous in declaring that he greatly overestimated the influence of ancestor worship.

The Japanese, like all gallant people, foster a deep reverence for their heroic ancestors. Secluded from the rest of the world for centuries, all their hero-worship had been devoted to their own nationality; but practical, hard-headed, material-minded, pushing forward in every direction, grasping the necessities that the competitive struggle of modern civilisation has forced upon them, keeping in the van by every means inculcated by cleverness and shrewdness—arguing by analogy, it is not likely that a people, living intensely in the present, clutching at every opportunity as it passes, would nourish a feeling such as Hearn describes for " millions long buried "—for " the nameless dead."

Nature worship, the worship of the Sun, that gave its name to the ancient kingdom, the natural phenomena of their volcanic mountains Fuji-no-yama or Asama-yama, inspired feelings of reverence in the ancient Japanese, far more potent than any idea connected with their " ancestral spirits."

In Shinto there is no belief in the passage of " mind essence " from form to form, as in Buddhism; the spirits of the dead, according to the most ancient Japanese religion, continue to exist in the world, they mingle with the viewless forces of Nature and act through them, still surrounding the living, expecting daily offerings and prayers. What a charm and mysticism is imparted to all the literary work done by Hearn in Japan by the Shinto idea of ancestral ghosts, which he really seems for a time to have adopted, woven into the Buddhist belief in pre-existence, the continuity of mind connected again with the scientific theory of Evolution.

"He stands and proclaims his mysteries," says an American critic, "at the meeting of Three Ways. To the religious instinct of India,—Buddhism in particular,—which history has engrafted on the æsthetic heart of Japan, Hearn brings the interpreting spirit of Occidental science; and these three traditions are fused by the peculiar sympathies of his mind into one rich and novel compound,—a compound so rare as to have introduced into literature a psychological sensation unknown before. More than any other living author he has added a new thrill to our intellectual experience."

When at Tokyo, if you find your way into the street called Naka-dori where ancient curios and embroideries are to be bought,—you will perchance be shown a wonderful fabric minutely intersected with delicate traceries on a dark-coloured texture. If you are accompanied by any one who is acquainted with ancient Japanese embroidery, they will show you that these traceries are fine Japanese ideographs; poems, proverbs, legends, embroidered by the laying on of thread by thread all over the tissue, producing a most harmonious and beautiful effect. Thus did Hearn, like these ancient artificers, weave ancient theories of pre-existence and Karma into spiritual fantasies and imaginations. Ever in consonance with wider interests his work opened up strange regions of dreamland, touched trains of thought that run far beyond the boundaries of men's ordinary mental horizon. In his sketch, for instance, called the "Mountain of Skulls," [1] how weirdly does

[1] *In Ghostly Japan:* Little, Brown & Co.

he make use of the idea of pre-existence. A young man and his guide are pictured climbing up a mountain, where was no beaten path, the way lying over an endless heaping of tumbled fragments.

Under the stars they climbed, aided by some super-human power, and as they climbed the fragments under their feet yielded with soft dull crashings. . . . And once the pilgrim youth laid hand on something smooth that was not stone—and lifted it—and was startled by the cheekless gibe of death.

In his inimitable way, Hearn tells how the dawn breaks, casting a light on the monstrous measureless height round them. "All of these skulls and dust of bones, my son, are your own!" says his guide, "each has at some time been the nest of your dreams and delusions and desires."

The Buddhist idea of pre-existence has been believed in by Orientals from time immemorial; in the Sacontala the Indian poet, Calidas, says: "Perhaps the sadness of men, in seeing beautiful forms and hearing sweet music, arises from some remembrance of past joys, and the traces of connections in a former state of existence." The idea has been re-echoed by many in our own time, but by none more exquisitely and fancifully than by Lafcadio Hearn.

In one of his sketches, entitled "A Serenade," his prose is the essence of music, weird and pathetic as a nocturne by Chopin; setting thrilling a host of memories and dreams, suggesting hints and echoes of ineffable things. You feel the violet gloom, the warm air, and see the fire-flies, the plumes of the palms, and the haunting circle of the sea beyond, the silence only broken by the playing of flutes and mandolines.

" The music hushed, and left me dreaming and vainly trying to explain the emotion that it had made. Of one thing only I felt assured,—that the mystery was of other existences than mine." [1]

Then he brings forward his favourite theme, that our living present is the whole dead past. Our pleasures and our pains alike are but products of evolution— created by experiences of vanished being more countless than the sands of a myriad seas. . . . Echoing into his own past, he imagines the music startling from their sleep of ages countless buried loves, the elfish ecstasy of their thronging awakening endless remembrance, and with that awakening the delight passed, and in the dark the sadness only lingered—unutterable—profound.

[1] *Exotics and Retrospectives :* Little, Brown & Co.

CHAPTER XIV

WEST INDIES

" Ah ! the dawnless glory of tropic morning ! The single sudden leap of the giant light over the purpling of a hundred peaks,—over the surging of the Mornes ! and the early breezes from the hills—all cool out of the sleep of the forest, . . . and the wild high winds that run roughling and crumpling through the cane of the mountain slopes in storms of papery sound. And the mighty dreaming of the woods,— green drenched with silent pouring of creepers . . . and the eternal azure apparition of the all-circling sea. . . . And the violet velvet distances of evening, and the swaying of palms against the orange-burning sunset,—when all the heavens seem filled with vapours of a molten sun ! "

In the early part of June, 1887, Hearn left New Orleans, and made his way to New York via Cincinnati. He went to see no one in the Western city, where he had been so well known, but his old friend Mr. Watkin. Seated in the printing-office, then situated at 26, Longworth Street, they chatted together all day to the accompaniment of the ticking of the tall clock, loud and insistent, like the footstep of a man booted and spurred. We can imagine their discussions and arguments on the subject of Herbert Spencer and Darwin, Esoteric Buddhism, and " that which the Christian calls soul,—the Pantheist Nature,—the philosopher, the Unknowable."

Hearn took his departure from Cincinnati late in the evening. A delightful trip, he wrote to Mr. Watkin, had brought him safe and sound to New York, where his dear friend Krehbiel was waiting to receive him and take him as a guest to his cosy home. "I cannot tell you," he adds, "how our little meeting delighted me, or how much I regretted to depart so soon. . . . I felt that I loved you more than I ever did before; feel also how much I owed you and will always owe you."

Mr. Watkin, who died this spring, aged eighty-six, spent the last years of his life in the "Old Men's Home" in Cincinnati. I received a letter from him a few months before his death relating to his friend Lafcadio Hearn. After this meeting in 1887, he was never fated to see his "Raven," but the old man kept religiously all the letters written to him by the odd little genius, who forty years before had so often sat with him in his printing-office, pouring forth his hopes and ambitions, his opinions and beliefs, his wild revolts and despairs. Loyally did the old printer add his voice to Krehbiel's and Tunison's in defence of his reputation after Hearn's death in 1904.

The Krehbiels lived at a flat, 438, West Fifty-seventh Street, New York, and Lafcadio had arranged to stop with them there before he left New Orleans.

Krehbiel's position as leading musical critic to the *Tribune* necessitated his frequenting busy literary and social circles; it is easy to imagine how Hearn, just arrived from the easy-going, loafing life of New Orleans, must have suffered in such a *milieu*.

Gould, in his "Biography," notes with "sorrow and pain" that Hearn's letters to Krehbiel suddenly ceased in 1887. "One may be sure," he adds, "that it was not Krehbiel who should be blamed." Without blaming either Krehbiel or Hearn, it is easy to see many reasons for the break-off of the close communion between the friends. For a person of Hearn's temperament, innumerable sunken rocks beset the waters in which he found himself in New York City. Before starting on his journey thither he told Krehbiel that the idea of mixing in society in a great metropolis was a horrible nightmare, that he had been a demophobe for years, hating crowds and the heterogeneous acquaintances of ordinary city life. "Here I visit a few friends for months, then disappear for six. Can't help it;—just a nervous condition that renders effort unpleasant. So I shall want to be very well hidden away in New York, —to see no one except you and Joe."

It was hardly a prudent step on Krehbiel's part to subject this sensitive, excitable spirit to so great a trial of temper as caging him in a flat in the very midst of the "beastly machinery." He and Hearn had not met personally since Cincinnati days, many divergencies of sentiment and feeling must have arisen between them in that space of ten years, subtle antagonisms of personal habit and manner of life, formed in the passage of the years, that would not have revealed themselves in letters transmitted across thousands of miles.

Hearn, like many Irishmen, was intemperate in argument. Testiness in argument is a quality peculiar to the Celt, and in the Hearn family was inordinately developed. Richard Hearn, Lafcadio's uncle, the warmest and gentlest-hearted of men, would sometimes become quite unmanageable in the course of a political or artistic discussion. Old Mrs. Hearn, Lafcadio's grandmother, a person far superior to any of the Hearns of her day in mental calibre, was wont to declare that the only way she had lived in peace and amity with her husband and his relations was, that for thirty years she had never ventured to express an opinion.

Krehbiel was a Teuton, a Northerner; Hearn was an Oriental with Oriental tendencies and sympathies. Continually in the course of the Krehbiel correspondence, Hearn reminds his friend that his ancestors were Goths and Vandals—and he tells him that he still possesses traces of that Gothic spirit which detests all beauty that is not beautiful with the fantastic and unearthly beauty that is Gothic. . . . This is a cosmopolitan Art Era, he tells him again, and you must not judge everything that claims Art merit by a Gothic standard.

From the fine criticisms and essays that have been given to the public by Henry Krehbiel, it is apparent that his musical taste was entirely for German music. Above all, he was an enthusiast upon the subject of the Modern School, the Music of the Future, as it was called; Hearn, on the other hand—no musician from a technical point of view—frankly declared that he preferred a folk-song or negro melody, to a Beethoven's Sonata or an opera by Wagner. Krehbiel, in an article written after his death, entitled "Hearn and Folk Music," declares that it would have broken Hearn's heart had he ever told him that any of the music which he sent him or of which he wrote descriptions showed no African, but Scotch and British characteristics, or sophistications from the civilised art. "He had heard from me of Oriental scales, and savage music, in which there were fractional tones unknown to the Occidental system. These tones he thought he heard again in negro and Creole melodies, and he was constantly trying to make me understand what he meant by descriptions, by diagrams, he could not record rhythms in any other way. The *glissando* effect which may be heard in negro singing, and the use of tones not in our scales, he described over and over again as ' tonal splinterings.' They had for him a great charm."

Miss Elizabeth Bisland was in New York, acting as sub-editor of the *Cosmopolitan Review*. Lafcadio made an unsuccessful attempt to see her. " Nobody can find anybody, nothing seems to be anywhere, everything seems to be mathematics, and geometry, and enigmatics, and riddles and confusion worse confounded. . . . I am sorry not to see you—but since you live in Hell what can I do? " This is his outburst to Tunison.

To Harper's, the publishers, he offered to go where they would send him, so long as it was South, taking an open engagement to send letters when he could. They suggested a trip to the West Indies and British Guiana. In the beginning of June, 1887, he started on the *Barracouta* for Trinidad. His account of his " Midsummer Trip to the West Indies," a trip that only lasted for three months, from July to September, appeared originally in *Harper's Monthly*. It was afterwards incorporated in his larger book, *Two Years in the French West Indies*.

Hearn's more intimate life, during this, his first visit to the tropics, is to be found recounted in his letters to Dr. Matas, the New Orleans physician. They reveal the same erratic, unpractical, wayward being as ever, beset by financial difficulties, carried away by unbalanced enthusiasms.

He had been without a cent of money, he said, for

four months, and, unacquainted with any one, he could not get credit, yet starvation at Martinique was preferable to luxury in New York. "The climate was simply heaven on earth, no thieves, no roughs, no snobs; everything primitive and morally pure. Confound fame, wealth, reputation and splendour! Leave them all, give up New Orleans, these things are superfluous in the West Indies, obsolete nuisances." All ambition to write was paralysed, "but nature did the writing in green, azure, and gold, while the palms distilled Elixir Vitæ." [1]

There is only one letter to Krehbiel from the West Indies, published in the series edited by Miss Bisland. Krehbiel was apparently leaving for Europe to attend the Wagner Festival at Bayreuth. Hearn expresses a hope that before his departure from New York he would arrange with Tunison or somebody to put the things left in his charge by Hearn, in a place of safety until some arrangement had been come to with Harper's, the publishers. Though there is no record of a broken friendship, the two comrades had apparently drifted apart. All the old spontaneity, the close communion of mind with mind was gone. You cannot help feeling as if you had personally lost a valued and sympathetic companion.

During the course of the month of September, Hearn found himself back in the United States. His stay, however, only lasted a week. He arrived on the 21st, and on the 28th of the same month returned to the tropics on board the *Barracouta*, on which he had

---

[1] Dr. George Milbury Gould's book, *Concerning Lafcadio Hearn*, published by Messrs. Fisher Unwin.

returned. *Two Years in the French West Indies*,
though it has not the poetic pathos, the weird atmosphere, that make his Japanese books so arresting and
original, is a delightful collection of pictures taken
absolutely fresh from the heart of tropical nature with
its luxuriant and exotic beauty. Had he never written
anything but this, Hearn would have been recognised
as one, at least, of the striking figures in the prose
literature of the latter end of the nineteenth century.
To appreciate the beauty of its style, it is well to compare it with books on the same subject, Froude's *West
Indies*, for instance, or Sir Frederick Treves's *Cradle of
the Deep*, written, both of them, in sonorous, vigorous
English. You are interested, carried along in the flow
of chapter and paragraph, suddenly you come upon a
few sentences that take your senses captive with the
music of their eddying ripple. You feel as if you had
been walking through a well-cultured upland country,
when from under a hidden bank the music of a running
stream falls upon your ear with the soothing magic of
its silvery cadence; looking at the foot of the page
you see it is a quotation from Lafcadio Hearn. For
instance : —

" Soundless as a shadow is the motion of all these
naked-footed people. On any quiet mountain way,
full of curves, where you fancy yourself alone, you may
often be startled by something you *feel*, rather than
hear behind you,—surd steps, the springy movement
of a long lithe body, dumb oscillations of raiment,—
and ere you can turn to look, the haunter swiftly
passes with Creole greeting of ' bon-jou ' or ' bonsoue,
missie.' . . ."

Two Years in the French West Indies was dedicated

"À mon cher ami,

LÉOPOLD ARNOUX

Notaire à Saint Pierre, Martinique.

Souvenir de nos promenades, de nos voyages, de nos causeries, des sympathies échangées, de tout le charme d'une amitié inaltérable et inoubliable, de tout ce qui parle à l'âme au doux Pays des Revenants."

Arnoux is mentioned subsequently in one or two of Hearn's letters. He alludes to suppers eaten with him at Grande Anse, in a little room opening over a low garden full of banana-trees, to the black beach of the sea, with the great voice thundering outside so that they could scarcely hear themselves speak, and the candle in the verrine fluttering like something afraid.

In 1902, in a letter written to Ellwood Hendrik from Tokyo, shortly after the great eruption of Mt. Pelée that destroyed Saint Pierre, he alludes to Arnoux' garden, and speaks of a spray of arborescent fern that had been sent him. In the fragment also, called "Vanished Light," he describes the amber shadows and court-yard filled with flickering emerald and the chirrup of leaping water. A little boy and girl run to meet him, and the father's voice, deep and vibrant as the tone of a great bell, calls from an inner doorway, "Entrez donc, mon ami!" "But all this was—and is not! . . . Never again will sun or moon shine upon the streets of that city; never again will its ways be trodden, never again will its gardens blossom . . . except in dreams."

Hearn definitely left Martinique in 1889, bound for America; having completed the task he had undertaken to do. Much as he loved the lazy, easy tropical life, "the perfumed peace of enormous azured noons, and the silent flickering of fire-flies through the lukewarm distance, the turquoise sky and the beautiful brown women," he began, before the end of his stay to acknowledge that the resources of intellectual life were lacking; no libraries, no books in any language; a mind accustomed to discipline became, he said, like a garden long uncultivated, in which rare flowers returned to their primitive savage forms, smothered by rank, tough growths, which ought to be pulled up and thrown away. "Nature does not allow serious study or earnest work, and if you revolt against her, she leaves you helpless and tortured for months. One must not seek the Holy Ghost, the world is young here,—not old and wise and grey as in the North. . . . The material furnished by the tropics could only," he said, "be utilised in a Northern atmosphere. . . ." The climate numbed mental life, and the inspiration he hoped for wouldn't come.

During his stay in New York, while preparing *Youma* (a story written in the West Indies) for press and going over the proofs of *Chita* before its appearance in book form, he seems to have been in a pitiable state of destitution, obliged to make a translation of Anatole France's *Le Crime de Sylvestre Bonnard* to keep bread in his mouth.

"So you read my translation of *Sylvestre Bonnard?*" he says to his sister, writing from Japan. "I made it in two weeks, the Publishers paying me only $100. Of course the translation was too quickly done to be very good. I could not have written it all in the prescribed time, so a typewriter was hired for me. She was a pretty girl and I almost fell in love with her."

In 1889, Hearn made that ill-advised visit to Philadelphia, to Dr. George Milbury Gould. He had only known this gentleman hitherto through an interchange of letters. Gould had written to him at New Orleans, expressing delight with some of Hearn's translations from the French, upon which Hearn, in his usual impulsive way rushed into a correspondence. This was in April, 1887. Gould had written several pamphlets on the subject of myopia and defective sight, these he sent to Hearn, and Hearn had responded, touching as usual on every sort of philosophical and literary subject. When he returned to the United States, after his two years in the French West Indies, he thought he would like to consult Gould on the subject of his eyesight. He therefore wrote, suggesting that if a quiet room could be found for him in Philadelphia he would try his luck there.

Gould's account of his first appearance in his consulting-room is familiar to all who have read his book. "The poor exotic was so sadly out of place, so wondering, so suffering and shy, that he would certainly have run out of the house if by a tone of voice I had betrayed any curiosity or a doubt." [1]

Being extremely hard-up, Hearn was glad to accept an arrangement to stop in Gould's house for a while, sharing the family meals, but spending the greater part of the day at work on his proof-correcting in a room set apart for him. An incident, related by Gould,

[1] *Concerning Lafcadio Hearn :* Messrs. Fisher Unwin.

shows Hearn's extraordinary shyness and dislike to make the acquaintance of strangers. He was desirous of giving an idea of the music of Creole songs in his book on the West Indies, but because of his ignorance of technical counterpoint, was unable to do so. Gould made an arrangement with a lady, an acquaintance, to repeat the airs on her piano as he whistled them. An appointment was made for a visit, but on their way to the house Hearn gradually became more and more silent, and his steps slower and slower. When at last he reached the doorstep and the bell had been rung, his courage failed, and before the servant appeared he had run, as if for life, and was half a square away.

Gould claims to have made noteworthy changes in Hearn's character during the summer he stayed with him at Philadelphia. He declares that he first gave him a " soul," taught him the sense of duty, and made him appreciate the beauties of domestic life! A very beautiful story entitled " Karma," published in *Lippincott's Magazine* after Hearn had left for Japan, certainly shows that a change of some sort was being wrought. "I never could find in the tropics that magnificent type of womanhood, which in the New England girl makes one afraid even to think about sex, while absolutely adoring the personality. Perfect nature inspires a love that is fear. I don't think any love is noble without it. The tropical woman inspires a love that is half compassion; this is always dangerous, untrustworthy, delusive."

Gould also, much to the indignation of Hearn's friends, claims to have been the first person who definitely turned his thoughts to the Far East. Inasmuch as Hearn's mind had been impregnated with Japan from

New Orleans days, this seems an unlikely statement; but of all unprofitable things in this world is the sifting of literary wrangles; Hearn's intimacy with George Milbury Gould has led to lawsuits, recriminations, and many distasteful and painful episodes between Gould and some of Hearn's friends. It is as well perhaps, therefore, to go into detail as little as possible.

A passage occurs in one of Hearn's letters to Ellwood Hendrik which disposes of the matter. "Of course we shall never see each other again in this world, and what is the use of being unkind after all? . . . The effect is certainly to convince a man of forty-four that the less he has to do with his fellow-men the better, or, at least, that the less he has to do with the so-called 'cultured' the better. . . ."

From the city of doctors and Quakers Hearn wrote several letters to Miss Bisland, at first entirely formal upon literary subjects. He couldn't say when he was going to New York, as he was tied up by business muddle, waiting for information, anxious beyond expression about an undecided plan, shivering with cold, and longing for the tropics.

Lights are thrown upon his emotional and intellectual life in letters written in the autumn to Dr. Gould from New York.

Japan was looming large on the Oriental horizon. A book by Percival Lowell, entitled *The Soul of the Far East*, had just appeared. It apparently made a profound impression upon Hearn; every word he declared to be dynamic, as lucid and philosophical as Schopenhauer. All his former enthusiasm for Japan was aroused, he followed her progress with the deepest interest. The Japanese Constitution had been promulgated in 1889, the first Diet had met in Tokyo in 1890, the simultaneous reconstruction of her army, and creation of a navy, was gradually placing her in the van of Far Eastern nations; and what was more important to commercial America, her trade had enormously developed under the new régime.

Harper's, the publishers, came to the conclusion that it would be expedient to send one of their staff to Tokyo as regular correspondent; Hearn had succeeded in catching the attention of the public by his story of *Chita* and a *Midsummer Trip*, that had both been published serially in their magazine. With his graphic and picturesque pen he would adequately, they thought, fill the post.

In an interview with the managing director he was approached upon the subject, and, needless to say, eagerly accepted the offer. It was arranged, therefore, that, accompanied by Charles Welton, one of Harper's artists, he was to start in the beginning of the March of 1890 for the Far East.

Little did Hearn realise that the strange land for which he was bound was to receive him for ever, to make him one with its religion, its institutions, its nationality, and that as he closed the door of the publisher's room that day, he was closing the door between himself and Western civilisation for ever.

CHAPTER XV

JAPAN

" . . . Yes—for no little time these fairy-folk can give you all the soft bliss of sleep. But sooner or later, if you dwell long with them, your contentment will prove to have much in common with the happiness of dreams. You will never forget the dream,—never; but it will lift at last, like those vapours of spring which lend preternatural loveliness to a Japanese landscape in the forenoon of radiant days. Really you are happy because you have entered bodily into Fairyland, into a world that is not and never could be your own. You have been transported out of your own century, over spaces enormous of perished time, into an era forgotten, into a vanished age,—back to something ancient as Egypt or Nineveh. That is the secret of the strangeness and beauty of things, the secret of the thrill they give, the secret of the elfish charm of the people and their ways. Fortunate mortal! the tide of Time has turned for you! But remember that all here is enchantment, that you have fallen under the spell of the dead, that the lights and the colours and the voices must fade away at last into emptiness and silence."

MRS. WETMORE is inaccurate in stating that Lafcadio Hearn started for Japan on May 8th, 1890. She must mean March, for he landed in Yokohama on Good Friday, April 13th, after a six weeks' journey. His paper, entitled "A Winter Journey to Japan," contributed to *Harper's*, describes a journey made in the depth of winter.

He stepped from the railway depot, "not upon Canadian soil, but upon Canadian ice. Ice, many inches thick, sheeted the pavement, and lines of sleighs, instead of lines of hacks, waited before the station for passengers. . . . A pale-blue sky arched cloudlessly overhead; and grey Montreal lay angled very sharply in the keen air over the frozen miles of the St. Lawrence; sleighs were moving,—so far away that it looked like a crawling of beetles; and beyond the farther bank where ice-cakes made a high, white ridge, a line of purplish hills arose into the horizon. . . ."

Hearn's account of his journey through wastes of snow, up mountain sides, through long chasms, passing continually from sun to shadow, and from shadow to sun, the mountains interposing their white heads, and ever heaping themselves in a huge maze behind, are above the average of ordinary traveller's prose, but there is no page that can be called arresting or original. The impressions seem to be written to order, written in fact as subordinate to the artist's illustrations. So irksome did this necessity of writing a text to Welton's illustrations become, that it is said to have been one of the reasons for the rupture of his contract with Harper almost immediately after his arrival in Japan.

The seventeen days that he passed on the Northern Pacific with their memories of heavy green seas and ghostly suns, the roaring of the rigging and spars against the gale, the steamer rocking like a cradle as she forced her way through the billowing waves are well described. There is a weird touch, too, in his description of the Chinese steerage passengers, playing the game of " Fan-Tan " by the light of three candles at a low table covered with a bamboo mat.

Deep in the hold below he imagines the sixty square boxes resembling tea-chests, covered with Chinese lettering, each containing the bones of a dead man, bones being sent back to melt into that Chinese soil from whence by nature's vital chemistry they were shapen . . . and he imagines those labelled bones once crossing the same ocean on just such a ship, and smoking or dreaming their time away in just such berths, and playing the same strange play by such a yellow light in even just such an atmosphere, heavy with vaporised opium.

"Meanwhile, something has dropped out of the lives of some of us, as lives are reckoned by Occidental time, —a day. A day that will never come back again, unless we return by this same route,—over this same iron-grey waste, in the midst of which our lost day will wait for us,—perhaps in vain."

Not from the stormy waters of the Pacific, how-ever, not from gleaming Canadian pinnacles, or virgin forests, or dim cañons, was this child of the South and the Orient, this interpreter of mankind in all his exotic and strange manifestations to draw his inspiration, but from the valleys and hill-sides of that immemorial East that stretched in front of him, manured and fructified by untold centuries of thought and valour and belief.

The spell fell on him from the moment that through the transparent darkness of the cloudless April morning he caught sight of the divine mountain. The first sight of Fuji, hanging above Yokohama Bay like a snowy ghost in the arch of the infinite day, is a sight never to be forgotten, a vision that, for the years Hearn was yet to traverse, before the heavy, folded curtain fell on his stage of life, was destined to form the background of his poetic dreams and imaginings.

Mr. Henry Watkin appears to have been the first

person to whom Hearn wrote from Japan. So great was the charm of this new country that he seems irresistibly called to impart some of the delight to those he had left behind in America. He tells him that he passes much of his time in the temples, trying to see into the heart of the strange people surrounding him. He hoped to learn the language, he said, and become a part of the very soul of the people. He rhapsodises on the subject of the simple humanity of Japan and the Japanese. . . . He loved their gods, their customs, their dress, their bird-like, quavering songs, their houses, their superstitions, their faults. He was as sure as he was of death that their art was as far in advance of our art, as old Greek art was superior to that of the earliest art groupings. There was more art in a print by Hokousai, or those who came after him, than in a $100,000 painting. Occidentals were the barbarians.

Most travellers when first visiting Japan see only its atmosphere of elfishness, of delicate fantasticality. The queer little streets, the quaint shops where people seem to be playing at buying and selling, the smiling, small people in " geta " and " kimono," the mouldering shrines with their odd images and gardens; but to Hearn a transfiguring light cast a ghostly radiance on ordinary sights and scenes, opening a world of suggestion, and inspiring him with an eloquent power of impressing upon others, not only the visible picturesqueness and oddity of Japanese life, but that dim surmise of another and inscrutable humanity, that atmosphere of spirituality so inseparably a part of the religion Buddha preached to man. With almost sacramental solemnity, he gazed at the strange ideographs, wandered about the temple gardens, ascended the stairways leading to ancient shrines. What these experiences did for his genius is to be read in the first book inspired by the Orient while he was still under the glamour of enchantment. Amidst the turmoil, the rush, the struggle of our monster City of the West, if you open his *Glimpses of Unfamiliar Japan*, and read his description of his first visit to a Buddhist temple, you will find the silence of centuries descending upon your soul, the thrill of something above and beyond the commonplace of this everyday world. The bygone spirit of the race, with its hidden meanings and allegories, its myths and legends, the very essence of the heart of the people, that has lain sleeping in the temple gloom, will reveal itself, the faint odour of incense will float to your nostrils, the shuffling of pilgrim feet to your ear; you will see the priests sliding back screen after screen, pouring in light on the gilded bronzes and inscriptions; involuntarily you will look for the image of the Deity, of the presiding spirit between the altar groups of convoluted candelabra, and you will see " Only a mirror! Symbolising what? Illusion? Or that the universe exists for us solely as the reflection of our own souls? Or the old Chinese teaching that we must seek the Buddha only in our hearts? "

A storm soon passed across the heaven of his dreams. He suddenly terminated his contract with Harper's. " I am starved out," he wrote to Miss Bisland. " Do you think well enough of me to try to get me employment at a regular salary, somewhere in the United States? " . . .

It is said that his reason for breaking with Harper's was a difference of opinion as to the relative position of himself and their artist, Mr. C. P. Welton. Hearn was expected to write up to the illustrations of the articles sent to the magazine, instead of the illustrations being done for Hearn's letterpress. Besides which, the fact transpired that the artist was receiving double Hearn's salary.

The little Irishman was a mixture of exaggerated humility and sensitive pride on the score of his literary work; always in extremes in this, as in all else. He was also, as we have seen, extremely unbusinesslike; he never attempted to enter into an agreement of any kind. It seems difficult to accept his statement that his publishers, having made a success with *Chita* and *Youma* and *Two Years in the French West Indies*, paid him only at the rate of five hundred dollars a year. No doubt Harper's might have been able to put a very different complexion on the matter. As a proof of the difficulty in conducting affairs with him, when he threw up his Japanese engagement he declined to accept royalties on books already in print. Harper's were obliged to make arrangements to transmit the money through a friend in Japan, and it was only after considerable persuasion and a lapse of several years that he was induced to accept it. So often in his career through life Hearn proved an exemplification of his own statement. Those who are checked by emotional feeling, where no check is placed on competition, must fail. Uncontrolled emotional feeling was the rock on which he split, at this and many other critical moments in his career.

He had brought a letter of introduction, presumably from Harper's, the publishers, to Professor Basil Hall Chamberlain, Professor of English Literature at the Tokyo University, the well-known author of *Things*

Japanese. On his arrival, Hearn thought of obtaining a position as teacher in a Japanese family, so as to master the spoken language. Simply to have a small room where he could write would satisfy him, he told Professor Chamberlain, and so long as he was boarded he would not ask for remuneration. He knew also that he could not carry out his fixed determination of writing a comprehensive book on Japan, without passing several years exclusively amongst Japanese people.

Chamberlain, however, saw at once that Hearn's capacities were far superior to those necessary for a private tutorship. Having been so long resident in Japan, and written so much upon the country, as well as occupying a professorship in Tokyo Imperial University, his influence in Japanese official life was considerable; he now bestirred himself, and succeeded in getting Hearn an appointment as English teacher in the Jinjo Chugakko, or ordinary Middle School, at Matsue, in the province of Izumo, for the term of one year.

A week or two later Hearn was able to announce to his dear sister Elizabeth that he was going to become a country schoolmaster in Japan.

On several occasions Professor Chamberlain held out the kindly hand of comradeship to Lafcadio; to him Hearn owed his subsequent appointment at the Tokyo University.

For five or six years the two men were bound together in a close communion of intellectual enthusiasms and mutual interests, as is easy to see by the wonderful correspondence recently published. To him and to Paymaster Mitchell McDonald, Lafcadio dedicated his *Glimpses of Unfamiliar Japan.*

TO THE FRIENDS

WHOSE KINDNESS ALONE RENDERED POSSIBLE

MY SOJOURN IN THE ORIENT

PAYMASTER MITCHELL McDONALD, U.S.N.

AND

BASIL HALL CHAMBERLAIN, ESQ.

EMERITUS PROFESSOR OF PHILOLOGY AND

JAPANESE IN THE IMPERIAL UNIVERSITY

OF TOKYO

I DEDICATE THESE VOLUMES

IN TOKEN OF

AFFECTION AND GRATITUDE

Then came a sudden break.

After Hearn's death, Chamberlain, in discussing the subject, lamented "the severance of a connection with one so gifted." He made one or two attempts at renewal of intercourse, which were at first met with cold politeness, afterwards with complete silence, causing him to desist from further endeavours. The key, perhaps, to Hearn's course of action, is to be found in some observations that he addresses to Professor Chamberlain just before the close of their friendship. They had been in correspondence on the subject of the connection of the tenets of Buddhism and scientific expositions of Evolutionary Science in England.

"DEAR CHAMBERLAIN: In writing to you, of course, I have not been writing a book, but simply setting down the thoughts and feelings of the moment as they come. . . .

"I write a book exactly the same way; but all this

has to be smoothed, ordinated, corrected, toned over twenty times before a page is ready. . . . I cannot help fearing that what you mean by ' justice and temperateness' means that you want me to write as if I were you, or at least to measure sentence or thought by your standard. . . . If I write well of a thing one day, and badly another, I expect my friend to discern that both impressions are true, and solve the contradiction—that is, if my letters are really wanted."

The fact is that if Hearn took up a philosophic or scientific opinion he was determined to make all with whom he held converse share them, and if they did not do so at once, like the despotic Oriental monarch, he would overturn the chessboard.

" The rigid character of his philosophical opinions," says Chamberlain, " made him perforce despise as intellectual weaklings all those who did not share them, or shared them in a lukewarm manner, and his disillusionment with a series of friends in whom he had once thought to find intellectual sympathy is seen to have been inevitable."

It was principally during the last fourteen years of his life that Hearn acquired the unenviable name of being ungrateful, inconstant and capricious. To those friends made in his youthful days of struggle and adversity he remained constant, but with the exception of Mitchell McDonald, Nishida Sentaro and Amenomori, it is the same story of perversity and estrangement.

An unceremonious entry into his house, without deference to ancient Japanese etiquette, which enjoined the taking off of boots and the putting on of sandals, a sneer at Shinto Ancestor Worship, a difference of

opinion on Herbert Spencer, and Hearn would disappear
actually and metaphorically. This proves his want of
heart, you say. But a careful study of Hearn's *Wesen*
will show that his apparent inconstancy did not arise
from a change of affection, but because his very affection for the people he had turned from made the taut
strands of friendship more difficult to reunite, especially
for a person of his shy temperament. Which of us
has not recognised the greater difficulty of making up
a " tiff " with a friend for whom you care deeply than
with a person to whom you are indifferent? The
tougher the stuff the more ravelled the edges of the
tear, and the more difficult to join together.

At Kobe, an incident was related to us by Mr.
Young, his chief on the *Kobe Chronicle* and a person
to whom Hearn owed much and was attached by many
ties of gratitude and friendship. A guest at dinner
ventured to dissent from Hearn's opinion that the
reverential manner in which people prostrated themselves before the Mikado was in no way connected
with religious principles. Hearn shrugged his shoulders, rose, walked away from the table and nothing
would induce him to return. He did not, indeed,
enter Mr. Young's house again for some days, though
doing his work at the office for the newspaper as
usual.

When Hearn left Tokyo to take up his appointment
at Matsue he was accompanied by his friend Akira, a
young student and priest, who spoke English and could
therefore act as interpreter. At Kobe they left the
railway and continued their journey in jinrikishas, a
journey of four days with strong runners, from the
Pacific to the Sea of Japan.

" Out of the city and over the hills to Izumo, the Land of the Ancient Gods! " The incantation is spoken, we find ourselves in the region of Horai—the fairyland of Japan—with its arch of liquid blue sky, lukewarm, windless atmosphere, an atmosphere enormously old, but of ghostly generations of souls blended into one immense translucency, souls of people who thought in ways never resembling Occidental ways.

Writing later to Chamberlain, Hearn acknowledged that what delighted him those first days in Japan was the charm of nature in human nature, and in human art, simplicity, mutual kindness, child-faith, gentleness, politeness . . . for in Japan even hate works with smiles and pretty words.

For the first time Hearn was not merely describing a sensuous world of sights and sounds, but a world of soft domesticity, where thatched villages nestled in the folds of the hills, each with its Buddhist temple, lifting a tilted roof of blue-grey tiles above a congregation of thatched homesteads. Can anything be more delightful than his description of one of the village inns, with its high-peaked roof of thatch, and green-mossed eaves, like a coloured print out of Hiroshige's picture-books, with its polished stairway and balconies, reflecting like mirrored surfaces the bare feet of the maid-servants; its luminous rooms fresh and sweet-smelling as when their soft mattings were first laid down. The old gold-flowered lacquer ware, the diaphanous porcelain wine-cups, the teacup holders, which are curled lotus leaves of bronze; even the iron kettle with its figurings of dragons and clouds, and the brazen hibachi whose handles are heads of Buddhist lions; distant as it was from all art-centres, there was

no object visible in the house which did not reveal the
Japanese sense of beauty and form. "Indeed, wherever to-day in Japan one sees anything uninteresting
in porcelain or metal, something commonplace and
ugly, one may be almost sure that detestable something has been shaped under foreign influence. But
here I am in Ancient Japan, probably no European
eyes ever looked upon these things before."

After he had submitted to being bathed by his
landlord, as if he had been a little child, and eaten
a repast of rice, eggs, vegetables and sweetmeats, he
sat smoking his kiseru until the moon arose, peeping
through the heart-shaped little window that looked out
on the garden behind, throwing down queer shadows
of tilted eaves, and horned gables, and delightful
silhouettes. Suddenly a measured clapping of hands
became audible, and the echoing of *geta*, and the
tramping of wooden sandals filled the street. His companion, Akira, told him they were all going to see
the dance of the Bon-odori at the temple, the dance
of the Festival of the Dead, and that they had better
go too. This dance of the Festival of the Dead he
describes in his usual graphic way; the ghostly weaving of hands, the rhythmic gliding of feet, above all,
the flitting of the marvellous sleeves, apparitional,
soundless, velvety as the flitting of great tropical bats.
In the midst of the charmed circle there crept upon
him a nameless, tingling sense of being haunted, until
recalled to reality by a song full of sweet, clear quavering, gushing from some girlish mouth, and fifty other
voices joined in the chant. "Melodies of Europe,"
he ends, "awaken within us feelings we can utter,
sensations familiar as mother-speech, inherited from

all the generations behind us. But how explain the emotion evoked by a primitive chant, totally unlike anything in Western melody, impossible even to write in those tones which are the ideographs of our music-tongue? ''

" And the emotion itself—what is it? I know not; yet I feel it to be something infinitely more old than I, something not of only one place or time, but vibrant to all common joy or pain of being, under the universal sun. Then I wonder if the secret does not lie in some untaught spontaneous harmony of that chant with Nature's most ancient song, in some unconscious kinship to the music of solitudes,—all trillings of summer life that blend to make the great sweet Cry of the Land.''

CHAPTER XVI

MATSUE

" Far underlying all the surface crop of quaint superstitions and artless myths and fantastic magic there thrills a mighty spiritual force, the whole soul of a race with all its impulses and powers and intuitions. He who would know what Shinto is must learn to know that mysterious soul in which the sense of beauty and the power of art and the fire of heroism and magnetism of loyalty and the emotion of faith have become inherent, immanent, unconscious, instinctive."

THE year spent in the quaint old city of Matsue—birth-place of the rites, mysteries and mythologies of the ancient religion—was one of the happiest and most productive, intellectually, of Hearn's career.

His *Glimpses of Unfamiliar Japan* was the result. It is perhaps not as finished as some of his later Japanese studies. Writing some years afterwards he said that when he wanted to feel properly humbled he read about half a page of *Glimpses of Unfamiliar Japan;*—then he howled and wondered how he ever could have written so badly, and found that he was only really a very twenty-fifth-rate workman, and that he ought to be kicked. Like some of the early poems of celebrated poets, however, though now and then lacking in polish and reticence, the glow of enthusiasm, of surprised delight, that illumines every page, will always make this book, in spite of the vogue of much of his subsequent work, the one which is most read and by which he is best known.

Here amongst this bizarre people he found his

predilection for the odd, the queer, the strange, satisfied beyond his utmost desires. Matsue was not the tourists' Japan, not the Japan of bowler hats and red-brick warehouses, but the Japan where ancient faiths were still a living force, where old customs were still followed, and ancient chivalry still an animating power.

How fresh and picturesque is his record of the experiences of every day and every hour as they pass. We hear it, and see it all with him : the first of the noises that waken a sleeper . . . the measured, muffled echoing of the ponderous pestle of the cleaner of rice, the most pathetic of the sounds of Japanese life : the beating, indeed, of the pulse of the land. The booming of the great temple bell, signalling the hour of Buddhist morning prayer, the clapping of hands, as the people saluted the rising of the sun, and the cries of the earliest itinerant vendors, the sellers of *daikon* and other strange vegetables . . . and the plaintive call of the women who hawked little thin slips of kindling-wood for the lighting of charcoal fires.

Sliding open his little Japanese window, he looked out. Veiled in long nebulous bands of mist, the lake below looked like a beautiful spectral sea, of the same tint as the dawn-sky and mixing with it . . . an exquisite chaos, as the delicate fogs rose, slowly, very slowly, and the sun's yellow rim came into sight.

From these early morning hours until late at night every moment was packed full of new experiences, new sensations. Not only was the old city itself full of strange and unexpected delights, but the country round was a land of dreams, strange gods, immemorial temples.

One day it was a visit to the Cave of the Children's

Ghosts, where at night the shadowy children come to build their little stone-heaps at the feet of Jizo, changing the stones every night. Doubtless in the quaint imagination of the people there still lingers the primitive idea of some communication, mysterious and awful, between the world of waters and the world of the dead. It is always over the sea, after the Feast of Souls, that the spirits pass murmuring back to their dim realm, in those elfish little ships of straw which are launched for them upon the sixteenth day of the seventh moon. The vague idea behind the pious act is that all waters flow to the sea and the sea itself unto the " Nether-distant Land."

Then a visit to Kitzuki to visit the Buddhist temple, into whose holy precincts no European had hitherto been admitted. Senke Takamori, the spiritual governor of Kitzuki, whose princely family dated back their ancestry to the goddess of the sun, received him with extraordinary urbanity. Senke, it appears, was connected with the Koizumis, the family to which Hearn's future wife belonged.

To see the ancient temple of Kitzuki at that time was to see the living centre of Shinto, to feel the life pulse of the ancient cult throbbing in the nineteenth century as in the unknown past—that religion that lives not in books, nor ceremonial, but in the national heart. The magnetism of another faith, polarised his belief. The forces about him, working imperceptibly, influenced him and drew him towards the religion of those amongst whom he lived, moulding and forming that extraordinary mixture of thought and imagination that enabled him to enter into the very heart and soul of Ancient Japan.

If ever a man was, as religious people term it,

"called," Hearn was called to the task of interpreting the superstitions and beliefs of this strange people. "Putting jesting on one side," he once said, "if he could create something unique and rare he would feel that the Unknowable had selected him for a mouth-piece for a medium of utterance in the holy cycle of its eternal utterance."

The half-blind, vagrant little genius had at last found the direction in which the real development of his genius lay; the loose, quivering needle of thought that had moved hither and thither, was now set in one direction. The stage he was treading, though at first he did not realise it, was gradually becoming the sphere of a drama with eternal and immutable forces as scene-shifters and curtain-raisers. The qualities that had enabled Japan to conquer China, and had placed her practically in the forefront of Far Eastern nations, he was called upon to analyse and explain; to interpret the curious myths of this great people of little men, who, shut off from the rest of the world for hundreds of years, had, out of their own inner consciousness, built up a code of discipline and behaviour that in its self-abnegation, its sense of cohesion, and fidelity to law, throws our much-vaunted Western civilisation into the shade. Hearn brought to bear upon the interpretation a rare power of using words, sympathetic insight, an earnest and vivid imagination that enabled him to comprehend the strongly accentuated characteristics of a race living close to the origins of life; barbaric, yet highly refined; super-stitious, yet capable of adapting themselves to modern thought; playful as children, yet astounding in their heroic gallantry and patriotism. His genius enabled him to catch a glimpse of the indisputable truth that legend and tradition are a science in themselves, that however grotesque, however fantastic primeval myths and allegories may be, they are indicative of the gradual evolution of the heart and mind of generations as they arise and pass away.

An idea, he said, was growing upon him about the utility of superstition, as compared with the utility of religion. In consequence of his having elected to live the everyday life, and enter into the ordinary interests and occupations of this strange people, as no Occidental ever had before, he was enabled to see that many Japanese superstitions had a sort of shorthand value in explaining eternal and valuable things. When it would have been useless to preach to people vaguely about morality, or cleanliness, or ordinary rules of health, a superstition, a belief that certain infringements of moral law will bring direct corporal punishment, that maligned spirits will visit a room that is left unswept, that the gods will chastise over-excess in eating or drinking, are related to the most inexorable and highest moral laws, it is easy to understand how invaluable is the study of their superstitions in analysing and explaining so enigmatical a people as the Japanese.

" Hearn thought a great deal of what we educated Japanese think nothing," said a highly-cultured Tokyo professor to me, with sarcastic intonation. Hearn, on the other hand, maintained that not to the educated Japanese must you go to understand the vitality of heart and intelligence which through centuries of the Elder Life has evolved so remarkable a nationality. To set forth the power that has moulded the character of this Far Eastern people, material must be culled from the unsophisticated hearts of the peasants and the common folk. "The people make the gods, and the gods the people make are the best." Hearn did not attempt, therefore, a mechanical repetition of social and religious tenets; but in the mythological beliefs, in the legendary lore that has slumbered for generations in simple minds he caught the suggestion of obedience and fidelity to authority, the strenuous industry and self-denial that endowed these quaint superstitions with a potency far beyond the religion and meaning, or the primitive idea that caused their inception. Merely accurate and erudite students would call the impressions that he collected here, in this unfamiliar Japan, trifling and fantastic, but he is able to prove that the details of ordinary intercourse, however trifling, the way in which men marry and bring up their children, the very manner in which they earn their daily bread, above all, the rules they impose, and the punishment and rewards they invoke to have them obeyed, reveal more of the manner by which the religion, the art, the heroism of this Far Eastern people have been developed, than hundreds of essays treating of dynasties, treaties and ceremonials.

Aided by that very quality, which some may look upon as a mental defect, Hearn's tendency to over-emphasise an impressive moment at the expense of accuracy, stood him now in good stead. Physical myopia, he maintained, was an aid to artistic work from one aspect: "the keener the view, the less depth in the impression produced. There is no possibility of attraction in wooded deeps or mountain recesses for the eye that, like the eye of a hawk, pierces shadow and can note the separate quiver of every leaf." So mental myopia united with the shaping power of imagination was more helpful in enabling him to catch a glimpse of the trend of thought and characteristics of the folk, whose country he adopted, than the piercing judgment that saw faults and intellectual short-comings.

Many people, even the Japanese themselves, have said that Hearn's view in his first book of things in their country, was too roseate. Others have declared that he must have been a hypocrite to write of Japan in so enthusiastic a strain when in private letters, such as those to Chamberlain and Ellwood Hendrik, he expresses so great a detestation for the people and their methods. Those who say so do not know the nature of the man whom they are discussing; compromise with those in office was entirely antagonistic to his mode of thought. His life was composed of passing illusions and disillusions. That he, with his artistic perception, should have been carried off his balance by the quaintness and mysticism that he encountered in the outlying portions of the country was but natural. Go into the Highlands of Japan amongst the simple folk, where primitive conditions still reign, where the ancient gods are still believed to haunt the ancient shrines, where the glamour and the grace of bygone civilisation still lingers, you will yield to the same charm, and as Hearn himself says, better the sympathetic than the critical attitude. Perhaps the man who comes to Japan full of hate for all things Oriental may get nearer the truth at once, but he will make a kindred mistake to him who views it all, as I did at first almost with the eyes of a lover.

CHAPTER XVII

MARRIAGE

" ' Marriage may be either a hindrance or help on the path,' the old priest said, ' according to conditions. All depends upon conditions. If the love of wife and child should cause a man to become too much attached to the temporary advantages of this unhappy world, then such love would be a hindrance. But, on the contrary, if the love of wife and child should enable a man to live more purely and more unselfishly than he could do in a state of celibacy, then marriage would be a very great help to him in the Perfect Way. Many are the dangers of marriage for the wise; but for those of little understanding, the dangers of celibacy are greater, and even the illusion of passion may sometimes lead noble natures to the higher knowledge.' "

Hearn's marriage, as his widow told us, took place early in the year 1891, "23rd of Meiji." That on either side it was one of passionate sentiment is doubtful. Marriages in Japan are generally arranged on the most businesslike footing. By the young Japanese man, it is looked upon as a natural duty that has duly to be performed for the perpetuation of his family. Passion is reserved for unions unsanctioned by social conventions.

Dominated as he was by the idea that his physical deficiencies rendered a union with one of his own nationality out of the question, he yet knew that at his time of life he had to enter into more permanent conditions with the other sex, than hitherto, or face a future devoid of settled purpose, or stability. His state of health also demanded domestic comfort and feminine care. The only alternative that presented itself to a celibate life was to choose a wife from amongst the people with whom his lines were cast.

From the first moment of his arrival, Hearn had been carried away by enthusiasm for the gentleness, the docility, of the women of Japan. He compares them much to their advantage, with their American sisters. " In the eternal order of things, which is the highest being, the childish, confiding, sweet Japanese girl, or the Occidental Circe women of artificial society, with their enormous power of evil and their limited capacity for good ? " In his first letter to Miss Bisland, he writes : " This is a domesticated nature, which loves man and makes itself beautiful for him in a quiet grey and blue way like the Japanese women."

It seems an unromantic statement to make with regard to an artist, who has written such exquisite passages on the sentiment that binds a man to a woman, but Hearn in spite of his intellectual idealism, had from certain points of view a very material outlook. All considerations,—even those connected with the deepest emotions that stir the human heart, were secondary to the necessities of his genius and artistic life.

His intimacy with Althea Foley in Cincinnati was prompted and fostered by gratitude for her care in preparing his meals, and nursing him when ill, thus saving him from the catastrophe of relinquishing his position on the staff of the *Enquirer* newspaper, which meant not only the loss of all means of subsistence, but also the possibility of prosecuting the ambition of his life,—a literary career.

Now, at Matsue, after a touch of somewhat severe illness obliging him to pass some weeks in bed, it became really a matter of life or death that he should give up living from hand to mouth in country inns.

With the Japanese teacher of English at the Matsue College, an accomplished English scholar, Hearn had formed a close intimacy from the moment of his arrival, an intimacy indeed only broken by Nishida Sentaro's death in 1898.

"His the kind eyes that saw so much for the stranger, his the kind lips that gave him so much wise advice, helping him through the difficulties that beset him, in consequence of his ignorance of the language." At the beginning of his first term Hearn found the necessity of remembering or pronouncing the names of the boys, even with the class-roll before him, almost an insurmountable difficulty. Nishida helped him; gave him all the necessary instructions about hours and text-books, placed his desk close to his, the better to prompt him in school hours, and introduced him to the directors and to the governor of the province. *Out of the East*, the volume written later at Kumamoto, was dedicated to Nishida Sentaro, "In dear remembrance of Izumo days."

"Hearn's faith in this good friend was something wonderful," his wife tells us. "When he heard of Nishida's illness in 1897, he exclaimed, 'I would not mind losing everything that belongs to me if I could make him well.' He believed in him with such a faith only possible to a child."

Nishida Sentaro was also one of the ancient lineage and caste, and an intimate friend of the Koizumi family.

Matsue had been at one time almost exclusively occupied by the Samurai feudal lords. After throwing open her doors to the world, and admitting Western civilisation, Japan found herself obliged to accept, amongst other democratic innovations, the sweeping away of the great feudal and military past, reducing families of rank to obscurity and poverty. Youths and maidens of illustrious extraction, who had only mastered the "arts of courtesy," and the "arts of war," found themselves obliged to adopt the humblest occupations to provide themselves and their families with the means of livelihood. Daughters of men once looked upon as aristocrats had to become indoor servants with people of a lower caste, or to undertake the austere drudgery of the rice-fields or the lotus-ponds. Their houses and lands were confiscated,—their heirlooms, costly robes, crested lacquer ware, passed at starvation prices to those whom "misery makes rich." Amongst these aristocrats the Koizumis were numbered. Nishida Sentaro, knowing their miserable circumstances, and seeing how advisable it would be, if it were Hearn's intention to remain in Japan, to have a settled home of his own, formed the idea of bringing about a union between Setsu and the English teacher at the Matsue College.

On his own initiative he undertook the task of approaching his foreign friend. Finding him favourably inclined, he suggested the marriage as a suitable one to Setsu's parents.

It is supposed that marriage in Japan must be solemnised by a priest, but this is not so. A Japanese marriage is simply a legal pledge, and is not invested with any of the solemnity and importance cast around it in Occidental society. A union between an Englishman and a Japanese woman can be dissolved with the greatest facility; in fact, it is seldom looked upon as an obligatory engagement. It is doubtful if Nishida, when he undertook to act as intermediary, or *Nakodo*, as they call it in Japan, looked upon the contract entered into by Lafcadio Hearn and Setsu Koizumi as a permanent affair. Hearn from the first took it seriously, but it was certainly not until after the birth of his first child that the marriage was absolutely legalised according to English notions, and then only by his nationalising himself a Japanese citizen.

One of Hearn's saving qualities was compassion for the weak and suffering. The young girl's surroundings were calculated to inspire the deepest pity in the hearts of those admitted,—as he was,—behind the closely drawn veil of pride and reserve that the Samurai aristocrats drew between their poverty and public observation.

What the Samurai maiden,—brought up in the seclusion of Matsue,—may have thought of the grey-haired, odd-looking little Irishman of forty-four (a patriarchal age in Japan), who was offered to her as a husband we know not. She accepted her fate, Japanese fashion, and as the years went by and she began to appreciate his gentlemanly breeding and chivalry, inherited as was hers from generations of well-bred ancestors, the fear and bewilderment with which he filled her during these first years of marriage, changed to a profound and true affection, indeed to an almost reverential respect for the *Gakusha* (learned person) who kept the pot boiling so handsomely, and was run after by all the American and English tourists at Tokyo.

So far as we can judge now, Setsu Koizumi can never have had any of the exotic charm of the butterfly maidens of Kunisada, or the irresistible fascination ascribed to her countrywomen by foreign male visitors

to Japan. The Izumo type is not a good-looking one,
—the complexion darker and less fresh than that of the
Tokyo women,—but comely, with the comeliness of
truth, common-sense and goodness she always must
have been.

Tender and true, as her *Yerbina*, or personal,
name, "Setsu," signifies, she had learned in self-
denial and poverty the virtues of patience and self-
restraint. A daughter of Japan—one of a type fast
becoming extinct—who deemed it a fault to allow her
personal trials to wound other hearts.

She may not have been obliged to submit to the
trials of most Japanese wives, the whims and tyranny,
for instance, of her father and mother-in-law, or the
drudgery to provide for, or wait upon a numerous
Japanese household; but from many indications we
know that her life sometimes was not by any means a
bed of roses. Humorous, and at the same time
pathetic, are her reminiscences of these first days of
marriage, as related in later life.

"He was such an intense nature," she says, "and
so completely absorbed in his work of writing, that it
made him appear strange and even outlandish in ordinary life. He even acknowledged himself that he must
look like a madman."

During the course of his life when undergoing any
severe mental or physical strain, Hearn was subject to
periods of hysterical trance, during which he lost consciousness of surrounding objects. There is a host of
superstitions amongst the Japanese connected with
trances or fainting fits. Each human being is supposed
to possess two souls. When a person faints they believe
that one soul is withdrawn from the body, and goes on

all sorts of unknown and mysterious errands; while the other remains with the envelope to which it belongs, but when this takes place a man goes mad; mad people are those who have lost one of their souls. On first seeing her husband in this condition, the little woman was so terrified that she hastened to Nishida Sentaro to seek advice. "He always acted for us as middle-man in those Matsue days, and I confess I was afraid my husband might have gone crazy. However, I found soon afterwards that it was only the time of enthusiasm in thought and writing; and I began to admire him more on that account."

The calm and material comforts of domestic life gave Hearn, for a time, a more assured equilibrium, but these trances returned again with considerable frequency in later days.

Amenomori, his secretary at Tokyo, tells a story of waking one night and seeing a light in Hearn's study. He was afraid Hearn might be ill, and cautiously opened the door and peeped in. There he saw the little genius, absorbed in his work, standing at his high desk, his nose almost touching the paper on which he wrote. Leaf after leaf was covered with his small, delicate handwriting. After a while, Amenomori goes on, he held up his head, "and what did I see? It was not the Hearn I was familiar with; his face was mysteriously white; his eyes gleamed. He appeared like one in touch with some unearthly presence."

Many other peculiarities and idiosyncrasies used to cause his wife much perturbation of soul. "He had a rare sensibility of feeling," [1] she says, "also peculiar

---

[1] It is well to remember that Mrs. Hearn cannot speak or write a word of English; all her *Reminiscences* are transcribed for her by the Japanese poet, Yone Noguchi.

tastes." One of his peculiar tastes, apparently, was his love of cemeteries. She could not find out what he found so interesting in ancient epitaphs and verses. When at Kumamoto he told her that he had "found a pleasant place." When he offered to take her there, she found that it was through a dark path leading to a cemetery. He said, "Stop and listen. Do you hear the voices of the frogs and the Uguisu singing?" The poor little woman could only tremble at the dark and the eeriness.

She gives a funny picture of herself and Lafcadio, in a dry-goods store, when clothes had to be bought "at the changing of the season," he selecting some gaudy garment with a large design of sea-waves or spider-nests, declaring the design was superb and the colour beautiful.

"I often suspected him," the simple woman adds, "of having an unmistakable streak of passion for gay things—however his quiet conscience held him back from giving way to it."

His incurable dislike, too, to conform to any of the rules of etiquette—looked upon as all-important in Japan, especially for people in official positions—was a continual source of trouble to the little woman. She could hardly, she says, induce him to wear his "polite garments," which were *de rigueur* at any official cere-mony. On one occasion, indeed, he refused to appear when the Emperor visited the Tokyo College because he would not put on his frock coat and top hat.

The difficulty of language was at first insuperable. After a time they instituted the "Hearn San Kotoba," or Hearnian language, as they called it, but in these Matsue days an interpreter had to be employed. The "race problem," however, was the real complication that beset these two. That comradeship such as we comprehend it in England could exist between two nationalities, so fundamentally different as Setsu Koizumi's and Lafcadio Hearn's, is improbable if not impossible. "Even my own little wife," Hearn writes years afterwards, "is somewhat mysterious still to me, though always in a lovable way—of course a man and a woman know each other's hearts; but outside of personal knowledge, there are race tendencies difficult to understand."

CHAPTER XVIII

THE KATCHIU-YASHIKI

" The real charm of woman in herself is that which comes after the first emotion of passionate love has died away, when all illusions fade to reveal a reality lovelier than any illusion which has been evolved behind the phantom curtain of them. And again marriage seems to me a certain destruction of all emotion and suffering. So that afterwards one looks back at the old times with wonder. One cannot dream or desire anything more after love is transmuted into marriage. It is like a haven from which you can see currents rushing like violet bands beyond you out of sight. It seems to me (though I am a poor judge of such matters) that it does not make a man any happier to have an intellectual wife, unless he marries for society. The less intellectual, the more capable, so long as there is neither coarseness nor foolishness ; for intellectual converse a man can't really have with women. Woman is antagonistic to it. An emotional truth is quite as plain to the childish mind, as to the mind of Herbert Spencer or of Clifford. The child and the God come equally near to the Eternal truth. But then marriage in a complex civilisation is really a terrible problem ; there are so many questions involved."

As summer advanced Hearn found his little two-storeyed house by the Ohasigawa,—although dainty as a birdcage,—too cramped for comfort, the rooms being scarcely higher than steamship cabins, and so narrow that ordinary mosquito nets could not be suspended across them.

On the summit of the hill above Matsue stood the ancient castle of the former Daimyo of the province. In feudal days, when the city was under military sway, the finest homesteads of the Samurai clustered round

215

its Cyclopean granite walls; now owing to changed conditions and the straitened means of their owners, many of these Katchiu-yashiki were untenanted. Hearn and his wife were lucky enough to secure one. Though he no longer had his outlook over the lake, with the daily coming and going of fishing-boats and sampans, he had an extended view of the city and was close to the University. But above all he found compensation in the spacious Japanese garden, outcome of centuries of cultivation and care.

The summer passed in this Japanese Yashiki was as happy as any in Hearn's life, and one to which he perpetually looked back with longing regret. Wandering from room to room, sitting in sunned spaces where leaf shadows trembled on the matting, or gazing into the soft green, dreamy peace of the landscape garden, he found a sanctuary where the soul stopped elbowing and trampling, and being elbowed and trampled—a free, clear space, where he could see clearly, breathe serenely, fully. Discussions with publishers, differences of opinion with friends were soothed and forgotten; his domestic arrangements seemed all that he could have expected, and, as he was receiving a good salary, and life was not expensive in the old city, money difficulties for the moment receded into the background. His health improved. He weighed, he said, twenty pounds more than he did when he first arrived . . . but, he adds, this is perhaps because I am eating three full meals a day instead of two.

Echoes from the outer world reached him at intervals, such as the announcement of the marriage of Miss Elizabeth Bisland.

He describes himself as dancing an Indian war-dance

of exultation in his Japanese robes, to the unspeakable astonishment of his placid household. After which he passed two hours in a discourse in "The Hearnian Dialect." Subject of exultation and discourse,—the marriage of Miss Elizabeth Bisland.

Hearn's description of the old Yashiki garden is done with all the descriptive charm of which he was a master. Many others have described Japanese gardens, but none have imparted the mental "atmosphere," the special peculiarities that make them so characteristic of the genius of the people that have originated them. It is impossible to find space to follow him into all the details of his "Garden Folk Lore" as he calls it; of "Hijo," things without desire, such as stones and trees, and "Ujo," things having desire, such as men and animals, the miniature hills clothed with old trees, the long slopes of green, shadowed by flowering shrubs, like river banks, verdant elevations rising from spaces of pale yellow sand, smooth as a surface of silk, miming the curves and meanderings of a river course. Much too beautiful, these sanded spaces, to be trodden on; the least speck of dirt would mar their effect, and it required the trained skill of an experienced native gardener,—a delightful old man,— to keep them in perfect form.

Lightly and daintily as the shadows of the tremulous leaves of the bamboo-grove, and the summer light that touches the grey stone lanterns, and the lotus flowers on the pond, so does his genius flit from subject to subject, conjuring up and idealising ancient traditions and superstitions. The whole of his work seems transfused with mystic light.

We can hear him talking with Kinjuro, the venerable

gardener; we can catch the song of the caged Uguisu, an inmate of the establishment, presented to him by one of the sweetest ladies in Japan, the daughter of the Governor of Izumo.

The Uguisu, or Japanese nightingale, is supposed to repeat over and over again the sacred name of the Sutras, " Ho-ke-kyo," or Buddhist Confession of Faith. First the warble; then a pause of about five seconds, then a slow, sweet, solemn utterance of the holy name.

They planted, his wife tells us, some " Morning Glories " in summer. He watched them with the greatest delight, until they bloomed, and then was equally wretched when he saw them withering.

One early winter morning he noticed one tiny bloom, in spite of the sharp frost; he was delighted and surprised, and exclaimed in Japanese, " Utsukushii yuki, anata, nanbo shojik " (What a lovely courage, what a serious intention).

When the next morning the old gardener picked it, Hearn was in despair. " That old man may be good and innocent, but he was brutal to my flower," he said. He was depressed all day after this incident.

He had already, he declared, become a little too fond of his dwelling-place; each day after returning from his College duties and exchanging his teacher's uniform for the infinitely more comfortable Japanese robe he found more than compensation for the weariness of five class-hours in the simple pleasure of squatting on the shady verandah overlooking the gardens. The antique garden walls, high mossed below their ruined coping of tiles, seemed to shut out even the murmur of the city's life. There were no sounds but the voices of birds, the shrilling of *semi*, or, at intervals, the solitary

splash of a diving frog, and those walls secluded him
from much more than city streets; outside them
hummed the changed Japan of telegraphs, and newspapers, and steam-ships. Within dwelt the all-reposing
peace of nature, and the dreams of the sixteenth century; there was a charm of quaintness in the very air,
a faint sense of something viewless and sweet; perhaps
the gentle beauty of dead ladies who lived when all
the surroundings were new. For they were the gardens
of the past. The future would know them only as
dreams, creations of a forgotten art, whose charm no
genius could produce.

The working of Hearn's heart and mind at this time
is an interesting psychological study. He had been
wont to declare that his vocation was a monastic one.
He now initiated an asceticism as sev're in its discipline
as that of St. Francis of Assisi on the Umbrian Hills.
The code on which he moulded his life was formulated
according to the teaching of the great Gautama. If
the soul is to attain life and effect progress, continual
struggle against temptation is necessary. Appetites
must be restrained. Indulgence means retrogression.

It is not without a sense of amusement that we
observe the complex personality, Lafcadio Hearn, in
the Matsue phase of self-suppression and discipline.
Well might Kinjuro, the old gardener, tell him that he
had seven souls. A dignified University professor had
taken the place of the erratic Bohemian, who frequented
the Levee at Cincinnati, and of the starving little
journalist, who, arrayed in reefer coats, flannel shirt, and
outlandish hat, used to appear in the streets of New
Orleans. Now clad in official robes, he passed out
through a line of prostrate servants on his way to

College, each article of clothing having been handed to him, as he dressed, with endless bows of humility and submission by the daughter of a line of feudal nobles.

He gives his sister the same account of his austere, simple day, as to Basil Hall Chamberlain, the early morning prayer and greeting of the sun, his meals eaten alone before the others, the prayers again at eventide, some of them said for him as head of the house. Then the little lamps of the kami before the shrine were left to burn until they go out; while all the household waited for him to give the signal for bedtime, unless, as sometimes, he became so absorbed in writing as to forget the hour.

Sometimes, however, in spite of severe discipline and mortification of the flesh, ghostly reminders returned to prove that the old self was very real indeed.

The " Markham Girl " is certainly well done. " I asked myself : ' If it was I ? ' and conscience answered : ' If it was you, in spite of love, and duty, and honour, and Hell fire staring you in the face, you would have gone after her. . . .' " Then he adds a tirade as to his being a liar and quibbler when he attempts to contradict the statement, and that's why I am poor and unsuccessful, void of mental balance, and an exile in Japan.

Or a sinister note is struck, as in a letter to Basil Hall Chamberlain, alluding to a story in Gœthe's *Wilhelmmeister,* " The New Melusine," of which the application is apparent. A man was loved by a fairy; and she told him she must either say good-bye, or that he must become little like herself and go to dwell with her in her father's kingdom. She put a gold ring on his finger that made him small, and they entered into their tiny world. The man was greatly petted by the fairy folk, and had everything given to him which he could desire. In spite of it all, however, although he had a pretty child too, he became ungrateful and selfish and got tired, and dreamed of being a giant. He filed the ring off his finger, and became big again, and ran away to spend the gold in riotous living. " The fairy was altogether Japanese—don't you think so? And the man was certainly a detestable fellow."

Though the little man permitted himself such outbursts as this on paper, he soon crept back to the grim reality of a wooden pillow and Japanese food; back to a kingdom undisturbed by electrical storms of passion, to interviews with College students and communion with a wife whose knowledge was circumscribed by Kanbara's *Greater Knowledge for Women*.

" Never be frightened at anything but your own heart," he writes to one of these Matsue pupils, when giving him good advice some years later. Poor Lafcadio! Good reason had he to be frightened of that wild, wayward, undisciplined heart that so often had betrayed him in days gone by.

When in Japan we heard whispers of Hearn having fallen a victim to the wiles of the accomplished ladies who abide in the street of the Geisha. After his marriage to Setsu Koizumi, however, not even from his enemies, and their name was legion, at Kumamoto, Kobe, or Tokyo, did we ever hear the faintest suggestion of scandal connected with his name. In Japan, where there is no privacy of any sort in everyday life, where, if a man is faithless to his wife, all the quarter where he lives knows of it, and the wife accepts it as her *Ingwa*,—or sin in a former state of existence,— it would have been impossible for Hearn to have stepped over the line, however tentatively, without its being known and talked about.

A pleasant vision is the one we conjure up of him on the verandah of the old Yashiki, squatted, Buddhawise, smoking a tiny long-stemmed Japanese pipe, his little wife seated near him, relating, by the aid of the interpreter, the superstitions and legends of the ancient Province of the Gods.

She tells us how he took even the most trivial tale to heart, murmuring " How interesting," his face sometimes even turning pale while he looked fixedly in front of him.

Under these conditions of tranquillity and well-being his genius seemed to expand and develop. The " Shira-byoshi," [1] or Dancing Girl, the finest piece of imaginative work he ever did, was conceived and written during the course of the summer passed in the old " Yashiki." Its first inception is indicated in a letter to Basil Hall Chamberlain, in 1891. " There was a story some time ago in the *Asahi-shimbun* [2] about a ' Shira-byoshi,' that brought tears to my eyes, as slowly and painfully translated by a friend."

The *Dancing Girl* has been translated into four foreign languages—German, Swedish, French and Italian—a writer in the *Revue des Deux Mondes* declares it to be one of the love-stories of the world. The only remarkable fact is, that it has not made more of a stir in England.

The hero is the well-known Japanese painter Buncho; the heroine a Geisha. There is some-

---

[1] *Glimpses of Unfamiliar Japan :* Houghton, Mifflin & Co.

[2] The *Asahi-shimbun* was one of the principal Japanese illustrated daily papers, printed and published at Osaka.

thing simple, natural, tragic and yet intangible and ethereal in the manner in which Hearn tells it; the presence of a vital spirit, the essential element of passion and regret, the throb of warm human emotion, in spite of its exotic setting, brings it into kinship with the human experience of all times and countries. There is no attempt at scenery, only a woman hidden away in the heart of nature, in a lonely cottage amongst the hills, with her love, her memory, her regret. Into this solitary life enters youth, attractive, beautiful, the possibility of further romance; but no romance other than the one she cherishes is for her.

Unfortunately it is only possible to give the merest sketch of the story that Hearn unfolds with consummate artistic skill. He begins with an account of dancing-girls, of the education they have to undergo, how they use their accomplishments to cast a web of enchantment over men.

It is one of these apparently soulless creatures, a dancing-girl, a woman of the town, wearing clothes belonging neither to maid nor wife, that he makes the central figure of his story; and by her constancy to ideal things, her pure and simple passion he thrills us through with the sense of the impermanence of humanity and beauty, and the strength of love overcoming and conquering the tragedy of life.

How different the manner in which he treats the scenes between the young man and the beautiful dancing-girl, compared to the manner in which his French prototypes,—in which Pierre Loti, for instance, whom Hearn declared to be one of the greatest living artists,—would have treated it. Far ahead has he passed beyond them; the moral, the life of the soul, is never lost sight of, in not one line does he play on the lower emotions of his readers.

A young artist was travelling on foot over the mountains from Kyoto to Yeddo, and lost his way. . . . He had almost resigned himself to passing the night under the stars, when, down the farther slope of the hill, a single thin yellow ray of light fell upon the darkness. Making his way towards it, he found that it was a small cottage, apparently a peasant's house. . . . Not until he had knocked and called several times, did he hear any stir. At last, however, a feminine voice asked what he wanted. He told her, and after a brief delay the storm doors were pushed open and a woman appeared with a paper lantern. She scrutinised him in silence, and then said briefly, " Wait, I will bring water." Having washed from his feet the dust of travel, he was shown into a neat room, and a brazier was set before him, and a cotton *zabuton* for him to kneel upon. He was struck by the beauty of his hostess, as well as by her goodness, when she told him that he might stay there that night. . . . " I will have no time to sleep to-night," she said, " therefore you can have my bed and paper mosquito curtain."

After he had slept a while, the mysterious sound of feet moving rapidly fell upon his ears; he slipped out of bed, and creeping to the edge of the screen, peeped through. There before her illuminated *Butsudan*, he saw the young woman dancing. Turning suddenly she met his eyes, but before he had time to speak, she smiled : " You must have thought me mad when you saw me dancing, and I am not angry with you for trying to find out what I was doing." Then she went on to tell him how a youth and she had fallen in love with one another, and how they had gone away and built the cottage in the mountains, and each evening she had danced to please him. One cold winter he fell sick and died; since then she had lived alone with nothing to console her but the memory of her lover, laying daily before his tablet the customary offerings, and nightly dancing to please his spirit.

After she had told her tale, she begged the young man to go back and try again to sleep.

On leaving next morning, he wanted to pay for the hospitality he had received. "What I did was done for kindness alone, and it certainly was not worth money," she said, as she dismissed him. Then, pointing out the path he had to follow, she watched him until he passed from sight, his heart, as he went, full of the charm and beauty of the woman he had left behind.

Many years passed by; the painter had become old, and rich, and famous. One day there came to his house an old woman, who asked to speak with him. The servants, thinking her a common beggar, turned her away, but she came so persistently, that at last they had to tell their master. When, at his order, the old woman was admitted, she began untying the knots of a bundle she had brought with her; inside were quaint garments of silk, a wonderful costume, the attire of a Shirabyoshi.

With many beautiful and pathetic touches, Hearn tells how, as he watched her smooth out the garments with her trembling fingers, a memory stirred in the master's brain; again in the soft shock of recollection, he saw the lonely mountain dwelling in which he had received unremunerated hospitality, the faintly burning light before the Buddhist shrine, the strange beauty of a woman dancing there alone in the dead of the night.

"Pardon my rudeness for having forgotten your face for the moment," he said, as he rose and bowed before her, "but it is more than forty years since we last saw each other; you received me at your house. You gave up to me the only bed you had. I saw you dance and you told me all your story."

The old woman, quite overcome, told him that in the course of years, she had been obliged, through poverty, to part with her little house, and becoming weak and old, could no longer dance each evening before the *Butsudan*. Therefore she had sought out the master, since she desired for the sake of the dead a picture of herself in the costume and attitude of the dance that she might hang it up before the *Butsudan*. "I am not now as I was then," she added. "But, oh, master, make me young again. Make me beautiful that I may seem beautiful to him, for whose sake I, the unworthy, beseech this!"

He told her to come next day, and that he only would be too delighted to thus repay the debt he had owed her for so many years. So he painted her, as she had been forty years before. When she saw the picture, she clasped her hands in delight, but how was she ever to repay the master? She had nothing to offer but her Shirabyoshi garments. He took them, saying he would keep them as a memory, but that she must allow him to place her beyond the reach of want.

No money would she accept, but thanking him again and again, she went away with her treasure. The master had her followed, and on the next day took his way to the district indicated amidst the abodes of the poor and outcast. He tapped on the door of the old woman's dwelling, and receiving no answer pushed open the shutter, and peered through the aperture. As he stood there the sensation of the moment, when, as a tired lad, forty years before, he had stood, pleading for admission to the lonesome little cottage amongst the hills, thrilled back to him.

Entering softly, he saw the woman lying on the floor seemingly asleep. On a rude shelf he recognised the ancient *Butsudan* with its tablet, and now, as then, a tiny lamp was burning; in front of it stood the portrait he had painted.

" The master called the sleeper's name once or twice. Then suddenly, as she did not answer, he saw that she was dead, and he wondered while he gazed upon her face, for it seemed less old. A vague sweetness, like the ghost of youth, had returned to it; the wrinkles and the lines of sorrow had been strangely smoothed by the touch of a phantom Master mightier than he."

CHAPTER XIX

KUMAMOTO

" Of course Urashima was bewildered by the gods. But who is not bewildered by the gods? What is Life itself but a bewilderment? And Urashima in his bewilderment doubted the purpose of the gods, and opened the box. Then he died without any trouble, and the people built a shrine to him as Urashima Mio-jin. . . .

" Things are quite differently managed in the West. After disobeying Western gods, we have still to remain alive and to learn the height and the breadth and the depth of superlative sorrow. We are not allowed to die quite comfortably just at the best possible time: much less are we suffered to become after death small gods in our own right. How can we pity the folly of Urashima after he had lived so long alone with visible gods?

" Perhaps the fact that we do may answer the riddle. This pity must be self-pity; wherefore the legend may be the legend of a myriad souls. The thought of it comes just at a particular time of blue light and soft wind,—and always like an old reproach. It has too intimate relation to a season and the feeling of a season not to be also related to something real in one's life, or in the lives of one's ancestors.

ONLY for a year did Hearn's sojourn in Fairyland last. The winter following his arrival was a very severe one. The northern coast of Japan lies open to the Arctic winds blowing over the snow-covered plains of Siberia. Heavy falls of snow left drifts five feet high round the Yashiki on the hill. The large rooms, so delightful in the summer with their verandah opening on the garden, were cold as " cattle barns " in winter, with nothing but charcoal braziers to heat them. He dare not face another such experience, and asked, if possible, to be transferred to warmer quarters. Aided again by his friend Professor Chamberlain, the authorities at Tokyo were induced to give him the Professorship of English at the Imperial University at Kumamoto.

Kumamoto is situated in Kyushu, facing Formosa and the Chinese coast, the climate therefore is much milder than that of Matsue. Here, however, began Hearn's first disillusionment; like Urashima Taro, having dwelt within the precincts of Fairyland he felt the shock of returning to Earth again. The city struck him as being ugly and commonplace, a half-Europeanised garrison town, resounding to the sounds of bugles and the drilling of soldiers, instead of pilgrim songs and temple bells. "But Lord! I must try to make money; for nothing is sure in Japan and I am now so tied down to the country that I can't quit it, except for a trip, whether the Government employs me or not."

He began to look back with regret to the days passed at Matsue. "You must travel out of Izumo," he said, "after a long residence, and find out how unutterably different it is from other places,—for instance, this country . . . the charming simplicity of the Izumo folk does not here exist."

All his Izumo servants had accompanied him to his new quarters, and apparently all his wife's family, for he mentions the fact that he has nine lives dependent upon him: wife, wife's mother, wife's father, wife's adopted mother, wife's father's father, then servants, and a Buddhist student.

This wouldn't do in America, he says to Ellwood Hendrik, but it is nothing in Japan. The moral burden, however, was heavy enough; he indulged in the luxury of filial piety, and it was impossible to let a little world

grow up round him, to depend on him, and then break
it all up—the good and evil results of "filial piety"
are only known to Orientals, and an Oriental he had
now become. His people felt like fish out of water,
everything surrounding them was so different from their
primitive home in Izumo. A goat in the next yard,
"mezurashii kedamono," filled his little wife with an
amused wonder. Some geese and a pig also filled her
with surprise, such animals did not exist in the highlands
of Japan.

The Kumamoto Government College was one of
the largest in Japan,—came next, indeed, to the Imperial
University in Tokyo in importance. It was run on
the most approved Occidental lines. A few of the boys
still adhered to their Japanese dress, but most of them
adopted the military uniform now as a rule worn in
Japanese colleges. There were three classes, correspond-
ing with the three higher classes of the Jinjo Chugakko
—and two higher classes. He did not now teach on
Saturdays. There were no stoves—only hibachi. The
library was small, and the English books were not good.
There was a building in which Jiu-jitsu was taught;
and separate buildings for sleeping, eating, and bathing.
The bath-room was a surprise. Thirty or forty students
could bathe at the same time; and four hundred could
sit down to meals in the great dining-hall. There was
a separate building also for the teaching of chemistry,
natural history, etc.; and a small museum.

Hearn apparently foregathered with none of the
masters of the college, except the old teacher of
Chinese. The others he simply saluted morning and
evening, and in the intervals between classes sat in
a corner to himself smoking his pipe.

" You talk of being without intellectual companion-
ship! " he writes to Hendrik. " OH YE EIGHT
HUNDRED MYRIADS OF GODS! What would
you do if you were me? Lo! The illusion is gone!
Japan in Kyushu is like Europe,—except I have no
friend. The differences in ways of thinking, and the
difficulties of language, render it impossible for an
educated Japanese to find pleasure in the society of a
European. My scholars in this great Government
school are not boys, but men. They speak to me
only in class. The teachers never speak to me at all.
I go to the college and return after class,—always alone,
no mental company but books. But at home everything is sweet."

In consequence of this isolation, or because of the
softening influence of matrimony, here at Kumamoto
he seemed for the first time to awake to the fact of
having relations in that distant Western land he had
left so many years before. " Our soul, or souls, ever
wanders back to its own kindred," he says to his sister.

His father, Charles Bush Hearn, had left three
children by his second wife (daughters), all born in
India. Invalided home, Charles Hearn had died in the
Red Sea of Indian fever; the three orphan children and
his widow continued their journey to Ireland.

At their mother's death which occurred a few years
later, the girls were placed under the guardianship of
various members of the family; two of them ultimately
married; one of them a Mr. Brown, the other a Mr.
Buckley Atkinson. The unmarried one, Miss Lillah
Hearn, went out to Michigan in America, to stop with
Lafcadio's brother, and her own half-brother, Daniel
James Hearn, or Jim as he was usually called.

Public interest was gradually awakening with regard to Japanese affairs. Professor Basil Hall Chamberlain's and Satow's books were looked upon as standard works to refer to for information concerning the political and social affairs of the extraordinary little people who were working their way to the van in the Far East. But, above all, Lafcadio Hearn's articles contributed to the *Atlantic Monthly*, afterwards published under the title of *Glimpses of Unfamiliar Japan*, had claimed public attention.

Miss Lillah Hearn was the first member of the family to write to this half-brother, who was becoming so famous, but received no answer. Then Mrs. Brown, the other sister, approached him, silence greeted her efforts as well. On hearing of his marriage to a Japanese lady, Mrs. Atkinson, the youngest sister, wrote. Whether it was that she softened the exile's heart in his expatriation by that sympathy and innate tact, which are two of her distinguishing qualities, it is impossible to say, but her letter was answered.

This strange relative of theirs who had gone to Japan, adopted Japanese dress and habits, and married a Japanese lady, had become somewhat of a legendary character to his quiet-going Irish kindred. The arrival of the first letter, therefore, was looked upon as quite an event and was passed from house to house, and hand to hand, becoming considerably mutilated in its journeyings to and fro. The first page is entirely gone, and the second page so erased and torn, that it is only decipherable here and there. We are enabled to put an approximate date to it by his reference to Miss Bisland's marriage, of which he had heard towards the end of his stay at Matsue.

" I have written other things, but am rather ashamed of them," he adds. " So Miss Bisland has married and become Mrs. Wetmore. She is as rich at least as she could wish to be, but I have not heard from her for more than a year. I suppose friendship ends with marriage. If my sister was not married, I think—I only think—I would feel more brotherly.

" Well, I will say *au revoir*. Many thanks for the letter you wrote me. I would like   Please give me   you can. Don't think busy to write—much   I teach for a week—English   and Elementary Latin :   the time I study   and write for pleasure, not for profit. There isn't much profit in literature unless, as a novelist, one happens to please a popular taste,—which isn't good taste. Some exceptions there are, like Rudyard Kipling; but your brother has not his inborn genius for knowing, seizing and painting human nature.

" Love to you and yours—from

" LAFCADIO HEARN.

" *Tetorihomnatu* 34,
" *Kumamoto, Kyushu,*
" *Japan.*"

Mrs. Atkinson replied immediately, thus beginning a series of delightful letters, which alas! relate, so many of them, to intimate family affairs that it is impossible to publish them in their original form.

" My sweet little sister," he wrote in answer, " your letter was more than personally grateful : it had also an unexpected curious interest for me, as a revelation of things I did not know. I don't know anything of my relations—their names, places, occupations, or even number : therefore your letter interested me in a peculiar way, apart from its amiable charm. Before I talk any more, I thank you for the photographs. They have made me prouder than I ought to be. I did not know that I had such nice kindred and such a fairy niece. My wife stole your picture from me almost as soon as I had received it, to caress it, and pray to Buddha and all the ancient gods to love the original : she has framed it in a funny little Japanese frame, and suspended it in that sacred part of the house, called the Toko, a sort of alcove, in which only beautiful things are displayed. Formerly the gods were placed there (many hundred years ago); but now the gods have a separate shrine in the household, and the Toko is only the second Holy place. . . ."

The next letter is dated June 7th, '92, 25th year of Meiji.

" Dear sister, I love you a little bit more on hearing that you are little. The smaller you are the more I will be fond of you. As for marriage being a damper upon affection between kindred, it is true only of Occidental marriages. The Japanese wife is only the shadow of her husband, infinitely unselfish and naïve in all things. . . .

" If you want me to see you soon, you must pray to the Occidental Gods to make me suddenly rich. However, I doubt if they have half as much influence as the Gods of Japan,—who are helping me to make a bank account as fast as honest work can produce such a result. I have no babies; and don't expect to have, and may be able to cross the seas one of

MRS. ATKINSON (HEARN'S HALF-SISTER)

these days to linger in your country a while. But
really I don't know. I drift with the current of events.

"As for my book on Japan,—my first book,—there
is much to do yet,—it ought to be out in the Fall.
It will be called: *Glimpses of Unfamiliar Japan*, and
will treat of strange things.

"I would like to see you very much; for you are
too tantalizing in your letters, and tell me nothing
about your inner self. I want to find out what the
angel shut up in your heart is like. No doubt very
sweet, but I would like to pull it out, and stroke its
wings, and make it chipper a little. As for the little
ones, make them love me; for if they see me without
previous discipline, they will be afraid of my ugly face
when I come—I send you a photo of one half of it,
the other is not pleasant, I assure you: like the moon,
I show only one side of myself. In Spanish countries
they call me Leucadio—much easier for little folk to
pronounce. By the way, you never gave me your
address,—sign of impulsive haste, like my own.

"With best love,
"LAFCADIO HEARN."

Then in January 1903 he writes again, "Your kind
sweet letter reached me at Christmas time, where there
is no Christmas. Don't you know that you are very
happy to be able to live in England? I am afraid you
do not. Perhaps you could not know without having
lived much elsewhere. . . . Your photo has come.
The same eyes, the same chin, brow, nose: we are
strangely alike—excepting that you are very comely,
and I very much the reverse—partly by exaggeration
of the traits which make your face beautiful, and partly

because I am disfigured by the loss of an eye—punched out at school. . . . Won't you please give my kindest thanks to your husband for the pains he has taken to please me! I hope to meet him some day, and thank him in person, if I don't leave my bones in some quaint and curious Buddhist cemetery out here. . . ."

The wonderful series of letters to Professor Hall Chamberlain, recently published by Miss Bisland, are also written from Kumamoto and Kobe, and to a great extent run simultaneously with those to his sister. He had a habit of repeating himself; the same expressions, the same quotations, appear in both series, and sometimes are again repeated in his published essays. When struck by an idea or incident, it seems as if he must impart it as something noteworthy to every one with whom he was holding communion. He gives, for instance, the same account to his sister of the routine of his Japanese day as related to Professor Hall Chamberlain and Ellwood Hendrik.

We can imagine his rigidly Protestant Irish relations amidst the conventional surroundings of an Irish country house, following minutely the services of the Established Church as preached to them by their local clergyman, utterly bewildered in reading the description of the outlandish cult to which he, their relation, subscribed in Japan. The awakening to the rising of the sun with the clapping of hands of servants in the garden, the prayers at the Butsudan, the putting out the food for the dead, all the strange quaint customs that mark the passing of the day in the ancient Empire of Nippon. Not by thousands of miles only was he separated from his Occidental relations, but by immemorial centuries of thought.

On May 21st, 1893, there is another letter to his sister, Mrs. Atkinson, in which he first announces his expectation of becoming a father. It is so characteristic of Lafcadio to take it for granted that the child would be a boy, and already to make plans for his education abroad.

> " *Tsuboi, Nichihorabata* 35, *Kumamoto,*
> " *Kyushu, Japan.*
> " *May* 21*st,* '93.

" MY DEAR MINNIE,

" (I think ' sister ' is too formal, I shall call you by your pet name hereafter.) First let me thank you very, very much for the photographs. I was extremely pleased with that of your husband;—and thought at once, ' Ah! the lucky girl! ' For your husband, my dear Sis, is no ordinary man. There are faces that seen for the first time leave an impression which gives the whole of the man, *ineffaceably*. And they are rare. I think I know your husband already, admire him and love him,—not simply for your sake, but for his own. He [is] all man,—and strong,—a good oak for your ivy. I don't mean physical strength, though he seems (from the photograph) to have an uncommon amount of it, but strength of character. You can feel pretty easy about the future of your little ones with such a father. (Don't read all this to him, though,—or he will think I am trying to flatter either him or you,—though, of course, you can tell him something of the impression his photo gives me, in a milder form.) And you don't know what the real impression is,—nor how it is enhanced by the fact that I have been for three years isolated from all English or European intercourse,—

never see an English face, except that of some travelling missionary, which is apt to be ignoble. The Oriental face is somewhat inscrutable,—like the faces of the Buddhist gods. In youth it has quite a queer charm, —the charm of mysterious placidity, of smiling calm. (But among the modernised, college-bred Japanese this is lost.) What one never—or hardly ever—sees among these Orientals is a face showing strong character. The race is strangely impersonal. The women are divinely sweet in temper; the men are mysteries, and not altogether pleasant. I feel myself in exile; and your letters and photographs only make me homesick for English life,—just one plunge into it again.

" —Will I ever see you? Really I don't know. Some day I should like to visit England,—provided I could assure myself of sufficient literary work there to justify a stay of at least half-a-year, and the expense of the voyage. Eventually that might be possible. I would never go as a mere guest—not even a sister's; but I should like to be able to chat with the sister occasionally on leisure-evenings. I am quite a savage on the subject of independence, let me tell you; and would accept no kindnesses except those of your company at intervals. But all this is not of to-day. I cannot take my wife to Europe, it would be impossible to accustom her to Western life,—indeed it would be cruel even to try. But I may have to educate my child abroad,—which would be an all-powerful reason for the voyage. However, I would prefer an Italian, French, or Spanish school-life to an English one.

" —Oh yes, about the book—*Glimpses of Unfamiliar Japan* is now in press. It will appear in two volumes, without illustrations. The publishers are

Houghton, Mifflin & Co., of Boston,—the best in America. Whether you like the book or no, I can't tell. I have an idea you do not care much about literary matters;—that you are too much wife and mother for that;—that your romances and poetry are in your own home. And such romance and poetry is the best of all. However, if you take some interest in trying to look at ME between the lines, you may have patience to read the work. Don't try to read it, if you don't like.

" —But here is something you might do for me, as I am not asking for certain friendly offices. When the book is criticised, you might kindly send me a few of the best reviews. Miss Bisland, while in London, wrote me the reviews of some of my other books had been very kindly; but she never dreamed of supplementing this pleasant information by cutting out a few specimens for me.—By the way, she has married well, you know,—has become awfully rich and fashionable, and would not even condescend to look at me if she passed me in Broadway—I *suppose*. But she well deserved her good fortune; for she was certainly one of the most gifted girls I ever knew, and has succeeded in everything—against immense obstacles—with no help except that of her own will and genius.

" —And now I must give you a lecture. I don't want more than one sister,—haven't room in my heart for more. All appear to be as charming as they are sweet looking. I am interested to hear how they succeed, etc., etc. But don't ask me to write to everybody, and don't show everybody my letters. I can't diffuse myself very far. You said you would be ' my favourite.' A nice way you go about it! Suppose I tell you that I am a very jealous, nasty brother; and that if I can't have one sister by herself I don't want any sister at all! Would that be very, very naughty? But it is true. And now you can be shocked just as much as you please.

" —Yes, I have lost an eye, and look horrible. The operation in Dublin did not cause the disfigurement, but a blow, or rather the indirect results of a blow, received from a play-fellow.

" —You ask me if I should like a photograph of father. I certainly should, if you can procure me one without trouble. I hope—much more than to see England,—to visit India, and try to find some tradition of him. I did not know positively, until last year, that father had been in the West Indies. When I went there, I had the queerest, ghostliest sensation of having seen it all before. I think I should experience even stranger sensations in India! The climate would be agreeable for me. Remember, I passed fourteen years of my life south of winter. The first snow I saw from 1876 to 1890 was on my way through Canada to Japan. Indeed, if ever I become quite independent, I want to return to the tropics.

" Enough to tire your eyes,—isn't it?—for this time.

" Ever affectionately,
" LAFCADIO HEARN.

" In the names of the eight hundred myriads of Gods, —do give me your address. The only way I have been able to write you is by finding the word *Portadown* in *Whittaker's Almanac*. You are a careless, naughty ' Sis.'

" I enclose my name and address in Japanese.

"YAKUMO KOIZUME,

" *Tsuboi,*

" *Nichihorabata* 35,

" *Kumamoto, Kyushu.*"

All the women are making funny little Japanese baby-clothes, and all the Buddhist Divinities, who watch over little children, are being prayed to. . . . "Letters of congratulation," he said, "were coming from all directions, for the expectation of a child is always a subject of great gladness in Japan. . . . Behind all this there is a universe of new sensations, revelations of things in Buddhist faith which are very beautiful and touching. About the world an atmosphere of delicious, sacred naïveté,—difficult to describe because resembling nothing in the Western world. . . ."

Hearn's account of his home before the birth of his son throws most interesting lights on Japanese methods of thought and daily life. He refers to the pretty custom of a woman borrowing a baby when she is about to become a mother. It is thought an honour to lend it. And it is extraordinarily petted in its new home. The one his wife borrowed was only six months old, but expressed in a supreme degree all the Japanese virtues; docile to the degree of going to sleep when bidden, and of laughing when it awakened. The eerie wisdom of its face seemed to suggest a memory of all its former lives. The incident he relates also of a little Samurai boy whom he and his wife had adopted is interesting as showing the Spartan discipline exercised over Japanese children from earliest youth, enabling them in later life to display that iron self-control that has astonished the world; interesting also as showing how nothing escaped Hearn's quick observation and assiduous intellect. Hearn, at first, wanted to fondle the child, and make much of him, but he soon found that it was not in accordance with custom. He therefore ceased to take notice of him; and left him under the control of the women of the house. Their treatment of him Hearn thought peculiar; the little fellow was never praised and rarely scolded. One day he let a little cup fall and broke it. No notice was taken of the accident for fear of giving him pain. Suddenly, though the face remained quite smilingly placid as usual, he could not control his tears. As soon as they saw him cry, everybody laughed and said kind things to him, till he began to laugh too. But what followed was more surprising. Apparently he had been distantly treated. One day he did not return from school until three hours after the usual time; suddenly the women began to cry—they were indeed more deeply affected than their treatment of the boy would have justified. The servants ran hither and thither in their anxiety to find him. It turned out that he had only been taken to a teacher's house for something relating to school matters. As soon as his voice was heard at the door, every one was quiet, cold, and distantly polite again.

On September 17th he writes again to his sister, thanking her for a copy she had sent him of the *Saturday Review*. "You could send me nothing more pleasing, or more useful in a literary way. It is all the more welcome as I am really living in a hideous isolation, far away from books, and book-shops, and Europeans. When I can get—which I hope is the next year— into a more pleasant locality, I shall try to pick out

some pretty Oriental tales to send to the little ones."
He was not able, he goes on, to go far from Kumamoto, not liking to leave his little wife too long alone;
so his vacation was rather monotonous. He travelled
only as far as Nagasaki. It was quaint and pretty, but
hotter than any West Indian port in the hot season.
He was economising, he said, and had saved nearly
three thousand five hundred dollars. Once he had provided for his wife he hoped to be able to make a few
long voyages to places east of Japan. " You are much
to be envied," he goes on to his sister, " for your
chances of travel. What a pity you are not able to
devote yourself to writing and painting in a place like
Algiers—full of romance and picturesqueness. If you
go there, don't fail to see the old Arab part of the city
—the Kasbah, I think they call it. How about the
Continent? Have you tried Southern Italy? And
don't you think that one gets all the benefit of travel
only by keeping away from fashion-resorts and places
consecrated by conventionalism? Nothing to me is
more frightful than a fashionable seaside resort—such
as those of the Atlantic Coast. My happiest sojourns
of this sort have been in little fishing villages, and little
queer old unknown towns, where there are no big vulgar
hotels, and where one can dress and do exactly as one
pleases.

" What will you do with your little man when he
grows up? Army, or Civil Service? Whatever you
do, never let him go to America, and lose all his traditions. Australia would be far better. I expect he will
be gloriously well able to take care of himself anywhere,
—judging by his father, but I have come to the belief
that one cannot too soon begin the cultivation of a

single aim and single talent in life. This is the age of specialism. No man can any longer be successful in many things. Even the 'general practitioner' in medicine has almost become obsolete.

"Nothing seems to me more important now for a little boy than the training of his linguistic faculties,—giving him every encouragement in learning languages by ear—(the only natural way); and your travelling sometimes with him will help you to notice how his faculties are in that direction. But perhaps it will be possible for him to pass all his life in England. (For me England, Ireland and Scotland mean the same thing.) That would be pleasant indeed. . . . When I think of your little man with the black eyes, I hope that his life will always be in the circle of English traditions, wherever the English Flag flies, there remain.

"I suppose you know that in this Orient the construction of the family is totally different to what it is in Europe. . . . We are too conceitedly apt to think that what is good for Englishmen is good for all nations, —our ethics, our religion, our costumes, etc. The plain facts of the case are that all Eastern races lose, instead of gaining, by contact with us. They imitate our vices instead of our virtues, and learn all our weaknesses without getting any of our strength. Already statistics show an enormous increase of crime in Japan as the result of 'Christian civilisation'; and the open ports show a demoralisation utterly unknown in the interior of the country, and unimaginable in the old feudal days before 1840 or 1850. . . ."

In the next letter he gives his sister a minute account of his Japanese manner of life on the floor without chairs or tables. It has been described so often by

visitors to Japan, and by Hearn himself, that it is
unnecessary to repeat it here. He ends his letter : —

"I am now so used to the Japanese way of living,
that when I have to remain all day in Western clothes,
I feel very unhappy; and I think I should not find
European life pleasant in summer time. Some day, I
will send you a photograph of my house.

"I wish you much happiness and good health and
pleasant days of travel, and thank you much for the
paper.

"This letter is rather rambling, but perhaps you
will find something interesting in it.

"Ever affectionately,

"LAFCADIO."

In September comes another letter to Mrs. Atkinson : "You actually talk about writing too often,
—which is strange! There is only this difficulty about
writing,—that we both know so little of each other
that topics interesting to both can be only guessed at.
That should be only a temporary drawback.

"The more I see your face in photos, the more I feel
drawn toward you. Lillah and the other sister represent different moods and tenses pictorially. You seem
most near to me,—as I felt on first reading your letter.
You have strength, too, where I have not. You are
certainly very sensitive, but also self-repressed. I
think you are not inclined to make mistakes. I think
you can be quickly offended, and quick to forgive—if
you understand the offence to be only a mistake. You
would not forgive at all should you discern behind the
fault a something much worse than mistake,—and in
this you would be right. You are inclined to reserve,

and not to bursts of joy;—you have escaped my extremes of depression and extremes of exultation. You
see very quickly beyond the present relations of a fact
—I think all this. But of course you have been shaped
in certain things by social influences I have never had,
—so that you must have perfect poise where I would
flounder and stumble.

"But imagining won't do always. I should like to
know more of you than a photograph or a rare letter
can tell. I don't know, remember, anything *at all*
about you. I do not know where you were born, where
you were educated,—anything of your life; or what is
much more, infinitely more important, I don't know
your emotions and thoughts and feelings and experiences in the past. What you are now, I can guess.
But what *were* you,—long ago? What memories most
haunt you of places and people you liked? If you
could tell me some of these, how pleasantly we might
compare notes. Mere facts tell little: the interest of
personality lies most in the infinitely special way that
facts affect the person. I am very curious about you,
—but, don't take this too seriously; because though
my wishes are strong, my disinclination to cause you
pain is stronger; and you have told me that writing is
sometimes fatiguing to you. It were so much better
could we pass a day or two together.

"You must not underrate yourself as you did in
your last. Your few lines about the scenery,—short as
they were,—convinced me that you could do something literary of a very nice sort had you the time and
chance to give yourself to any such work. But I do not
wish that you would—except to read the result; for
literary labour is extremely severe work, even after

the secret of method is reached. I am only beginning
to learn; and to produce five pages means to write at
least twenty-five. Enthusiasms and inspirations have
least to do with the matter. The real work is condens-
ing, compressing, choosing, changing, shifting words
and phrases,—studying values of colour and sound and
form in words; and when all is done, the result satisfies
only for a time. What I wrote six years ago, I cannot
bear the sight of to-day. If I had been a genius, I
wonder whether I would feel the same.

"Romances are not in novels, but in lives. Can
you not tell me some of yours when you are feeling
very, very well, and don't know what to do? What
surprised me was your observation about 'sentimental'
in your last letter,—and that upon such a worthy topic!
What can you think of me? And here in this Orient,
where the spirit of more ancient faiths enters into one's
blood with the sense of the doctrine of filial piety, and
the meaning of ancestor worship,—how very, very
strange and cruel it seems to me that my little sister
should be afraid of being thought *sentimental* about
the photograph of her father! What self-repression
does all this mean, and what iron influences in Western
life—English life that I have almost forgotten! However, character loses nothing: under the exterior ice,
the Western could only gain warmth and depth if it be
of the right sort. I hope, nevertheless, my little sister
will be just as 'sentimental' as she possibly can when
she writes to Japan,—and feel sure of more than sympathy and gratitude. Unless she means by 'sentimental' only something in regard to style of writing—
in which case I assure her that she cannot err. If she
is afraid of being thought really sentimental, I should

be much more afraid of meeting her,—for I should wish to say sweet things and to hear them, too, should I deserve.

"At all events remember that you have given me something very precious,—not only in itself,—but precious because precious to you. And it shall never be lost,—in spite of earthquakes and possible fires."

The something he alludes to as "very precious" was a photograph of their father, Charles Hearn, that Mrs. Atkinson had sent him.

"—I wish I could talk to you more about Father and India. I wish to ask a hundred thousand questions. But on paper it is difficult to express all one wishes to say. And letters of mere questions carry no joy with them, and no sympathy. So I shall not ask *now* any more. And you must not tire your dear little aching head to write when you do not feel well. I shall write again soon. For a little while good-bye, with love and all sweet hope to you ever,

"LAFCADIO HEARN.

" *Kumamoto,*
" *Kyushu, Japan.*
" *Jan.* 30, '94."

On November 17th, 1893, at one o'clock in the morning, Hearn's eldest son, Leopold Kazuo Koizumi, was born.

He declared that the strangest and strongest sensation of his life was hearing for the first time the cry of your own child. There was a strange feeling of being double; something more also impossible to analyse—the echo in a man's heart of all the sensations felt by all the fathers and mothers of his race at a similar instant in the past.

A few weeks later he writes to his sister, giving her news about his son. "The physician says that from the character of his bones he ought to become very tall. He is very dark. He has my nose and promises to have the Hearn eyebrows; but he has the Oriental eye. Whether he will be handsome or ugly, I can't tell: his little face changes every day;—he has already looked like five different people. When first born, I thought him the prettiest creature I ever saw. But that did not last. I am so inexperienced in the matter of children that I cannot trust myself to make any predictions. Of course I find the whole world changed about me. . . .

"My wife," he goes on, "is quite well. Happily the old military caste to which she belongs is a strong one, but how sacred and terrible a thing is maternity. When it was all over I felt very humble and grateful to the Unknowable Power which had treated us so kindly. The possibility of men being cruel to the women who bear their children seemed at the moment to darken existence.

"I have received your last beautiful photograph— or I should say two:—the vignette is, of course, the most lovable, but both are very, very nice. I gave the full-figure one to Setsu. She would like to have her boy grow up looking either like you or like Posey —but most like you. (Thanks also for the pretty photo of yourself and Posey: Posey is decidedly handsome.) But I fear my son can never be like either of you. He is altogether Oriental so far,—looks at me with the still calm Buddhist eyes of the Far East, and the soul of another race. Even his nose will never declare his Western blood; for the finest class of the Japanese offer many strongly aquiline faces. Setsu is a Samurai, and though her own features are the reverse of aquiline, there are aquiline faces among the kindred.

"I am awfully anxious that the boy should get to be like you. I have had your most beautiful photograph copied by a clever photographer here and have sent the copies to friends, saying, ' this is my sister; and this is the boy. I want him to look like her.' You see I am proud of you,—not only as to the ghostly, but also as to the material part of you. Physiologically I am all Latin and Pagan,—even though my little boy's eyes are bright blue.

". . . It is really nonsense, sending such a thing as his photo at fifty-five days old, because the child changes so much every week. But you are my little sister. I have called him Leopold Kazuo Hearn— for European use and custom. Kazuo, in Japanese, signifies ' First of the Excellent.' I have not registered him under that name, however; because by the law, if I registered my wife or son in the Consulate, both become English citizens, and lose the right to hold any property, or do any business in Japan, or even to live in the interior without a passport. I have, therefore, stopped at the Japanese marriage ceremony, and a publication of the fact abroad. In the present order I dare not deprive my folks of their nationality."

Then some time later he writes:—

" You ask for all kinds of news about Kajiwo. Well, he is now able to stand well, and is tremendously strong to all appearance. He tries to speak. ' Aba ' is the first *word* spoken by Japanese babes: it means ' good-bye.' Here is a curious example of the contrast between West and East,—the child comes into the world saying farewell. But this would be in accordance with

Buddhist philosophy,—saying farewell to the previous life.

"You are right about supposing that the birth of a son in Japan is an occasion of special rejoicing. All the baby clothes are ready long before birth—(except the ornamental ones)—as the *Kimono* or little robe is the same shape for either sex (*of children*). But, when the child is born, if it be a girl, very beautiful clothes of bright colours, covered with wonderful pictures, are made for it. If it be a boy the colours are darker, and the designs different. My little fellow's silken Kimono is covered with pictures of tortoises, storks, pine, and other objects typical of long life, prosperity, steadfastness, etc. This subject is enormously elaborate and complicated,—so that I cannot tell you all about it in a letter.

"After the child is born, all friends and relatives bring presents,—and everybody comes to see and congratulate the mother. You would think this were a trial. I was afraid it would tire Setsu. But she was walking about again on the seventh day after birth. The strength of the boy is hers,—not mine.

"I was also worried about the physician. I wanted the chief surgeon of the garrison,—because I was afraid. He was a friend, and laughed at me. He said: 'If anything terrible should happen, call me, but otherwise don't worry about a doctor. The Japanese have managed these things in their own way for thousands of years without doctors: a woman or two will do.' So two women came, and all was well. I hated the old women first, but after their success, I became very fond of them, and hugged them in English style, which they could not understand."

The kind dull veil that nature keeps stretched between mankind and the Unknown was drawn again. The world became to Hearn nearly the same as it had been before the birth of his child, and he could plan, he said, for the boy's future. He was afraid he might be near-sighted, and wondered if he would be intellectual. " He was so proud of him," his wife says, " that whenever a guest, a student, or a fellow-professor called, he would begin talking about him and his perfections without allowing his friend to get a word in. He perfectly frightened me with a hundred toys he brought home when he returned."

After his son's birth, Hearn naturally became still more anxious to have Setsu registered legally as his wife, but he was always met by official excuses and delays. He was told that if he wished the boy to remain a Japanese citizen he must register him in the mother's name only. If he registered him in his own name his son became a foreigner. On the other hand, Hearn knew that if he nationalised himself his salary would be reduced to a Japanese level.

" I don't quite see the morality of the reduction," he says, "for services should be paid according to the market value at least;—but there is no doubt it would be made. As for America, and my relatives in England, I am married: that has been duly announced. Perhaps I had better wait a few years and then become a citizen. Being a Japanese citizen would, of course, make no difference whatever as to my relations in any civilised countries abroad. It would only make some difference in an uncivilised country,—such as revolutionary South America, where English or French, or American protection is a good thing to have. But the

KAZUO (HEARN'S SON) AND HIS NURSE

long and the short of the matter is that I am anxious about Setsu's and the boy's interests: my own being concerned only at that point where their injury would be Setsu's injury."

The only way out of the difficulty, he concluded, was to abandon his English nationality and adopt his wife's family name, Koizumi. As a prefix for his own personal use he selected the appellation of the Province of Izumo "Yakumo" ("Eight clouds," or the "Place of the Issuing of Clouds," the first word of the ancient, Japanese song "Ya-he-gaki").

On one of his letters he shows his sister how his name is written in Japanese.

Mrs. Atkinson's youngest child, Dorothy, was born in March, 1894. There is an interval of exactly four months between her and her cousin Kazuo. It is in reference to this event that the following letter was written:—

"How sweet of you to get Mrs. or Miss Wetherall to write me the dear news! You will be well by the time this reaches you, so that I may venture to write more than congratulations.

"I was quite anxious about you,—feeling as if you were the only real *fellow-soul* in my world but one:— and birth is a thing so much more terrible than all else in the universe—more so than death itself—that the black border round the envelope made my heart cold for a moment. I had forgotten the why. Now I hope you will not have any more sons or daughters; you have three,—and I trust you will have no more pain or trouble. As for me, I am very resolved not to become a father again.

"You will laugh at me, and perhaps think it very

strange that when only thirty-five I began to feel a kind of envy of friends with children. I knew their troubles, anxieties, struggles; but I saw their sons grow up, beautiful and gifted men, and I used to whisper to myself,—' But I never shall have a child.' Then it used to seem to me that no man died so utterly as the man without children: for him I fancied (like some folk still really think in other lands) that death would be utter eternal blackness. When I did, however, hear the first cry of my boy—*my* boy, dreamed about in forgotten years—I had for that instant the ghostly sensation of being *double*. Just then, and only then, I did not think,—but *felt*, ' I am TWO.' It was weird but gave me thoughts that changed all pre-existing thoughts. My boy's gaze still seems to me a queerly beautiful thing: I still feel I am looking at myself when he looks at me. Only the thought has become infinitely more complicated. For I think about all the dead who live in the little heart of him—races and memories diverse as East and West. But who made his eyes blue and his hair brown? And will he be like you? And will he ever see the little cousin who has just entered the world? The other day, for one moment, he looked just like your boy in the picture."

Mrs. Atkinson about this time went through private trials upon which it is unnecessary to touch here. The following letter of consolation and encouragement was written to her by her half-brother:—

" Well, you too have had your revelations,—which means deep pains. One must pay a terrible price to see and to know. Still, the purchase is worth making. You know the Emerson lines:—

" Though thou love her as thyself,
  As a self of purer clay ;
  Though her parting dims the day,
  Stealing grace from all alive,
      Heartily know
      When half-Gods go,
        The Gods arrive ! . . .

" Reverse the condition : the moral is the same,—
and it is eternal. By light alone one cannot see; there
must be shadows in multitude to help. What we love
is good, and exists, but often exists only in *us*,—then
we become angry at others, not knowing the illusion
was the work of the Gods. The Gods are always right.
They make us sometimes imagine that something we
love ever so much is in others, while it is only in our
own hearts. The reason they do this to some, like
you and me, is to teach us what terrible long, long mistakes we might have made without their help. Sometimes they really cause a great deal of more serious
trouble, and we can't tell why. We must wait and
believe and be quite sure the Gods are good.

" What is not always good is the tender teaching
we get at home. We are told of things so beautiful
that we believe everybody must believe them,—truth,
and love, and duty, and honour of soul, etc. We are
even taught the enormous lie that the world is entirely
regulated by these beliefs. I wonder if it would not be
much better to teach children the adult truth :—' The
world is thus and so :—those beliefs are ideal only which
do not influence the intellectual life, nor the industrial
life, nor the social life. The world is a carnival-ball;
and you must wear a mask thereat,—and never,
never doff it;—except to the woman or the man you
must love always. Learn to wear your mask with grace

—only keep your heart fresh in spite of all bitter know-ledge.' Wouldn't this be the best advice? As a mere commonplace fact,—the whole battle of life is fought in disguise by those who win. No man knows the heart of another man. No woman knows the heart of another woman. Only the woman can learn the man, and the man the woman;—and this only after years! What a great problem it is; and how utterly it is neg-lected in teaching the little human flowers that we set out in the world's cold without a thought!

"You are more and more like me in every letter; but you are better far. I have not learned reserve with friends yet: I supply the lack by a retreating dis-position,—a disinclination to make acquaintances. I love very quickly and strongly; but just as quickly dislike what I loved—if deceived, and the dislike does not die. My general experience has been that the love-able souls are but rarely lodged in the forms which most attract us: there *are* such exceptions on the woman's side as my dear little Sis,—and there are excep-tions on the male side of a particular order, and rare. But the rule remains. I wonder if all these jokes are not played on us by the Gods, who think,—' No!— you want the infinite! That can be reached later only, —after innumerable births. First learn, for a million years or so, just to love only *souls*. You *must !* for you will be punished if you try to obtain all perfections in one.' I think the Gods talk to us about that way; and when we leave the Spring season of life behind, we find the Gods were right after all.

"—Still, the great puzzle is in all these things there are no general rules solid enough to trust in. I fancy the best teaching for a heart would be,—' Always

caution,—but—believe the tendency of the world is to
good.' And *largeness* seems to be necessary,—never to
suffer oneself to see only one charm; but to train oneself to study combinations and understand them. Any
modern human nature is too complex to be otherwise
judged.

"Music,—yes! If I were near you I would be
always teasing you to play:—and would bring you all
kinds of queer exotic melodies to make variations on:
strange melodies from Spanish America and the Creole
Islands, and Japan, and China, and all sorts of strange
places. We should try to do very curious things in
the way of ballads and songs, and you would teach me
all sorts of musical things I don't know. By the way,
you will be shocked to learn, perhaps, that I have never
been able to appreciate the superiority of the new
German music: The Italian still seems to me the
divine: but that may be because I have never had time
to train myself to appreciate.

"—You do not know how much I sympathise with
all your anxieties and troubles, and how much I wish
for your strength and happiness. Would I not like to
be travelling with you to countries where you would
find all the rest and light and warmth you could enjoy!
Perhaps, some day that may be. Pray to the Gods for
my good fortune; and we shall share the pleasure together if They listen. If They do not, we must wait
as the Buddhists say until the future birth. Then I
want to be a very rich man, or woman, and you a very
dear little sister or brother;—and I want to have a
steam yacht of 30,000 horse-power.

"—Your sweetest little daughter, may you live to
see her happiness in all things! I am glad I have no

daughter. A boy can fight—must fight his way; but a daughter is the luxury of a rich man. Had I a daughter, she would be too dear; and I should feel inclined to say if dying :—' My child, I am unable to guard you longer, and the world is difficult : you would do better to come to Shadowland with me.' But your Marjory will be well guarded and petted, and have the world made sweet for her; and you will have no more grief. You have had all your disappointments and troubles in girlhood—childhood;—the future must be kind to you. As for me, I really think the Gods owe me some favours; they have ignored me so long that I am now all expectation."

Then again :—

" MY VERY SWEET LITTLE SISTER,

" Your dear letter came yesterday, and filled us all with gladness. You see I say US;—for my folks prayed very hard for you to the ancient Gods and to the Buddhas,—that I might not lose that little sister of mine.—And now to answer questions.

" Indeed, Setsu got the photos, and wondered at them, for she had never seen a carriage before of that kind, or a room like your room; and very childishly asked me to make her a room like yours. To which I said :—' The cost of such a room would buy for you a whole street in your native city of Matsue; and besides, you would be very unhappy and uncomfortable in such a room.' And when I explained, she wondered still more. (A very large Japanese house could be bought with the grounds for about £30—I mean a big, big merchant's house—in Izumo.) Another wonder was the donkey in the other photo, for none had ever seen such an animal.

" —As for your ever coming to Japan, my dear, if you do, you shall have a chair. But I fear—indeed I am almost certain—that the day is not very far away when I must leave Setsu and Kajiwo to the care of the ancient Gods, and go away and work bravely for them elsewhere, till Kajiwo is old enough to go abroad. The days of foreign influence and of foreign teaching in Japan are rapidly drawing to a close. Japan is learning to do well without us; and we have not been kind enough to her to win her love. We have persecuted her with hordes of fanatical missionaries, robbed her by unjust treaties, forced her to pay monstrous indemnities for trifling wrongs;—we have forced her to become strong, and she is going to do without us presently, the future is dark. Happily my folks will be provided for; and I expect to be able, if I must go, to return in a few years. It is barely possible that I might get into journalism in Japan,—but not at all sure. I suppose you know that is my living profession : I understand all kinds of newspaper work. But as I am no believer in conventions, I am not likely to get any of the big sinecures. To do that one must be a ladies' man, a member of some church, a social figure. I am no ladies' man : I am known to the world as an ' infidel,' and I hate society unutterably. Were I rich enough to live where I please, I should certainly (if unable to live in Japan) return to the tropics. Indeed, I have a faint hope of passing at least the winters of my old age near the Equator. Where the means are to come from I don't know; but I have a kind of faith in Goethe's saying, that whatever a man most desires in youth, he will have an excess of in his old age. Leisure to write books in a warm climate is all I ask. Pray to the Gods, if you believe in any Gods, to help the dream to be realised.

"Kajiwo is my nightmare. I am tortured all day and all night by the problem of how to set him going in life before I become dust. Sometimes I think how bad it was of me to have had a child at all. Yet before that, I did not really know what life was; and I would not lose the knowledge for any terms of gifts of years. Besides, I am beginning to think I am really a tolerably good sort of fellow,—for if I had been really such a monster of depravity as the religious fanatics declared, how could I have got such a fine boy. There must be some good in me anyhow. Nobody shall make a 'Christian' of Kajiwo if I can help it—by 'Christian' I mean a believer in absurd and cruel dogmas. The world talks much about Christianity, but no one teaches it.

"—So glad to hear you are able to go out a little again. Perhaps a long period of strong solid calm health is preparing for you. After the trials and worries of maternity such happy conditions often come as a reward. I hope to chat with you by a fire when we are both old, and Kaji has shot up into a man,—looking like his aunt a little—with a delicate aquiline face. But only the Eternities know what his face will be like. It is changeable as water now. I won't send another photo of him till he looks pretty again.

"With best love,
"LAFCADIO HEARN.

"June 24, '94.

"I must go off travelling in a couple of weeks. Perhaps there will be a little delay before my next letter reaches you."

In the next letter he touches upon these travels under-taken with his wife, mother-in-law, and Kaji (an abbre-viation of Kazuo, or Kajiwo, as Hearn was in the habit of calling him at first).

"How sweet of you," he says, "to send that charming photo of the children. It delighted us all. Setsu never saw a donkey—there are none in Japan; and all wondered at the strange animal. What I won-dered at was to see what a perfect pretty little woman the charming Marjory is. As for the boy, he is certainly what every parent wants a boy to be as to good looks; but I also think he must have a very sweet temper. I trust that you won't allow the world to spoil it for him. They do spoil tempers at some of the great public schools. I cannot believe it is necessary to let young lads be subjected to the brutality of places like Eton and Harrow. It hardens them too much. The answer is that the great school turns out the conquerors of the world,—the subalterns of Kipling,—the Clives, —the daring admirals and great captains, etc. Per-haps in this militant age it is necessary. But I notice the great thinkers generally come from other places. However, this is the *practical* age,—there is nothing for philosophers, poets, or painters to succeed in, unless they are independently situated. I shall try to make a good doctor out of Kaji, if I can. I could never afford to do more for him. And if possible I shall take him to Europe, and stay there with him for a couple of years. But that is a far-away matter."

Characteristically with that apprehensive mind of his, his son's future, as Hearn himself confesses, became a perfect nightmare. "I must make an Englishman of him, I fear. His hair has turned bright brown. He is so strong that I expect him to become a very powerful man : he is very deep-chested and thick-built and so heavy now, that people think I am not telling the truth about his age.

"Kajiwo's soul seems to be so English that I fancy his memory of former births would scarcely refer much to Japan. How about the real compound race-soul, though? One would have to recollect having been two at the same time. This seems to me a defect in the popular theory—still the Japanese hold, or used to hold, that the soul is itself a multiple—that each person has a *number of souls*. That would give an explanation. Scientifically it is true. We are all compounds of innumerable lives—each a sum in an infinite addition—the dead are not dead—they live in all of us and move us,—and stir faintly in every heart-beat. And there are ghostly interlinkings. Something of *you* must be in *me*, and of both of us in Kajiwo.

" —I wonder if this also be true of little Dorothy. It is a curious thing that you tell me about the change in colour of the eyes. I only saw that happen in hot climates. Creole children are not uncommonly born with gold hair and bright blue eyes. A few years later the skin, eyes, hair seem to have entirely changed,—the first to brown, the two last to coal-black.

" —I am writing all this dreamy stuff just to amuse my sweet little sister,—because I can't be near to pet her and make her feel very happy. Well, a little Oriental theory may have some caressing charm for you. It is a very gentle faith—though also very deep; and you will find in my book how much it interests me.

KAZUO (HEARN'S SON, AGED ABOUT SEVEN)

"Take very, very, *very* good care of your precious little self,—and do not try to write till you feel immensely strong. Setsu sends sweet words and wishes. And I——!

"With love,

"LAFCADIO HEARN.

"*Kumamoto, June 2, '94.*"

CHAPTER XX

OUT OF THE EAST

" So Japan paid to learn how to see shadows in Nature, in life, and in thought. And the West taught her that the sole business of the divine sun was the making of the cheaper kind of shadows. And the West taught her that the higher-priced shadows were the sole product of Western civilisation, and bade her admire and adopt. Then Japan wondered at the shadows of machinery and chimneys and telegraph poles; and at the shadows of mines and of factories, and the shadows in the hearts of those who worked there; and at the shadows of houses twenty storeys high, and of hunger begging under them; and shadows of enormous charities that multiplied poverty; and shadows of social reforms that multiplied vice; and the shadows of shams and hypocrisies and swallow-tail coats; and the shadow of a foreign God, said to have created mankind for the purpose of an auto-da-fe. Whereat Japan became rather serious, and refused to study any more silhouettes. Fortunately for the world, she returned to her first matchless art; and, fortunately for herself, returned to her own beautiful faith. But some of the shadows still cling to her life; and she cannot possibly get rid of them. Never again can the world seem to her quite so beautiful as it did before."

AFTER the lapse of a certain amount of time Hearn gradually became more reconciled to Kumamoto. The climate agreed with him, he put on flesh, all his Japanese clothes, he declared, even his kimono, had become too small. "I cannot say whether this be the climate, the diet, or what. Setsu says it is because I have a good wife: but she might be prejudiced, you know."

It is more likely that his well-being at this time arose from his having given up the experiment of living exclusively on a Japanese regimen. After his bout of

264

illness at Matsue, he found that he could not recuperate on the fare of the country, even when reinforced with eggs. Having lived for ten months thus, horribly ashamed as he was to confess his weakness, he found himself obliged to return to the flesh-pots of Egypt, and devoured enormous quantities of beef and fowl, and drank terrific quantities of beer. "The fault is neither mine nor that of the Japanese : it is the fault of my ancestors, the ferocious, wolfish hereditary instincts and tendencies of boreal mankind. The sins of the fathers, etc."

Meantime, his knowledge of the strange people amongst whom his lot was cast was deepening and expanding. *Out of the East*, the collection of essays— essence of experiences accumulated at this time, and the book, next perhaps to *Glimpses of Unfamiliar Japan*, by which he is best known—is typical of his genius at its best and at its worst. The first sketch, entitled, "The Dream of a Summer's Day," is simply a bundle of impressions of the journey to which he alludes when writing to his sister, made from Nagasaki to Kumamoto, along the shores of the Inland Sea. This journey, through some of the most beautiful scenery of Japan, after the horrors of a foreign hotel at an open port, was one of those experiences that form an epoch in an artist's life, touching him with the magic wand of inspiration. All the delightful impressions made by the poetry and the elusive beauty of old Japan seem concentrated into six pages of poetic prose. To the world it is known as "The Dream of a Summer's Day." [1] To those who have been in Japan, and love the delicate beauty of her mountain ranges, the green

---

[1] *Out of the East :* Houghton, Mifflin & Co.

of her rice-fields, and the indigo shadows of her crypto-
meria-groves, it summons up delightful memories, the
rapture felt in the crystalline atmosphere, its picturesque little people, its running waters, the flying gleams
of sunlight, the softly tolling bells, the distant ridges
blue and remote in the warm air. Like a bubbling
spring the sense of beauty broke forth from the caverns
of ancient memory, where, according to Lafcadio, it had
lain imprisoned for years, to ripple and murmur sweet
music in his ears. He went back to the days of his
childhood, back to dreams lying in the past in what
had become for him an alien land, the fragrance of
a most dear memory swept over his senses. The
gnat of the soul of him flitted out into the gleam of
blue 'twixt sea and sun, back to the cedarn balcony
pillars of the Japanese hotel, whence he could see the
opening of the bay and the horizon, haunted by mountain shapes, faint as old memories, and then again to
distant and almost forgotten memories of his youth by
Loch Corrib, in the West of Ireland, the result being as
beautiful a prose poem as Hearn ever wrote.

The last essay in the collection is called " Yuko," a
reminiscence.

There are many of Lafcadio Hearn's critics who say,
that in consequence of his ignorance of the Japanese
language, and the isolation in which he lived, he never
could have known anything really of the innermost
thoughts and feelings of the people to whom he professed to act as interpreter. Sometimes they maintain
that his views are unfavourable to an exaggerated
extent, at another too laudatory. His essay entitled
" Yuko " might certainly be taken as an example of
the manner in which he selected certain superficial mani-

festations as typical of the inner life of the Japanese,—
a people as reserved, as secretive, as difficult to follow
in their emotional aspects as the hidden currents to
which he compares them, quoting the words of Kipling's
pilot : " And if any man comes to you, and says, ' I know
the Javva currents,' don't you listen to him; for those
currents is never yet known to mortal man ! "

Yuko was a servant-maid in a wealthy family at
Kinegawa.   She had read in the daily newspaper the
account of the attempt on the life of the Czarevitch
during his visit to Japan in 1891.   Being an hysterical,
excitable girl, she was apparently wound up to the pitch
of temporary insanity.   Leaving her employer's home,
she made her way to Kyoto, and there, buying a razor,
she cut her throat opposite the gate of the Mikado's
palace.   Hearn writes of the incident as if the girl were
a Joan of Arc, obeying the dictates of the most fervent
patriotism.   He goes to the extent of describing the
Mikado, " The Son of Heaven," hearing of the girl's
death, and " augustly ceasing to mourn for the crime
that had been committed because of the manifestations
of the great love his people bore him."

Afterwards, Hearn admitted that his enthusiasm
was perhaps exaggerated, for revelations showed that
Yuko, in a letter she had left, had spoken of " a
family claim."   Under the raw strong light of these
commonplace revelations, he confessed that his little
sketch seemed for the moment much too romantic, and
yet the real poetry of the event remained unlessened,—
the pure ideal that impelled a girl to take her own life
merely to give proof of the love and loyalty of a nation.
No small, mean, dry facts could ever belittle that large
fact.

Let those, however, who say that Hearn did not understand the enigmatical people amongst whom his lines were cast, read his article on " Jiu-jitsu " in this same volume. It is headed by a quotation from the *Tao-Te-King*. " Man at his birth is supple and weak; at his death, firm and strong. So is it with all things. . . . Firmness and strength are the concomitants of death; softness and weakness are the concomitants of life. Hence he who relies upon his own strength shall not conquer." Preaching from this text Hearn writes a masterly article, showing how Japan, though apparently adopting Western inventions, preserves her own genius and mode of thought in all vital questions absolutely unchanged. The essay ends with a significant paragraph, showing how we Occidentals, who have exterminated feebler races by merely over-living them, may be at last exterminated ourselves by races capable of under-living us, more self-denying, more fertile, and less expensive for nature to support. Inheriting, doubtless, our wisdom, adopting our more useful inventions, continuing the best of our industries,—perhaps even perpetuating what is most worthy to endure in our sciences and our arts; pushing us out of the progress of the world, as the dinotherium, or the ichthyosaurus, were pushed out before us.

Towards the end of his stay at Kumamoto, he wrote one of his delightful, whimsically affectionate letters to his old friend, Mr. Watkin, in answer apparently to one from him, recalling their talks and expeditions in the old days at Cincinnati, and expressing his gratitude for the infinite patience and wisdom shown in his treatment of his naughty, superhumanly foolish, detestable little friend. " Well, I wish I were near you to love you, and make up for all old troubles." He then tells his dad that he has been able to save between $3,500 and $4,000, that he has placed in custody in his wife's name. The reaction, he said, against foreign influence was very strong, and the future looked more gloomy every day. Eventually, he supposed, he must leave Japan and work elsewhere, and he ends, " When I first met you I was nineteen. I am now forty-four—well, I suppose I must have lots more trouble before I go to Nirvana."

Towards the end of the Chinese-Japanese War Hearn was worried with anxiety on the subject of the non-continuance of his appointment at the Kumamoto College. "Government Service," he writes to Ameno-mori, " is uncertain to the degree of terror,—a sword of Damocles; and Government doesn't employ men like you as teachers. If it did, and would give them what they should have, the position of a foreign teacher would be pleasant enough. He would be among thinkers and find some kindness,—instead of being made to feel that he is the servant of petty political clerks." He approached Page Baker, his old New Orleans friend, asking him if he could get him anything if he started in the spring for America. Something good enough to save money at, not only for himself, but something that would enable him to send money to Japan; he was not desirous of seeing Boston, New York or Philadelphia, but would rather be in Memphis, Charlestown, or glorious Florida. Page Baker had apparently been sending him help, for on June 2nd Hearn writes acknowledging a draft for one hundred and sixty-three pounds, thanking him ten thousand times from the bottom of his much scarified heart.

"I am now forty-four," he adds, "and as grey as a badger. Unless I can make enough to educate my boy well, I don't know what I'm worth,—but I feel that I shall have precious little time to do it in; add twenty to forty-four, and how much is left of a man?"

In another letter he again alludes to the manner in which the Government are cutting down the number of employés: "My contract runs only until March," he ends, "and my chances are o."

At last, after many hesitations, he definitely decided to leave Government service, and in the autumn of 1894 accepted the offer of a position on the staff of the *Kobe Chronicle* made by Mr. Robert Young, proprietor and editor of the newspaper.

To his sister he wrote from the *Kobe Chronicle* office, Kobe, Japan:—

"My dear Minnie,

"I am too much in a whirl just now to write a good letter to you (whose was the little curl in your last?—you never told me). I am writing only to say that I have left the Government Service to edit a paper in one of the open ports. This is returning to my old profession, and is pleasant enough,—though not just now very lucrative.

"Best love to you. Perhaps we shall meet in a few years. My boy is well, beginning to walk a little. My book was to be issued on the 29th Sept.

"Ever affectionately,

"Lafcadio."

DOROTHY ATKINSON

CHAPTER XXI

KOBE

LAST spring I journeyed to Japan with Mrs. Atkinson, Lafcadio Hearn's half-sister, and her daughter. Mrs. Atkinson was anxious to make the acquaintance of her Japanese half-sister-in-law to ascertain the circumstances surrounding the family, also if it were possible to carry out her half-brother's wishes with regard to educating his eldest son, Kazuo—his Benjamin—in England.

The first place at which we landed was Kobe, situated on the eastern end of the Inland Sea, opposite Osaka, the Manchester of Japan.

Kobe is numbered among the open ports. Consuls can fly their country's flag and occupy offices on the " Bund." Surrounding the bay are a number of German, American and British warehouses. Foreigners also are allowed to reside in the city under Japanese law.

During the six weeks on board the P. and O. coming out, I had been reading Hearn's books, and was steeped in the legendary lore, the " hidden soul-life " of ancient Nippon. At Moji—gateway of the Inland Sea—it had blown a gale, and the Japanese steamer, the *Chikugo Maru*, to which we had transhipped at Shanghai, was obliged to come to anchor under the headland. The ecstasy, therefore, after rolling in a heavy sea all night, of floating into the calm, sun-bathed waters of the Inland

Sea, made the enchantment all the more bewitching. Reclining in our deck-chairs, we looked on the scene as it slowly passed before our eyes, and yielded, without a struggle, to the exquisite and fantastical charm of the spirit of Old Japan. For what seemed uncounted hours we crept between the dim boundaries of tinted mountains, catching glimpses here and there of mysterious bays and islands, of shadowy avenues, arched by symbolic Torii leading to ancient shrines, of groups of fishing villages that seemed to have grown on the shore, their thatched roofs covered with the purple flowers of the roof plant, the "Yane-shobu." At first we endeavoured to decipher in Murray the names of the enchanting little hamlets, with their cedarn balconies, high-peaked gables, and quaint terraced gardens, inhabited by a strange people in geta and kimono, like figures on a Japanese screen depicting a scene of hundreds of years ago. Across the mind of almost every one the magic of Japan strikes with a sensation of strangeness and delight,—a magic that gives the visitor a sense of great issues, and remote visions, telling of a kingdom dim and half-apprehended. Unsubstantial and fragile as all these villages looked, they were hallowed by memorable stories of heroism and self-sacrifice, either in the last war with Russia and China, or in her own internecine fights centuries ago; chronicles of men who had fought heroically and died uncomplainingly in defence of their country, chronicles of women who had scorned to weep when told of the death of husbands, fathers and brothers in the pest-stricken rice-fields of China, or in the trenches before Port Arthur.

A warm, perfect noon came and went, and the sun

that had poured himself from above into the earth as
into a cup, gradually descended, as we crept up the
waters of the Inland Sea, towards the shoulders of
the eastern peaks, until they turned saffron and then
flushed pink, and then paled to green.

There was no moon, but the night stretched in pale
radiance overhead. And as we watched the stars burn
with the extraordinary brilliancy peculiar to Japan, we
dreamed that we looked on the River Celestial, the
Ghost of Waters. We saw the mists hovering along
the verge, and the water grasses that bend in the winds
of autumn, and we knew that the falling dew was the
spray from the herdsman's oar. And the heavens
" seemed very near, and warm, and human; and the
silence about us was filled with the dream of a love
unchanging, immortal, for ever yearning and for ever
young, and for ever left unsatisfied by the paternal
wisdom of the Gods."

The open port of Kobe came like an awakening out
of a delicious dream. It was impossible not to feel
exasperated with the Germans, Englishmen and Ameri-
cans who have desecrated an earthly paradise with
red-brick erections, factory chimneys, and plate-glass
shop-fronts; easy was it to understand Hearn's railings
against the modernisation of the country.

Not far, however, had the foreign wedge been
driven in. After a short *kuruma* journey from the
landing-stage to the hotel, we were back again in the
era of Kusimoki Marahige.

Foreign names may have been given to the hills, and
stretches of sea coast,—Aden, Bismarck Hill, Golf
Links Valley;—ancient Nippon keeps them as her
own, with their Shinto and Buddhist temples, sur-

rounded by woods of cryptomeria and camphor-trees. Their emotional and intellectual life is no more altered by their Occidental neighbours than the surface of a mirror is changed by passing reflections, as says their interpreter, Lafcadio Hearn.

Next to the hotel,—as if to emphasise its nationality, —was an ancient pine-surrounded cemetery, set with tall narrow laths of unpainted wood; while behind, to the summit of the hill, stretched a blue-grey sea of tiles, a cedar world of *engawa* and *shoji*, indescribable whimsicalities, representing another world in its picturesqueness and grotesquery. But it was not only in these visible objects that a strange, unexpected life manifested itself. In the street, as you passed along, dim surmises of some inscrutable humanity—another race soul, charming, fascinating, and yet alien to your own, formulated itself to your Western consciousness. The bowing, the smiling, the arrangement of flowers in the poorest shanties, the banners and lanterns with marvellous drawings and ideographs; the children singing nursery rhymes in an unknown language; others sitting naked in hot tubs, a woman with elaborately dressed hair stuck over with large-headed pins, and rouged and powdered cheeks, cleansing her teeth over the street gutter, while behind were glimpses of curious interiors where men and women were squatting on the floor like Buddhas, some reading, some with brushes writing on long strips of paper from right to left.

Enigmatical, incomprehensible it might be, but there was nothing displeasing, nothing objectionable as in a native Arab town, or even in the streets of Canton or Shanghai. No unhappy children, or cross, red-faced women; no coarse, drunken men, no loud voices, no brawling. Though all was alien to your traditions, you were forced to acknowledge a charm, a refinement, a courtesy, a kindliness far superior to those to be found in European cities.

The conditions existing in Kobe when Hearn arrived in 1895 were not satisfactory from a sanitary point of view. Cholera had come with the victorious army from China, and had carried off, during the hot season, about thirty thousand people. The smoke and odour from the funeral pyres that burnt continually, came wind-blown into Hearn's garden down from the hills behind the town, just to remind him, as he says, " that the cost of burning an adult of my own size is 80 sen— about half a dollar in American money at the present rate of exchange."

From the upper balcony of his house the Japanese street, with its rows of little shops, was visible to the bay; from thence he watched the cholera patients being taken away, and the bereaved, as soon as the law allowed, flitting from their paper-shuttered abodes, while the ordinary life of the street went on day and night, as if nothing particular had happened. The itinerant vendors with their bamboo poles, and baskets or buckets, passed the empty houses and uttered their accustomed cry; the blind shampooer blew his melancholy whistle; the private watchman made his heavy staff boom upon the gutter-flags; and the children chased one another as usual with screams and laughter. Sometimes a child vanished, but the survivors continued their play as if nothing had happened, according to the wisdom of the ancient East.

A supersensitive man, not in robust health, must have felt acutely the depressing effects of this state of things. Sclerosis of the arteries and other symptoms of heart failure, warned him during this autumn of 1895 that he was "descending the shady side of the hill." An attack of inflammation of the eyes also gave him much trouble. He had been worried, he says in a letter to Page Baker, by the fear that either he or his friend might die before they met again. "I think of you a great deal. . . . You are a long-lived, tough race, you Bakers. Page Baker will be most likely writing some day things of Lafcadio Hearn that was, which the said Lafcadio never deserved, and never will deserve."

Death had no terrors for Lafcadio Hearn, but the premonitions of physical shipwreck that beset him now depressed him heart and soul because of the work still left undone.

He would like nothing so much, he said, as to get killed, if he had no one but himself in the world to take care of—which is just why he wouldn't get killed. He couldn't afford luxuries until his work was done.

To his sister he writes:—"I have been on my back in a dark room for a month with inflammation of the eyes, and cannot write much. Thanks for sweet letter. I received a *Daily News* from you,—many, many thanks. Did not receive the other papers you spoke of —probably they were stolen in Kumamoto. I fear I cannot do much newspaper work for some time. The climate does not seem to suit my eyes,—a hot climate would be better. I may be able to make a trip next winter to some tropical place, if I make any money out of my books. My new book—*Out of the East*—will be published soon after this letter reaches you.

"Future looks doubtful—don't feel very jolly about it. The mere question of living is the chief annoyance.

I am offered some further work in Kobe, that would leave me leisure (they promise) for my own literary work, but I am not sure. However, the darkest hour is before the dawn, perhaps.

" Kaji is well able to walk now, and talks a little. Every day his hair is growing brighter; a thorough English boy.

" Excuse bad eyes.

"Love to you,

"LAFCADIO."

Although more than twelve years had elapsed between our visit and the period when Hearn had resided in Kobe, nearly every one remembered the odd little journalist, who might be seen daily making his way, in his shy, near-sighted fashion, from his house in Kitinagasa Dori, to the office of the *Kobe Chronicle*.

Dr. Papellier of Kobe, who attended Hearn in a professional capacity at this time, was full of reminiscences. Long before meeting him at Kobe Dr. Papellier had been a great admirer of his genius, had, indeed, when surgeon on board a German vessel, translated *Chita* for a Nuremberg paper.

Being an oculist, one of his first injunctions, as soon as he examined Hearn's eyes, was cessation from all work and rest in a darkened room if he wished to escape total blindness. The right eye was myopic to an extent seldom seen, and at the moment was so severely inflamed by neuritis that the danger of an affection to the retina seemed imminent,—the left was entirely blind. For the purpose of keeping up his spirits, under this unwonted constraint, Dr. Papellier, in spite of his professional engagements, went out of his way to visit the little man frequently, and would stop hours chatting; showed him, indeed, a kindness and consideration that, we were told, was quite exceptional. Hearn, Dr. Papellier relates, was a good and fluent talker, content to keep the ball rolling himself and preferred an attentive listener, rather than a person who stated his own opinions.

Their topics of conversation circled round the characteristics of the civilisation in which they were living. Hearn's emotional enthusiasm for the Japanese, the doctor said, had cooled; he had received several shocks in dealing with officials at Kumamoto, and said his illusions were vanishing, and he wanted to leave the country; France, China, or the South Sea Islands seemed each in turn to attract his wayward fancy.

The account of Stevenson's life in Samoa had made a great impression on him. He declared that if he had not his Japanese family to look after he would pack up his books of reference and start at once for Samoa.

"His wife, who understood no English at all, seldom appeared, a servant girl usually attending to his wants when I was present.

"It struck me at the time that his knowledge of the Japanese vernacular was very poor for a man of his intelligence, who, for nearly four years, had lived almost entirely in the interior, surrounded by those who could only talk the language of the country.

"It was plain that what he knew about Japan must have been gained through the medium of interpreters. I was still more surprised when I discovered how extremely near-sighted he was. His impressions of scenery or Japanese works of Art could never have been obtained as ordinary people obtain them. The details had to be studied piece by piece with a small telescope, and then described as a whole."

His mode of life, Dr. Papellier said, was almost penurious, although he must have been receiving a good salary from the *Kobe Chronicle*, and was making something by his books. At home he dressed invariably in Japanese style; his clothes being very clean and neat. The furniture of his small house was scanty. His food, which was partly Japanese and partly so-called "foreign," was prepared in a small restaurant somewhere in the town. In his position as medical attendant Papellier regarded it as his duty to remonstrate on this point, impressing upon him that he ought to remember the drain on his constitution of the amount of brain work that he was doing, both at the *Kobe Chronicle* office and writing at home.

There were reasons for this that Hearn would not care to tell Papellier. Mrs. Koizumi was in delicate health, expecting her second child, and Hearn doubtless, with that consideration that invariably distinguished him in his treatment of his wife, had his food brought from outside so as to save her the trouble and exertion of cooking it at home. Only in one way, Papellier said, did he allow himself any indulgence, and that was in the amount he smoked. Although he seldom took spirits he smoked incessantly! Not cigars, but a small Japanese pipe—a *kizeru*—which he handled in a skilful way, lighting one tiny tobacco pellet in the glowing ashes of the one just consumed. One of his hobbies was collecting pipes, the other was collecting books. He had already got together a valuable library at New Orleans, he did the same in Japan. He was able to exercise these hobbies inexpensively, but they needed

knowledge, time and patience. At his death he possessed more than two hundred pipes, all shapes and
sizes.

Every one whom we met when we arrived at Kobe
advised us to call on the editor of the *Kobe Chronicle*
if we wanted information on the subject of Lafcadio
Hearn. We therefore made our way to the *Kobe
Chronicle* office as soon as we could. Mr. Young as
well as Mrs. Young, whose acquaintance we made
subsequently, were both full of reminiscences of the
odd little genius.

He generally made it a rule to drop into the Youngs'
house every Sunday for lunch; his particular fancy in
the way of food, or, at all events, the only thing he
expressed a fancy for, was plum-pudding,—a plum-
pudding therefore became a standing dish on Sundays,
so long as Hearn was in Kobe. "The Japanese," he
was wont to say, "are a very clever people, but they
don't understand plum-pudding."

Absence of mind, and inattention to events passing
around him, was very noticeable, the Youngs told us,
these days. Sometimes he seemed even to find a difficulty in fixing his thoughts on the identity of the
individual with whom he was conversing.

Mrs. Young, if she will permit me to say so, is an
extremely agreeable-looking, clear-complexioned, chest-
nut-haired Englishwoman. For some considerable
time Hearn always addressed her in Japanese. At last
one day she remarked: "You know, Mr. Hearn, I
am not Japanese." "Oh, really," was his reply, as if
for the first time he had realised the fact. From that
time forward he addressed her in English.

Mr. Young was kind enough to furnish me with

copies of Hearn's editorials during the seven or eight months he worked on the staff of the *Kobe Chronicle*. Though not coinciding with many of Hearn's opinions and conclusions, with regard to the Japanese and their religious and social convictions, Mr. Young gave him a free hand so far as subject-matter and expression of opinion were concerned. None of his contributions, however, are distinguished by Hearn's peculiar literary qualities. The flint-edged space of the newspaper column cramped and hampered his genius. Work with him, he declared, was always a pain, but writing for money an impossibility.

Of course, he said, he could write, and write, and write, but the moment he began to write for money the little special colour vanished, the special flavour that was within him evaporated, he became nobody again; and the public wondered why it paid any attention to so commonplace a fool. So he had to sit and wait for the gods. His mind, however, ate itself when unemployed. Even reading did not fill the vacuum. His thoughts wandered, and imaginings, and recollections of unpleasant things said or done recurred to him. Some of these unpleasant things were remembered longer than others, under this stimulus he rushed to work, wrote page after page of vagaries, metaphysical, emotional, romantic—and threw them aside. Then next day he rewrote them and rewrote them until they arranged themselves into a whole, and the result was an essay that the editor of the *Atlantic* declared was a veritable illumination, and no mortal man knew how or why it was written, not even he himself.

Two of Hearn's characteristics, both of which militated considerably against his being an effective newspaper correspondent, were his personal bias and want of restraint. A daily newspaper must, above all things, be run on customary and everyday lines, but Hearn did not possess the ordinary hold on the conventional methods and usages of life. For instance, when treating of the subject of free libraries he thus expresses himself: " A library is now regarded, not as a treasury of wisdom and beauty, but as a 'dumping-ground' for offal, a repository of human frivolity, insanity and folly. Newspapers, forsooth!—why not collect and store the other things that wise men throw away, cigar-ends and orange-peelings? Some future historian of the gutter might like to see them. No, I would give to all these off-scourings and clippings the same doom."

No consideration would deter him from flying in the face of the ordinary reader if it suited him so to do. He had always passionately resisted the Christianising of Japan, not only from a religious, but from an artistic point of view. He thus roused the wrath of the orthodox,—a wrath that pursued him from this year in Kobe until his death, and makes the very sound of his name detested in Christian religious circles in Japan.

" For myself," he says in one of the *Kobe Chronicle* leaders, " I could sympathise with the individual, but never with the missionary cause. Unconsciously, every honest being in the Mission Army is a destroyer, —and a destroyer only; for nothing can replace what they break down. Unconsciously, too, the missionaries everywhere represent the edge,—the *acies*,—to use the Roman word—of Occidental aggression. We are face to face here with the spectacle of a powerful and selfish civilisation, demoralising and crushing a weaker, and, in many ways a nobler one (if we are to judge by comparative ideals); and the spectacle is not pretty. We must recognise the inevitable, the Cosmic Law, if you like; but one feels and hates the moral wrong, and this perhaps blinds one too much to the sacrifices and pains accepted by the ' noble army.' "

Hearn's gradually-increasing disinclination to meet strangers was, at this time, indicative of a morbid condition of mind and body. He summarily refused to hold any intercourse with the foreign commercial element in Kobe, pronouncing them rough and common. After life in the interior, he declared life at an open port to be very unpleasant. The Germans represented the best of the foreign element, plain and homely, which at all events was a virtue. But he harked back to the life in Old Japan as being better, and cleaner, and higher in every way, with only the bare means of Japanese comfort, than the luxury and money-grabbing at Kobe; in his opinion, the Japanese peasant was ten times more of a gentleman than a foreign merchant could ever learn to be. . . . Then he indulges in one of his outbursts against carpets—pianos—windows—curtains—brass bands—churches! and white shirts! and "yofuku"! Would that he had been born savage; the curse of civilised cities was on him, and he supposed he couldn't get away permanently from them. "How much I could hate all that we call civilisation I never knew before. How ugly it is I never could have conceived without a long sojourn in Old Japan—the only civilised country that existed since Antiquity."

Kokoro, the book written at this time, is now celebrated, and justly so. Hearn himself called it a " crazy book." Crazy, it may be designated, from its very originality, its strange interpretation of strange things, the new note that it initiates, and the sympathetic power it displays of divining beliefs and mythologies, the "race ghost" of one of the most enigmatical people on earth. "The papers composing this volume," he says in his preface, "treat of the inner rather than of the outer life of Japan,—for which reason they have been grouped under the title 'Kokoro' (Heart)."

Written with the above character, this word signifies also mind, in the emotional sense; spirit; courage; resolve; sentiment; affection; and inner meaning,—just as we say in English, "the heart of things."

It is the quality of truthful work that it never grows old or stale; one can return to it again and again, and in interpreting the "heart" of Japan, Hearn's work is absolutely truthful. I know that this is contradicted by many. Professor Foxwell tells a story of a lady tourist who told him before she came to Japan she had read Hearn's books and thought they were delightful as literature, but added, "What a disappointment when you come here; the people are not at all like his descriptions!"

The lady had not perhaps grasped the fact that Hearn's principal book on Japan, the book that every tourist reads, is called *Glimpses of Unfamiliar Japan.* The conditions and people that he describes are certainly not to be found along the beaten tourist track that Western civilisation has invaded with webs of steel and ways of iron. He perhaps exaggerated some of the characteristics and beliefs of the strange people amongst whom he lived, and saw romance in the ordinary course of the life around him, where romance did not exist.

Dr. Papellier, for instance, said that he once showed him a report in the *Kobe Chronicle*, describing the suicide of a demi-mondaine and her lover in a railway tunnel. The incident formed the basis of " The Red Bridal," published in *Out of the East*, which Papellier declared to be an entirely distorted account of the facts as they really occurred. It is the old story of imaginative genius and ordinary commonplace folk. In discussing the question, Hearn insisted that every artist should carry out the theory of selection. A photograph would give the unessential and the essential; an artist picks out important aspects; the portrait-painter's work, though manifestly less exact, is incomparably finer because of its spirituality; though less technically correct, it has acquired the imaginative sentiment of the mind of the artist. When depicting the Japanese he felt justified in emphasising certain excellent qualities, putting these forward and ignoring the rest; choosing the grander qualities, as portrait-painters do, and passing over the petty frailties, the mean characteristics that might impress the casual observer. Nothing is more lovely, for instance, than a Japanese village amongst the hills, when seen just after sunrise,—through the mists of a spring or autumn morning. But for the matter-of-fact observer, the enchantment passes with the vapours : in the raw clear light he can find no palace of amethyst, no sails of gold, but only flimsy sheds of wood and thatch and the unpainted queerness of wooden junks.

He attained to a certainty and precision of form in these *Kokoro* essays, that places them above any previous work. Now we can see the benefit of his concentration of mind, of his earnestness of purpose and monastic withdrawal from things of the world; no outside influences disturbed his communing with himself, and it is this communing that imparts a vague and visionary atmosphere, a ghostly thrill to every page of the volume.

Yet here was he, in the forty-fifth year of his age, a master amongst masters, arguing with solemn earnestness upon the use or mis-use of the word " shall " and " will ", begging Professor Hall Chamberlain for information and guidance.

" You will scarcely be able to believe me, I imagine, but I must confess that your letter on ' shall ' and ' will ' is a sort of revelation in one sense—it convinces me that some people, and I suppose all people of fine English culture, really feel a sharp distinction of meaning in the sight and sound of the words ' will ' and ' shall.' I confess also that I never have felt such a distinction, and cannot feel it now. I have been guided chiefly by euphony, and the sensation of ' will ' as softer and gentler than ' shall.' The word ' shall ' in the second person especially has for me a queer identification with English harshness and menace,—memories of school perhaps. I shall study the differences by your teaching and try to avoid mistakes, but I think I shall never be able to feel the distinction. The tone to me is everything—the word nothing."

The best essays in *Kokoro* were inspired, not by Kobe, but by Kyoto, one of the most beautiful cities in Japan, seat of the ancient Government and stronghold of the ancient creeds. It lies only a short distance from Kobe, and many were the days and hours that Hearn spent dreaming in the charming old-fashioned hotel and picking up impressions amidst the Buddhist shrines and gardens of the surrounding country. *Notes from a Travelling Diary*, "Pre-existence," and the charming sketch "Kimiko," written on the text "To wish to be forgotten by the beloved is a soul-task harder far than trying not to forget," all originated in Kyoto.

In a letter to his sister dated March 11th, 1895, he alludes to his book *Kokoro*. "My sweet little beautiful sister, since my book is being so long delayed I may anticipate matters by telling you something of the so-called Ancestor-Worship of which I spoke in my last letter. The subject is not in any popular work on Japan, and I think should interest you, if for no other reason than that you are yourself such a sweet little mother.

"When a person dies in Japan, a little tablet is made which stands upon a pedestal, and is about a foot high. On this narrow tablet is inscribed either the real name of the dead, or the Buddhist name given to the soul. This is the Mortuary Tablet, or as you have sometimes seen it called in books, the Ancestral Tablet.

"If children die they also have tablets in the home, but they are not prayed to,—but prayed *for*. Nightly the Mother talks to her dead child, advising, reminding, with words of caress,—just as if the little one were alive, and a tiny lamp is lighted to guide the little ghostly feet home.

"Well, I do not want to write a dry essay for you, but in view of all the unkind things said about Japanese beliefs, I thought you might like to hear this, for I think you will feel there is something beautiful in the rule of reverence to the dead.

"I hope, though I am not at all sure, that you will

receive some fairy tales by this same mail,—as I have
trusted the sending of them to a Yokohama friend.
Here there are no book-houses at all—only shops for
the sale of school texts. Should you get the stories, I
want you to read the 'Matsuyama Mirror' first. There
is a ghostly beauty that I think you will feel deeply.
After all, the simplest stories are the best.

" I wanted to say many more things; but the mail
is about to leave, and I must stop to-day.

" My little fellow is trying hard to talk and to walk.
He is now very fair and strong.

" Tell me, dear little beautiful sister, how you are
always,—give me good news of yourself,—and love me
a little bit. I will write soon again.

"LAFCADIO HEARN."

In November, 1895, Professor Basil Hall Chamberlain
visited him at Kobe, and then probably the possibility
was discussed of Hearn's re-entering the Government
service as Professor of English in the Imperial
University at Tokyo. But as late as April, 1896, he
still seemed uncertain that his engagement under
Government was assured.

Professor Toyama wrote to him, saying that his
becoming a Japanese citizen had raised a difficulty,
which he hoped might be surmounted. Hearn replied,
that he was not worried about the matter, and had
never allowed himself to consider it very seriously—
hinting, at the same time, that he would not accept a
lower salary. If Matsue only had been a little warmer
in the winter, he would rather be teaching there than
in Tokyo, in any event he hoped some day to make
a home there.

About this time comes Hearn's last letter to his sister : —

" MY DEAR LITTLE SIS,

" What you say about writing for English papers, etc., is interesting, but innocent. Men do not get opportunities to dispose of any MS. to advantage without one of two conditions. Either they must have struck a popular vein—become popular as writers; or they must have *social* influence. I am not likely to become popular, and I have no social influence. No good post would be given me,—as I am not a man of conventions, and I am highly offensive to the Orthodoxies who have always tried to starve me to death—without success, happily, as yet. I am looking, however, for an English publisher, and hope some day to get a hearing in some London print. But for the time being, it is not what I wish that I can get, but what I can. Perhaps your eyes will open wide with surprise to hear that I shall get nothing, or almost nothing for my books. The contracts deprive me of all but a nominal percentage on the 2nd thousand.

" Well, this is only a line to thank you for your sweet little letter. I have Marjory's too, and shall write her soon. Love,

" LAFCADIO.

" Excuse eyes.

" P.S.—I reopened this letter to add a few lines on second thought.

" You wrote in your last about Sir F. Ball. His expression of pleasure about my books may have been merely politeness to a pretty lady,—my sweet little sister. But it may have been genuine—probably was partly so. He could very easily say a good word for me to the Editors of the great Reviews,—the *Fortnightly*, *Nineteenth Century*, etc.—though I am not sure whether his influence would weigh with them very greatly.

"At all events what I need is 'a friend at Court,' —and need badly. Perhaps, perhaps only, my little sis could help me in that direction. I think I might ask you,—when possible,—to try. The help an earnest man wants isn't money: it is opportunity.

"We have a cozy little home in Kobe, and Kobe is pretty, but I fear I shall have to leave it by the time this reaches you. Therefore perhaps it will be better to address me: 'c/o James E. Beale, *Japan Daily Mail*, Yokohama, Japan.' I shall soon send Kajiwo's last photo with some more fairy tales written by myself for your 'bairns.'

"Love to you,

"L. H."

As Lafcadio Hearn's biographer, I almost shrink from saying that this was the last letter of the series written to his sister, Mrs. Atkinson. It somehow was so satisfactory to think of the exile having resumed intercourse with his own people, and with his native land; but with however deep a feeling of regret, the fact must be acknowledged that he suddenly put an end to the intercourse for some unaccountable reason. He not only never wrote again, but returned her envelope, empty of its contents, without a line of explanation. Mrs. Atkinson has puzzled over the enigma many times, but has never been able to fathom the reason for such an action on the part of her eccentric half-brother. There was nothing, she declares, in her letter to wound even his irritable nerves. At one time she thought it might have been in consequence of the attempts of various other members of the family to open a correspondence with him; he reiterated several times to Mrs. Atkinson the statement that " one sister was enough." I, on the other hand, think the key may with more probability be found in a passage from one of his letters written at this time, saying he had received letters from relatives in England that had made his thoughts not blue, but indigo blue. A longing had entered his heart that each year henceforward became stronger, to return to his native land, to hold communion with those of his own race; this nostalgia was rendered acute by his sister's letters, his literary work was interfered with and his nerves upset; he therefore made up his mind suddenly to stop the correspondence.

The person who behaved thus was the same erratic creature, who, having previously made an appointment, on going to keep it, rang the bell and then, seized with nervous panic—ran away; or had fits of nervous depression lasting for days because a printer had put a few commas in the wrong place or misspelt some Japanese words. Hearn possessed supreme intellectual courage, would stick to his artistic " pedestal of faith " with a determination that was heroic, but where his nerves were concerned he was an arrant coward. If letters, or arguments with friends, flurried him, or awakened uncongenial thoughts or memories, he was capable of putting the letters away unread, and breaking off a friendship that had lasted for years.

Thinking his silence might be caused by ill-health, Mrs. Atkinson wrote several times, the only answer she received was from Mr. James Beale of the *Japan Mail*:—

"JAPAN MAIL *Office*,
"*Yokohama*,
"*July 9th*, 1896.

"DEAR MADAM,

"I hasten to relieve your anxiety in regard to your brother's health. I have just returned from an expedition in the North, and previous to leaving about a month ago, was on the point of asking Hearn if he could accompany me, because it was a part of the country which he has never visited, but about that time I received a letter from him in which he stated that he was very busy (I believe he has another book on the stocks), and I did not mention the matter when I wrote. His letter was written in a very cheerful strain and indicated no illness or trouble with his eyes. In regard to the latter I have heard nothing since the spring of '95, when, through rest from study, they had recovered their normal condition. As Hearn once lived in a very isolated town on the West Coast I used to receive letters and other postal matter for him and do little commissions for him here, and I remember at times English letters passing through my hands. These were all carefully reposted to him as they came, and I should say that your letters had undoubtedly reached him.

"No apology is necessary on your part, as I am pleased to afford you whatever consolation you may find in the knowledge of the fact that your brother is alive and well. I think I may venture to say that if he has neglected his friends it is due to being busy.

"I send you his address below.

"Yours faithfully,

"JAS. ELLACOTT BEALE.

" *No.* 16, *Zashiki,*
    " *Shichi-chome, Bangai,*
        " *Naka Zamate-dori,*
           " *Kobe, Japan.*

" Mrs. M. C. Buckley-Atkinson.

" Since writing the foregoing I have learned that your brother has been appointed to a post in the University. The announcement will appear in to-morrow's *Mail.*

" This appointment will necessitate Hearn's removal to the capital, and as the vacation expires on September 15, the address at Kobe I have given will not find him. As soon as his Tokyo address reaches me I will send it to you.

                            " J. E. B."

As a set-off to this unaccountable break in his correspondence with his sister, I would like to end this chapter with a touching and pathetic letter, addressed to Mrs. Watkin at Cincinnati, and another to his " Old Dad," friends of over twenty years' standing, but unfortunately am not able to do so. Hitherto Hearn's affection had been given to Mr. Watkin; of his female belongings he had seen but little. Now apparently, Mrs. and Miss Effie Watkin ventured to address the " great man," as their husband's and father's eccentric Bohemian little friend had become. To Mrs. Watkin he touches on the mysteries of spiritualism which were scarcely mysteries in the Far East, some day he hoped to drop in on all the circle he loved and talk ghostliness. Some hints of it appeared, he said, in a little book of his, *Out of the East.* He imagined Mr. Watkin to be more like Homer than ever. He himself had become grey and wrinkled, fat, too, and disinclined for violent exercise. In other words, he was getting down the shady side of the hill, the horizon before him was already darkening, and the winds blowing out of it cold. He was not in the least concerned about the enigmas, he said, except that he wondered what his boy would do if he were to die. To his "Old Dad" he writes a whimsically affectionate letter, his old and dearest friend, he calls him. Practical, material people predicted that he was to end in gaol, or at the termination of a rope, but his "Old Dad" always predicted he would be able to do something. He was anxious for as much success as he could get for his son's sake. To have the future of others to care for certainly changed the face of life; he worked and hoped, the best and only thing to do.

CHAPTER XXII

TOKYO

" . . . No one ever lived who seemed more a creature of circumstance than I ; I drift with various forces in the line of least resistance, resolve to love nothing, and love always too much for my own peace of mind,—places, things, and persons,—and lo ! presto ! everything is swept away, and becomes a dream, like life itself. Perhaps there will be a great awakening ; and each will cease to be an Ego: become an All, and will know the divinity of man by seeing, as the veil falls, himself in each and all."

ONE of the greatest sacrifices that Hearn ever made, —and he made many for the sake of his wife and family,—was the giving up of his life in the patriarchal Japan of mystery and tradition, with its *Yashikis* and ancient shrines—to inhabit the modernised metropolis of Tokyo. The comparative permanency of the appointment and the, for Japan, high salary of twenty pounds a year, combined with the fact that lecturing was less arduous for his eyesight than journalistic work on the *Kobe Chronicle*, were the principal inducements. Still, it was one of the ironies of Fate that this shy, irritable creature, who had an inveterate horror of large cities and a longing to get back to an ancient dwelling surrounded by shady gardens, and high, moss-grown walls, should have been obliged to spend the last eight years of his life in a place pulsating with life, amidst commercial push and bustle.

His wife, on the other hand, longed to live in the capital, as Frenchwomen long to live in Paris. Tokyo,

the really beautiful Tokyo,—of the old stories and
picture-books,—still existed in her provincial mind;
she knew all the famous names, the bridges, streets,
and temples.

Hearn appears to have made an expedition from
Kobe to Tokyo at the beginning of the year 1896, to
spy out the land and decide what he would do. To
his friend Ellwood Hendrik he writes, giving him a
description of the University, such a contrast in every
way to his preconceived ideas, with its red-brick
colleges and imposing façade, a structure that would
not appear out of place in the city of Boston or Philadelphia, or London.

After his final acceptance of the appointment, and
his move to the capital, he experienced considerable
difficulty in finding a house. 21, Tomihasa-chio,
Ichigaya, situated in Ushigome, a suburb of Tokyo,
was the one he at last selected. He describes it as a
bald utilitarian house with no garden, no surprises, no
delicacies, no chromatic contrasts, a "rat-trap," compared to most Japanese houses, that were many of
them so beautiful that ordinary mortals hardly dared
to walk about in them.

In telling the story of Lafcadio Hearn's life at
Tokyo, it is well to remember that he only occupied
the house where his widow now lives at Nishi Okubo
for two years before his death. The bulk of his literary
work was done at 21, Tomihasa-chio.

When I was at Tokyo I endeavoured to find the
house; but my ignorance of the language, the "fantastic
riddle of streets," that constitute a Tokyo suburb, to
say nothing of the difficulties besetting a stranger, in
dealing with Japanese jinrikisha men, obliged me at last

to abandon the quest as hopeless. I did not even succeed
in tracing the proprietor, a *sake*-brewer, who had owned
eight hundred Japanese houses in the neighbourhood,
or in locating the old Buddhist temple of Kobduera,
where Hearn spent so much of his time, wandering in
the twilight of the great trees, dreaming out of space,
out of time.

The suburb of Ushigome is situated at some distance from the University. One hour daily to go, and
one to return by jinrikisha. But Hearn had one joy;
he was able to congratulate himself on the absence
of visitors. Any one who endeavoured to invade the
solitude of his suburban abode, must have "webbed
feet and been able to croak and spawn!"

Hearn's description of Tokyo might be placed as a
pendant to his celebrated description of New York
City. To any one who has visited the Japanese metropolis during the last five years, it is most vividly
realistic,—the size of the place, stretching over miles
of country; here the quarter of the foreign embas-
sies, looking like a well-painted American suburb;—
near by an estate with quaint Chinese gates several
centuries old; a little farther, square miles of indescribable squalor; then miles of military parade-ground
trampled into a waste of dust, and bounded by hideous
barracks; then a great park full of weird beauty, the
shadows all black as ink; then square miles of streets
of shops, which burn down once a year—then more
squalor; then rice-fields and bamboo-groves; then more
streets. Gigantic reservoirs with no water in them,
great sewer pipes without any sanitation. . . . To think
of art, or time, or eternity, he said, in the dead waste
and muddle of this mess, was difficult. But Setsu was

happy—like a bird making its nest, she was fixing up her new home, and had not yet had time to notice what ugly weather it was.

In spite of grumbling and complaints about his surroundings at Tokyo, there were redeeming features that rendered the position comparatively tolerable. Some of his old pupils from Izumo were now students at the Imperial University; they were delighted to welcome their old Professor, seeking help and sympathy as in days gone by. Knowing Hearn's irritable and sensitive disposition, the affection and respect entertained for him by his pupils at the various colleges in which he taught, and the manner in which he was given his own way and his authority upheld, even when at variance with the Directors, speaks well both for him and his employers.

His work, too, was congenial. He threw himself into the preparation and delivery of his lectures heart and soul. To take a number of Orientals, and endeavour to initiate them into the modes of thought and feeling of a people inhabiting a mental and moral atmosphere as far apart as if England and Japan were on different planets, might well seem an impossible task.

In summing up the valuable work which Hearn accomplished in his interpretation of the West to the East, these lectures, delivered while Professor of English literature at Kumamoto and Tokyo, must not be forgotten. At the end of her two delightful volumes of *Hearn's Life and Letters*, Mrs. Wetmore gives us one of them, delivered at Tokyo University, taken down at the time by T. Ochiai, one of his students. Another is given by Yone Noguchi in his book on *Hearn in Japan*. They are fair examples of the manner

in which Hearn spoke, not to their intellects, but to
their emotions. His theory was that beneath the surface the hearts of all nationalities are alike. An
emotional appeal, therefore, was more likely to be
understood than a mechanical explanation of technique
and style.

The description of the intrigue and officialism,
the perpetual panic in which the foreign professors at
the University lived, given by Hearn in a letter to
Ellwood Hendrik, is extremely funny. Earthquakes
were the order of the day. Nothing but the throne
was fixed. In the Orient, where intrigue has been
cultivated as an art for ages, the result of the adoption
of Constitutional government, by a race accustomed
to autocracy and caste, caused disloyalty and place-
hunting to spread in new form, through every condition of society, and almost into every household.
Nothing, he said, was ever stable in Japan. The whole
official world was influenced by under-currents of all
sorts, as full of changes as a sea off a coast of tides,
the side-currents penetrating everywhere, swirling
round the writing-stool of the smallest clerk, whose
pen trembled with fear for his wife's and babies' rice.
. . . "If a man made an observation about facts, there
was instantly a scattering away from that man as from
dynamite. By common consent he was isolated for
weeks. Gradually he would collect a group of his own,
but presently somebody in another party would talk
about things as they ought to be,—bang, fizz, chaos and
confusion. The man was dangerous, an intriguer, etc.,
etc. Being good or clever, or generous or popular,
or the best man for the place, counted for nothing.
. . . And I am as a flea in a wash-bowl."

The ordinary functions and ceremonials connected
with his professorship were a burden that worried and
galled a nature like Hearn's.

Every week he was obliged to decline almost nightly
invitations to dinner. He gives a sketch of the ordinary
obligations laid upon a University Professor : fourteen
lectures a week, a hundred official banquets a year, sixty
private society dinners, and thirty to fifty invitations
to charitable, musical, uncharitable and non-musical
colonial gatherings, etc., etc., etc.

No, was said to everything, softly; but if he had
accepted, how could he exist, breathe, even have time to
think, much less write books?   At first the professors
were expected to appear in a uniform of scarlet and
gold at official functions.   The professors were restive
under the idea of gold—luckily for themselves.

He gives a description of a ceremonious visit paid by
the Emperor to the University; he was expected to
put on a frock-coat, and headgear that inspired the
Mohammedan curse, " May God put a Hat on you! "
All the Professors were obliged to stand out in the sleet
and snow—no overcoats allowed, though it was horribly
cold.   They were twice actually permitted to bow down
before his Majesty.   Most of them got cold, but
nothing more for the nonce.   " Lowell discovered one
delicious thing in the Far East—' The Gate of Everlasting Ceremony.'   But the ancient ceremony was
beautiful.   Swallow-tails and plugs are not beautiful.
My little wife tells me : ' Don't talk like that : even
if a robber were listening to you upon the roof of the
house, he would get angry.'   So I am only saying to
you : ' I don't see that I should be obliged to take cold,
merely for the privilege of bowing to H.M.'   Of

course this is half-jest, half-earnest. There is a reason for things—for anything except—a plug hat. . . ."

As nearly as we can make out his friend Nishida Sentaro died during the course of this winter. He was an irreparable loss to Hearn, representing as he did, all that constituted his most delightful memories of Japan. In his last book, *Japan, an Interpretation*, he alludes to him as the best and dearest friend he had in the country, who had told him a little while before his death : " When in four or five years further residence you find that you cannot understand the Japanese at all, then you may boast of beginning to know something about them."

With none of the Professors at the University at Tokyo does Hearn ever seem to have formed ties of intimacy. Curiously enough, the Professor of French literature, a Jesuit priest, was to him the most sympathetic. Hearn in some things was a Conservative, in others a Radical. During the Boer War he took up the cause of the Dutch against the English, only because he inaccurately imagined the Boers to have been the original owners of Dutch South Africa. Protestant missionaries he detested, looking upon them as iconoclasts, destroyers of the beautiful ancient art, which had been brought to Japan by Buddhism. The Jesuits, on the other hand, favoured the preservation of ancient feudalism and ecclesiasticism. Hearn's former prejudices, therefore, on the subject of Roman Catholicism were considerably mitigated during his residence in Japan. He describes his landlord, the old *sake*-brewer, coming to definitely arrange the terms of the lease of the house. When he caught sight of Kazuo he said, " You

are too pretty,—you ought to have been a girl. . . .
That set me thinking," Hearn adds, "if Kazuo feels
like his father about pretty girls,—what shall I do with
him? Marry him at seventeen or nineteen? Or send
him to grim and ferocious Puritans that he may be
taught the Way of the Lord? I am now beginning
to think that really much of ecclesiastical education (bad
and cruel as I used to imagine it) is founded upon the
best experience of man under civilisation; and I understand lots of things which I used to think superstitious
bosh, and now think solid wisdom."

He and the Jesuit Professor of French got into a religious discussion one day, and Hearn found him charming. Of course he looked upon Hearn as a heretic, and
considered all philosophy of the nineteenth century false,
—everything, indeed, accomplished by free thought and
Protestantism, folly, leading to ruin. But he and
Hearn had sympathies in common, contempt of conventional religion, scorn of missionaries, and recognition
of the naturally religious character of the Japanese.

After Nishida Sentaro's death, the only Japanese
friendship that Hearn retained was that for Amenomori
Nobushige, to whom *Kokoro* was dedicated:—

> "TO MY FRIEND
> AMENOMORI NOBUSHIGE
> POET, SCHOLAR AND PATRIOT."

We first find Amenomori's name mentioned in
Hearn's letters the year he left Kumamoto for Kobe.
When we were at Tokyo we were told that Amenomori's widow, who lives there, possesses a voluminous
correspondence that passed between her husband and

Hearn, principally on the subject of Buddhism. Some day I imagine it will be published. To Amenomori as to others, Hearn poured out his despair at the uncongenial surroundings of Tokyo; he wanted new experiences, and Tokyo was not the place for them. " Perhaps the power to feel a thrill dies with the approach of a man's fiftieth year—perhaps the only land to find the new sensation is in the Past,—floats blue peaked under some beautiful dead sun in the ' tropic clime of youth.' Must I die and be born again, to feel the charm of the Far East—or will Amenomori Nobushige discover for me some unfamiliar blossom growing beside the fountain of Immortality? Alas! I don't know. . . ."

Amenomori seems to have had a real affection for the eccentric little genius, and to have philosophically accepted his fits of temper and apparently unaccountable vagaries. In the company of all Japanese, however, even the most highly cultivated, Hearn declared that all Occidentals felt unhappy after an hour's communion. When the first charm of formality is over, the Japanese suddenly drifts away into his own world, as far from this one as the star Rephan.

Mitchell McDonald, Paymaster of the United States Navy, stationed at Yokohama, was apparently the only person for whom Hearn cherished a warm human sentiment at this time beyond his immediate family circle.

In Miss Bisland's account of her *Flying Trip Around the World* she mentions McDonald of Yokohama—in brown boots and corduroys—as escorting her to various places of interest during her short stay in Japan. It was apparently through her intervention that the introduction to Lafcadio Hearn was effected, and must have

taken place almost immediately on Hearn's arrival in
Japan, for he mentions McDonald in one of his first
letters to Ellwood Hendrik, and *Glimpses of Unfamiliar Japan* was dedicated to him, in conjunction with
Chamberlain.

" After all I am rather a lucky fellow," he writes to
McDonald, " a most peculiarly lucky fellow, principally
owing to the note written by a certain sweet young
lady, whose portrait now looks down on me from the
ceiling of No. 21, Tomihasa-chio."

Writing from Tokyo to Mrs. Wetmore, in January,
1900, he tells her that above the table was a portrait of
a young American officer in uniform,—a very dear
picture. Many a time, Hearn said, they had sat up till
midnight, talking about things.

The conversation at these dinners, eaten overlooking
the stretch of Yokohama Harbour, with the sound of
the waves lapping on the harbour wall beneath, and the
ships and boats passing to and fro beyond, never seems
to have been about literary matters, which perhaps
accounts for the friendship between the two lasting so
long. " Like Antæus I feel always so much more of
a man, after a little contact with your reality, not so
much of a *literary* man however."

The salt spray that Hearn loved so well seemed to
cling to McDonald, the breeziness of a sailor's yarning
ran through their after-dinner talks, the adventures of
naval life at sea, and at the ports where McDonald
had touched during his service. He was always urging
McDonald to give him material for stories, studies of
the life of the " Open Ports,"—only real facts,—not
names or dates—real facts of beauty, or pathos, or
tragedy. He felt that all the life of the open ports is

not commonplace; there were heroisms and romances in it; and there was really nothing in this world as wonderful as life itself. All real life was a marvel, but in Japan a marvel that was hidden as much as possible—"especially hidden from dangerous chatterers like Lafcadio Hearn."

If he could get together a book of short stories—six would be enough—he would make a dedication of it to M. McD. as prettily as he could.

Under the soothing influence of a good cigar, Hearn would even take his friend into his confidence about many incidents in his own past life—that past life which generally was jealously guarded from the outside world. He tells McDonald the pleasure it gives him, his saying that he resembles his father, but "I have more smallness in me than you can suspect. How could it be otherwise! If a man lives like a rat for twenty or twenty-five years he must have acquired something of the disposition peculiar to house rodents, mustn't he?"

The communion between these two was more like that between some popular, athletic, sixth-form boy at Eton, whose softer side had been touched by the forlornness of a shy, sickly, bullied Minor, than that between two middle-aged men, one representing the United States in an official capacity, the other one of the most famous writers of the day. The first letter relates to a visit that McDonald apparently paid to Ushigome, an audacious proceeding that few ventured upon.

Hearn expressed his appreciation of McDonald's good nature in coming to his miserable little shanty, over a muddy chaos of street,—the charming way in which he accepted the horrid attempt at entertainment, and his interest and sympathy in Hearn's affairs.

Iñ the house at Nishi Okubo mementoes are still preserved of McDonald's visits. A rocking-chair, —rare piece of furniture in a Japanese establishment,—a spirit lamp, and an American cigar-ash holder.

McDonald apparently saw, as Dr. Papellier had seen at Kobe, that Hearn was killing himself by his ascetic Japanese mode of life. Raw fish and lotus roots were not food suited for the heavy brain work Hearn was doing, besides his professional duties at the University. McDonald, therefore, insisted on being allowed to send him wine and delicacies of all sorts.

" With reference to the ' best,' " Hearn writes, " you are a dreadful man! How could you think that I have got even half way to the bottom? I have only drunk three bottles yet, but that is a shameful ' only.' "

They seemed to have exchanged books and discussed things, and laughed and made jokes school-boy fashion. Hearn talks of their sprees, their dinners, their tiffins, " irresistibles," and alludes to " blue ghost " and " blue soul "—names given to some potation partaken of at the club or at the hotel. It shows McDonald's powers of persuasion that Hearn was tempted out of his shell at Ushigome to pass two or three days at Yokohama. Sunlit hours were these in the exile's life. Three days passed with his friend at Yokohama were, Hearn declares, the most pleasurable in a pilgrimage of forty-seven years.

" What a glorious day we did have! " he says again. " Wonder if I shall ever be able to make a thumb-nail

literary study thereof,—with philosophical reflections.
The Naval Officer, the Buddhist Philosopher (Amenomori), and the wandering Evolutionist. The impression is altogether too sunny and happy and queer, to
be for ever lost to the world. I must think it up some
day. . . ." There is something pathetic in these
healthy-minded, healthy-bodied men petting and
making much of the little genius, half in pity, half in
admiration, recognising in an indefinite way that some
divine attribute was his.

McDonald, in his enthusiastic sailor fashion, used
to express his belief in Hearn's genius, telling him that
he was a greater writer than Loti. Being a practical
person, he was apparently continually endeavouring to
try and induce his little friend to take a monetary view
of his intellectual capacities. Hearn tells him that he
understands why he wished him to write fiction;—he
wanted him to make some profit out of his pen, and he
knew that "fiction" was about the only stuff that
really paid. Then he sets forth the reasons why men
like himself didn't write more fiction. First of all, he
had little knowledge of life, and by that very want of
knowledge was debarred from mixing with the life
which alone can furnish the material. They can *divine*,
but must have some chances to do that, for Society
everywhere suspected them. Men like Kipling belonged to the great Life Struggle, and the world
believed them and worshipped them; "but Dreamers
that talk about pre-existence, and who think differently
from common-sense folk, are quite outside of social
existence."

Then his old dream of being able to travel was again
adverted to, or even an independence that would liberate

him from slavery to officialdom,—but he had too many little butterfly lives to love and take care of. His dream of even getting to Europe for a time to put his boy to college there must remain merely a possibility.

The only interruption to the harmony of the communion between the two friends was Hearn's dislike to meeting the inquisitive Occidental tourist; this dislike attained at last the proportions of an obsession, and the more he withdrew and shut himself up, the more did legendary tales circle round him, and the more determined were outsiders to get behind the veil that he interposed between himself and them.

He went in and out the back way so as to avoid the risk of being seen from afar off. Thursday last, he tells McDonald, three enemies dug at his hole, but he zigzagged away from them.

He adverts, too, to a woman, who had evidently never seen or known him, who spelt his name Lefcardio, and pestered him with letters. " Wish you would point out to her somebody who looks small and queer, and tell her ' that is Mr. Hearn, he is waiting to see you.' "

The curiosity animating these people, he declared, was simply the kind of curiosity that impelled them to look at strange animals—six-legged calves, for instance. His friends, he declared, were as dangerous, if not more dangerous, than his enemies, for these latter, with infinite subtlety, kept him out of places where he hated to go, and told stories of him to people to whom it would be vanity and vexation to meet, and their unconscious aid helped him so that he almost loved them.

But his friends!—they were the real destroyers, they

praised his work, believed in it, and yet, not knowing
what it cost, would break the wings and scatter the
feather-dust, even as a child caressing a butterfly. Converse and sympathy might be precious things to others,
but to him they were deadly, for they broke up habits
of industry, and caused the sin of disobedience to the
Holy Ghost,—"against whom sin shall not be forgiven,
—either in this life, or in the life to come."

Sometimes he wished, he said, that he were lost upon
the mountains, or cast away upon a rock, rather than
in the terrible city of Tokyo. "Yet here I am,
smoking a divine cigar—out of my friend's gift-box—
and brutally telling him that he is killing my literary
soul, or souls. Am I right or wrong? I feel like
kicking myself. And yet I feel that I ought never
again in this world to visit the Grand Hotel." In
spite of these protestations, however, McDonald would
lure him to come down again and again to Yokohama,
and again and again make him smoke good cigars, drink
good wine, and eat nourishing food. Once, when the
little man had, with characteristic carelessness, forgotten to bring a great-coat, McDonald wrapped him
up in his own to send him home,—an incident which
Hearn declared he would remember for its warmth
of friendship until he died. Another time, when he
complained of toothache, McDonald got the navy
doctor to remove, as he thought, the primary cause.
Hearn gives a humorous account of this incident.
He found that when he returned home the wrong one
had been pulled. Its character, he said, had been
modest and shrinking, the other one, on the contrary,
had been Mount Vesuvius, the last great Javanese
earthquake, the tidal wave of '96, and the seventh

chamber of the Inferno, all in mathematical combination.

It was magnanimous of Hearn to dedicate *Gleanings in Buddha Fields* to the doctor after this incident. McDonald and his genial surroundings seemed to have thoroughly understood how to manage the little man. When he became irritable and unreasonable they apparently took not the least notice, and good-naturedly wheedled him back into a good temper again—treated him, in fact, as Mr. Watkin had treated him during his attacks of temper at Cincinnati.

So, without any real break, this friendship, as well as Mrs. Wetmore's, lasted until the end. Since Hearn's death, Captain McDonald has loyally stood by his widow and children, taking upon himself the self-imposed duties of executor, collecting together scattered MS., and arranging the sale of the copyright of his books in the United States.

CHAPTER XXIII

USHIGOME

" Every one has an inner life of his own,—which no other eye can see, and the great secrets of which are never revealed, although occasionally, when we create something beautiful, we betray a faint glimpse of it—sudden and brief, as of a door opening and shutting in the night. . . . Are we not all Dopplegangers ?—and is not the invisible the only life we really enjoy ? "

In spite of his railings against Tokyo, Hearn was probably happier at Ushigome and Nishi Okubo than he had ever been during his other sojournings in Japan, excepting always the enchanted year at Matsue.

To paraphrase George Borrow, there was day and night, both sweet things, sun, moon, and stars, all sweet things, likewise there was the wind that rustled through the bamboo-grove.

Hearn had all the Oriental's scorn of comfort : so long as he could indulge in the luxury of dreaming and writing, his pipe and *Webster's Dictionary* within reach, he asked for little else.

This master of impressionist prose confessed—in his diffident and humble manner where his art was concerned—that now for the first time he began to write English with ease. Roget's *Thesaurus*, and Skeat's *Etymological Dictionary* were definitely discarded. He recognised also that he had caught the ear of the public, not only in America but in England.

The manner of Hearn's life at this time entirely contradicts his pessimistic statements, that "the Holy Ghost had deserted him . . . ," that "he had lost his pen of fire . . . ," and that he was "like a caged cicada that could not sing."

No author who writes and publishes can ever really, in his heart of hearts, be a pessimist. There is no conviction so optimistic as thinking that your thoughts and opinions are worth setting forth for the benefit of the public.

Though he had not much sympathy with Japanese and foreign professors, and clashed now and then with the officials at the Imperial University, at home he enjoyed the most complete tranquillity; all is noiseless in a Japanese house, not a footfall audible on the soft matting, everything was favourable to absorption in his work.

He was an early riser, always at his desk by six o'clock, pipe in one hand and pen in the other. " Even when in bed with a cold, or not feeling well," his wife tells us, " it was always, write, write, write." Sometimes she found him in the library, jumping for joy because he had a new idea. She would ask him, " did you finish your last story? " Sometimes he would answer, " That story has to wait for some time. Perhaps a month,—perhaps a year,—perhaps five years! " He kept one story in his drawer for seven long years before it was finished. I believe that many stories of his were left unfinished in his drawer, or at least, in the drawer of his mind when he passed away.

Though perturbed every now and then by the little man's fits of excitement and temper—phases of mind unknown to her own countrymen—and though she shrinkingly recognised the neighbours' suspicion that he was slightly crazy, Setsu Koizumi nourished a deep affection for her foreign husband, and Hearn, on the other hand, though intellectually an abyss might yawn between them, had the greatest respect for his wife's common-sense.

"I have learnt to be guided by K.'s mamma," he says, writing eight years after his marriage,—" indeed, no Occidental-born could manage a purely Japanese household, or direct Japanese according to his own light, things are so opposite, so eccentric, so provoking at times,—so impossible to understand. . . . By learning to abstain from meddling, I have been able to keep my servants from the beginning, and have learned to prize some of them at their weight in gold."

Quaint and pathetic sidelights are cast upon this strange Anglo-Japanese union by Mrs. Hearn's recently-published *Reminiscences* and by various letters of his to friends. "I was reproached very justly on reaching home last night," Lafcadio tells Mitchell McDonald. "'But you did not bring your American friend's picture? . . . Forgot to put it into the valise? . . . Oh! but you *are* queer—always, always dreaming! And don't you feel just a little bit ashamed?'"

On another occasion, the little woman, seeing by the expression of his face that he was in a bad temper when writing to his publisher, got possession of the letter and "posted it in a drawer," asking him next day whether he would not like to withhold some of the correspondence. He acted on the hint thus wisely given, and the letter "was never sent."

She describes him blowing for fun into a conch shell he had bought one day at Enoshima, delighting, like a mischievous boy, in the billowy sound that filled the room; or holding it to his ear to " listen to the murmur of the august abodes from whence it came." Happy in his garden and simple things, " the poet's home is to him the whole world," as the Japanese poem says, we see him talking, laughing, and singing at meals. " He had two kinds of laughter," his wife says, " one being a womanish sort of laughter, soft and deep; the other joyous and open-hearted, a catching sort of laughter, as if all trouble were forgotten, and when he laughed the whole household laughed too."

His multiplying family was growing up healthy and intelligent. He was kept in touch with youth and vigorous life, through intercourse with them and his pupils at the University. The account given us of his merrymaking with his children puts a very different aspect on Hearn's nature and outlook on life. However crabbed and reserved his attitude towards the outside world might be, at home with his children he was the cheeriest of comrades, expansive and affectionate. Sometimes he would play " onigokko," or devil-catching play (hide-and-seek), with them in the garden. " Though no adept in the Japanese language, he succeeded in learning the words of several children's songs, the Tokyo Sunset Song, for instance—

> " Yu-yake !
> Ko-yake !
> Ashita wa tenki ni nare."
> " Evening-burning !
> Little-burning !
> Weather, be fair to-morrow ! "

or the Song of " Urashima Taro."

He was much given to drawing, making pen-and-ink sketches illustrating quotations from English poetry for his eldest boy, Kazuo. Some of these which have recently been published are quite suggestively charming, distinguished by that quaint sadness which runs through all his work. In one, illustrative of Kingsley's *Three Fishers*, though the lighthouse has a slight slant to leeward, the sea and clouds give an effect of storm and impending disaster which is wonderful.

He was too near-sighted to be allowed to walk alone in the bustling, crowded streets of Tokyo; he one day, indeed, sprained his ankle severely, stumbling over a heap of stones and earth that he did not see. But in Kazuo's and his wife's company, he explored every corner of the district where he lived. He very seldom spoke, she tells us, as he walked with bent head, and they followed silently so as not to disturb his meditations. There was not a temple unknown to him in Zoshigaya, Ochiai, and the neighbouring quarters. He always carried a little note-book, and frequently brought it out to make notes of what he saw as they passed along.

An ancient garden belonging to a temple near his house was a favourite resort, until one day he found three of the cedar trees cut down; this piece of vandalism, for the sake of selling the timber, made him so miserable, that he refused any longer to enter the precincts, and for some time contented himself with a stroll round the lake in the University grounds. One of his students describes Hearn's slightly stooping form, surmounted by a soft broad-brimmed hat, pacing slowly and contemplatively along the lake, or sitting upon a stone on the shore, smoking his Japanese pipe.

Though Hearn hated the ceremonious functions connected with his professional position, he was by no means averse during the first half of his stay at Tokyo, —whilst his health indeed still permitted the indulgences,—to a good dinner and cigar, in congenial company at the Club. He was often compelled, at dinner, we were told, to ask some one at his elbow what was in his plate; sometimes a friend would make jestingly misleading replies, to which he would cheerfully respond: " Very well, if you can eat it, so can I."

Professor Foxwell describes dining and then loafing and strolling and smoking with him. " It was not so much the dinner he enjoyed, as the twilight afterwards in Ueno Park, the soft night air romantic with fireflies hovering amongst the luxurious foliage. Our intercourse, though constant and not to be forgotten, was nothing to describe. I think we never argued or discussed the burning questions that divided the foreign community in Japan. We simply ate and drank and smoked, and in fact behaved as ' slackers.' We delighted in the air, the sunshine, the babies, the flowers, nothing but trifles, things too absurd to recall."

Various cultured people in foreign circles in Tokyo were anxious enough to initiate friendly relations with the literary man whose Japanese books were beginning to make such a stir in the world, but Hearn kept them rigidly at a distance; indeed, as time went on he became more and more averse to mixing with his countrymen and countrywomen at Tokyo. He imagined that they were all inimical to him, and that he was the victim of gross injustice, and organised conspiracy. These prejudiced ideas were really the outcome of a peculiarly sensitive brain, lacking normal mental balance. Nothing but " Old Japan " was admitted inside his garden fence.

A motley company! Well-cleaners, pipe-stem makers, ballad-singers, an old fortune-teller who visited Hearn every season.

We can see him seated beside Hearn in his study, telling his fortune, which he did four times, until, as Hearn tells us, his predictions were fulfilled in such-wise that he became afraid of them. A set of ebony blocks, which could be so arranged so as to form any of the Chinese hexagrams, were his stock-in-trade, and he always began his divination with an earnest prayer to the gods. In the winter of 1903 he was found frozen in the snow on the Izumo hills. "Even the fortune-teller knows not his own fate," is a Japanese saying quoted by Hearn in connection with the incident.

But it was at Yaidzu, a small fishing village on the eastern coast, where he generally spent his summer vacation with his two boys, for sea-bathing, that he was in his element.

The Yaidzu people had the deepest affection and respect for him, and during the summer vacation he liked to become one of them, dressing as they did, and living their simple patriarchal life. Indeed, he preferred the friendship of country barbers, priests and fishermen far more than that of college professors.

As there was no inn at Yaidzu, Hearn lodged at the house of Otokichi, who, as well as being a fisherman, kept a fish-shop, and cooked every description of fish in a wonderful variety of ways. Aided by Hearn's description, we can see Otokichi's shop, its rows of shelves supporting boxes of dried fish, packages of edible seaweed, bundles of straw sandals, gourds for holding *sake*, and bottles of lemonade, while surmounting all

was the kamidana,—the shelf of the gods,—with its
Daruma, or household divinity.

Many and fanciful were his dreams as he loafed and
lay on the beach at Yaidzu, sometimes thinking of the
old belief, that held some dim relation between the dead
and the human essence fleeting in the gale,—floating in
the mists,—shuddering in the leaf,—flickering in the
light of waters,—or tossed on the desolate coast in a
thunder of surf, to whiten and writhe in the clatter of
shingle. . . . At others, as when a boy at school, lying
looking at the clouds passing across the sky, and imagining himself a part of the nature that was living and
palpitating round him.

It is impossible in the space at my command to ex-
amine Hearn's work at Tokyo in detail; it consists of
nine books. The first one published after his appointment as Professor of English at the University was
*Gleanings in Buddha Fields: Studies of Hand and Soul
in the Far East.* Though it saw the light at Tokyo in
1897, the greater part of it is said to have been written
at Kobe. Henceforth all his Japanese literary work
was but *Gleanings*, gathered in the fields he had
ploughed and sown at Matsue, Kobe, Kumamoto and
Kyoto. Every grain of impression, of reminiscence,
scientific and emotional, was dropped into the literary
mill.

Amongst the essays comprising the volume entitled
Gleanings in Buddha Fields, there is nothing particularly arresting. His chapter on "Nirvana" is hackneyed and unsubstantial, ending with the vaporous
statement that "the only reality is One; all that we
have taken for substance is only shadow; the physical
is the unreal: *and the outer-man is the ghost.*"

In dealing with Hearn's genius we have to accept frequent contradictions and changes of statement. His deductions need classifying and substantiating, he often generalises from insufficient premises, and over-emphasises the impression of the moment at the expense of accuracy.

In his article on the "Eternal Feminine," he endeavours to prove that the Japanese man is incapable of love, as we understand it in the West. Having taken up an idea, he uses all his skill in the manipulation of words to support his view, even though in his inner consciousness he fostered a conviction that it was not exactly a correct one. The fact of Occidental fiction being revolting to the Japanese moral sense, is far-fetched. Many people amongst ourselves are of opinion that in much of our fictional work the sexual question is given a great deal too much prominence; what wonder, therefore, that the male Japanese, being bound by social convention to keep all feeling under restraint, from the first moment he can formulate a thought, should look upon it as indecorous, and, above all, inartistic, to express his sentiments unreservedly on the subject of the deeper emotions, but that does not for a moment prove that he was incapable of feeling them.

All Japanese art, poetry as well as painting, is impressionist and suggestive instead of detailed. "Ittakkiri" (entirely vanished, in the sense of "all told"), is a term applied contemptuously to the poet who, instead of an indication puts the emotion itself into words.

The art of writing poetry is universal in Japan; verses, seldom consisting of more than two lines, are to be found upon shop-signs, panels, screens and fans. They are printed upon towels, draperies, curtains and women's crêpe silk underwear, they are written by every one and for all occasions. Is a woman sad and lonely at home, she writes poems. Is a man unoccupied for an hour, he employs himself putting his thoughts into poetry. Hearn was continually on the quest of these simple poems: to Otani he writes, "Please this month collect for me, if you can, some songs of the sound of the sea and the sound of the wind." The translations given by him in his essay entitled "Out of the Street," contradict his statement that the Japanese are incapable of deep feeling, and prove that Love is as important an element in the Island Empire as with us, though the expression is less outspoken. Some of them are charming.

> "To Heaven with all my soul I prayed to prevent your going ;
> Already, to keep you with me, answers the blessed rain.
>
> Things never changed since the Time of the Gods :
> The flowing of water, the Way of Love."

His next book was *Exotics and Retrospectives;* he thought of dedicating this volume to Mrs. Wetmore (Elizabeth Bisland), but in a letter to Ellwood Hendrik he expresses a doubt as to the advisability of doing so, as some of the essays might be rather of a startling character. Ultimately he dedicated it to H. H. Hall, late U. S. Navy, "In Constant Friendship."

The prefatory note shows how permeated his mode of thought was at this time with Buddhistical theories. . . . "To any really scientific imagination, the curious analogy existing between certain teachings of Eastern faith,—particularly the Buddhist doctrine that all sense-life is Karma, and all substance only the phenomenal result of acts and thoughts,—might have suggested something much more significant than my cluster of ' Retrospectives.' These are offered merely as intimations of a truth incomparably less difficult to recognise than to define."

The first essay, describing his ascent of Fuji-no-yama, is as beautiful a piece of impressionist prose as Hearn ever wrote—the immense poetry of the moment as he stood on the summit and looked at the view for a hundred leagues, and the pilgrims poised upon the highest crag, with faces turned eastward, clapping their hands as a salutation to the mighty day.

The colossal vision had already become a memory ineffaceable,—a memory of which no luminous detail could fade, till the light from the myriad millions of eyes that had looked for untold ages from the summit supreme of Fuji to the rising of the sun, had been quenched, even to the hour when thought itself must fade.

Ghostly Japan, written in 1899, was dedicated

TO

MRS. ALICE VON BEHRENS

FOR AULD LANG SYNE.

We cannot trace any mention of this lady elsewhere, but conclude she was one of his New York acquaintances

" Think not that dreams appear to the dreamer only at night: the dream of this world of pain appears to

us even by day," is the translation of the Japanese poem
on the first page.

To Mitchell McDonald he wrote, saying that he did
not quite know what to do with regard to *Ghostly
Japan*. Then later he says, he has been and gone and
done it. In fifteen minutes he had the whole thing perfectly packed and labelled and addressed in various
languages, dedicated to Mrs. Behrens, but entrusted
largely to the gods. To save himself further trouble
of mind, he told the publishers just to do whatever they
pleased about terms—and not to worry him concerning them. Then he felt like a man liberated from prison
—smelling the perfumed air of a perfect spring day.

In 1900 came *Shadowings*, dedicated to Mitchell
McDonald. Some of the fantasies at the end are full
of his peculiar ghostly ideas. A statement of his belief
in previous existence occurs again and again: "The
splendour of the eyes that we worship belongs to
them only as brightness to the morning star. It is a
reflex from beyond the shadow of the Now,—a ghost
light of vanished suns. Unknowingly within that
maiden-face we meet the gaze of eyes more countless
than the hosts of Heaven,—eyes otherwhere passed
into darkness and dust. . . . Thus and only thus do
truth and delusion mingle in the magic of eyes—the
spectral past suffusing with charm ineffable the apparition of the present; and the sudden splendour in the soul
of the seer is but a flash, one soundless sheet lightning
of the infinite memory."

Shadowings was succeeded by a *Japanese Miscellany*,
dedicated to Mrs. Elizabeth Bisland Wetmore. Here
there is no reference to "Auld Lang Syne," nor is
there a touch of sentiment from beginning to end.

The book is perhaps more intensely Japanese and fanciful than any yet written, and to Occidental readers the least interesting. One of the sketches, inspired by his sojournings in the village of Yaidzu, is a pæan, as it were, sung to the sea. Another on *Dragon-Flies* is delightful because of its impressionist translations of Japanese poems.

> " Lonesomely clings the dragon-fly to the under side of the leaf. . . . Ah ! the autumn rains ! "

And a verse written by a mother, who, seeing children chasing butterflies, thinks of her little one who is dead : —

> " Catching dragon-flies ! . . . I wonder where he has gone to-day."

CHAPTER XXIV

NISHI OKUBO

" From the foot of the mountain, many are the paths ascending in
shadow ; but from the cloudless summit all who climb behold the
self-same Moon."—*Buddhist poem translated by* LAFCADIO HEARN.

IT was on the 19th March, 1902, that the Koizumi
family removed from 21, Tomihasa-chio, Ichigaya,
Ushigome, to 266, Nishi Okubo.

Hearn had purchased the house out of his savings
and settled it on his wife according to English law, as
no woman can hold property in Japan. It is there that
Mrs. Hearn now lives, sub-letting half of it to Captain
Fujisaki,—one of Hearn's Matsue students, who has
remained an intimate friend of his widow and children.
Nishi Okubo is known as the Gardeners' Quarter
where the celebrated Tokyo azaleas are grown, and
where a show of azaleas is held once a year.

After he took possession, Hearn added on the library,
or Buddha-room, as it is now called,—and a guest-room,
which was assigned to Mrs. Koizumi for her occupation.

Had Hearn at this time managed his affairs with
the least businesslike acumen, he might have enjoyed
the comfortable competency which his widow now
receives from the royalties and sales of his books, which
have most of them been translated into German, Swedish
and French, and achieved a considerable circulation in
England.

There is little doubt he was lamentably wanting in

the most rudimentary knowledge of practical business affairs, and was entirely to blame for the difficulties in which he so repeatedly found himself. " I have given up thinking about the business side of literature, and am quite content to obtain the privilege of having my books produced according to my notions of things," he writes to Mitchell McDonald.

On the day of his arrival in the new house, while, —assisted by his wife,—he was arranging his books in the shelves in the library, he suddenly heard an " uguisu " (nightingale) singing in the bamboo-grove outside. He stopped to listen, then " How delightful! " he said to his wife, " Oh! how I hope I will live here for years until I have made enough for you and the children."

During the last two years of his life he suffered a great deal from his eyes; each month more powerful glasses had to be used; and he was obliged to stand writing at a high desk, his face almost touching the paper. Yet what a beautiful handwriting it is! almost as plain as copper-plate. Composition was easy for him, but the mechanical labour of setting down his thoughts became very irksome. Many were the kind offers of help that he received; Mr. Mason, for instance, proposed to do any necessary copying he wanted, but he was too irritable to do work in conjunction with any one, and was never able to dictate successfully.

The absence of intellectual communion with his own compatriots would have been a cruel test for most writers. His manuscript had to float round half a world before it met with sympathetic understanding. Surrounded by complete spiritual solitude, a voluntary outlaw from the practical thought of his time, the current of emotional and practical life which bore most of his contemporaries to affluence and popularity flowed entirely outside his mental boundary. Yet, is it not most probable that this aloofness and seclusion from the world invested his Tokyo work with its unique and original quality? "The isolation ought," he writes, "unless you are physically tired by the day's work,— to prove of value. All the best work is done this way by tiny, tireless and regular additions, preserving in memory what you think and see. In a year you will be astounded to find them self-arranging, kaleidoscopically, into something symmetrical,—and trying to live. Then pray God, and breathe into their nostrils,—and be astonished and pleased."

"You will remember," he says elsewhere, "my philosophical theory that no two living beings have the same voice . . . and it is the uniqueness of each that has its value. . . . I simply now try to do the best I can, without reference to nationalities or schools."

Strangeness, we are told by the romantic school, is essential for the highest beauty; it was a theory Hearn always maintained, but his strangeness now became spiritualised, instead of the oddness of a Creole song, or a negro "roustabout," it was the oddness of the ethics and religious superstitions of the genius of a remarkable people.

At this time Hearn had a recurrence of the emotional trances he had suffered from at various times in his life, a state of mental anæmia common to brain-workers of no great physical stamina. "He saw things," as his wife says, "that were not, and heard things that were not." Absence of mind was a peculiarity inherited with his Hearn inheritance. Sometimes, when called to

supper, he would declare he had had it already, and
continue writing instead of joining his family, or if he
did join them, he would make all sorts of blunders,
putting salt instead of sugar in his coffee, and eating
sugar with his fish. When his brain thus went "argo-
nauting," as Ruskin expresses it, practical consistency
was forgotten, even the sense of personal identity.
He beheld ghostly apparitions in the surrounding air,
he held communion with a multitude of supernatural
visions, a procession stretching back out of life into
the night of forgotten centuries. We can see him
seated in his library, weaving his dreams while all the
household slept, so absorbed in his work as to have forgotten bedtime, the stillness only broken by the rapping
of his little pipe against the *hibachi*, the intermittent
scratch of his pen, and the rustle of the leaves as he
threw them down, while the bronze figure of Buddha
on his lotus-stand, stood behind with uplifted hand and
enigmatic smile.

Richard Jefferies was wont to say that all his best
work was done from memory. The "Pageant of
Summer" with its vivid descriptions and realised visions
of country meadows and hedgerows was written in his
curtained sick-room at the seaside village of Goring.
So Hearn in his house at Tokyo, his outlook bounded
by the little plot of garden beneath his study window,
recalled all he had seen and felt during his wanderings
amongst the hills and by the seashore in distant
parts of Japan. The laughter of streams and whisper
of leaves, the azure of sky and sea; the falling of
the blossoms of the cherry-trees, the lilac spread of
the *myiakobana*, the blazing yellow of the *natalé*, the
flooded levels of the lotus-fields, and the pure and

tender green of the growing rice. Again he watched the flashing dragon-flies, the long grey sand-crickets, the shrilling *semi*, and the little red crabs astir under the roots of the pines; again he heard the croaking of the frogs, that universal song of the land in Japan, the melody of the *uguisu* and the moan of the surf on the beach at Yaidzu.

Hearn is principally known in England by his letters and essays on the social and political development of Japan. Cultured people who have Charles Lamb, De Quincey, or Robert Louis Stevenson at their fingers' ends will open eyes of wonder if you venture to suggest that Hearn's incidental sketches represent some of the best work of the kind done by any of our English essayists.

Fresh, spontaneous and unconventional, the whole of his genius seems suddenly poured forth in an impulse of sadness, pity or humour. After some grim Japanese legend, we are greeted by one of these dainty fancies when his acute sensibility, touched and awakened, concentrated itself on the trifle of a moment. With the mastery of words that he had attained after years of hard work, he was enabled to catch the evanescent inspiration, and set it down, preaching from the significance of small things an infinite philosophy. A dew-drop hanging to the lattice of his window; the sighing of the wind in the bamboo-grove, the moon rising above his garden fence, were all full of soul secrets, soul life.

In a sketch entitled " Moon Desire," for instance, he begins playfully, almost trivially, and ends with a fine burst of eloquence on the subject of human desire and attainment.

" He was two years old when—as ordained in the law of perpetual recurrence—he asked me for the Moon.

" Unwisely I protested :—

" ' The Moon I cannot give you because it is too high up. I cannot reach it.'

" He answered :—

" ' By taking a very long bamboo, you probably could reach it, and knock it down.'

". . . Whereat I found myself constrained to make some approximately truthful statements concerning the nature and position of the moon.

" This set me thinking. I thought about the strange fascination that brightness exerts upon living creatures in general,—upon insects and fishes and birds and mammals,—and tried to account for it by some inherited memory of brightness as related to food, to water, and to freedom. . . .

" Have we any right to laugh at the child's wish for the Moon? No wish could be more natural; and as for its incongruity,—do not we, children of a larger growth, mostly nourish wishes quite as innocent,—longings that if realised could only work us woe,—such as desire for the continuance after death of that very sense-life, or individuality, which once deluded us all into wanting to play with the Moon, and often subsequently deluded us in far less pleasant ways?

" No, foolish as may seem to merely empirical reasoning, the wish of the child for the Moon, I have an idea that the highest wisdom commands us to wish for very much more than the Moon,—even for more than the Sun and the Morning-Star, and all the Host of Heaven."

He suffered much from depression of spirits towards

the end, his wife tells us, and a Celtic tendency to vague
and wistful dreaminess became more strongly developed,
things full of unexplained meanings, supernatural, outside the experience of all ages, filled his mind. He
had been wont to talk of himself as "A Voice" in
past New York days. Now the sense of disembodi-
ment, of having sloughed his mortal envelope and
become " *one* " with every gloom of shadow and flicker
of sun, one with the rapture of wind and sea—was his.
The fact of his own existence was so strange and
unrealisable that he seemed always touching the margin
of life, meditating on higher conditions than existence
here below.

" In the dead of the night! So black, chill, and still,—
that I touch myself to find out whether I have yet a
body. . . . A clock strikes three! I shall see the sun
again!

" Once again, at least. Possibly several thousand
times. But there will come a night never to be broken
by any dawn— . . . Doubt the reality of substance
. . . the faiths of men, the gods,—doubt right and
wrong, friendship and love, the existence of beauty, the
existence of horror;—there will always remain one thing
impossible to doubt,—one infinite blind black certainty.
. . . And vain all human striving not to remember, not
to think : the Veil that old faiths wove, to hide the Void,
has been rent for ever away;—the Sheol is naked before
us,—and destruction hath no covering.

" So surely as I believe that I exist, even so surely
must I believe that I shall cease to exist—which is
horror! . . . But—

" *Must I believe that I really exist?* . . ."

Out of this idea he weaves a chapter of thrilling

possibilities, and ends, "I am awake, fully awake! . . . All that I am, is all that I have been. Before the beginnings of time I was;—beyond the uttermost circling of the Eternities I shall endure. In myriad million forms I but seem to pass : as form I am only Wave; as essence I am Sea. Sea without shore I am;—and Doubt and Fear are but duskings that fleet on the face of my depth. . . .

"Then a sparrow twittered from the roof; another responded. Shapes of things began to define in a soft grey glimmering;—and the gloom slowly lightened. Murmurs of the city's wakening came to my ears and grew and multiplied. And the dimness flushed.

"Then rose the beautiful and holy Sun, the mighty Quickener, the mighty Purifier,—symbol sublime of that infinite Life whose forces are also mine! . . ."

All his life Hearn had had a singular tenderness for animals. Mrs. Hearn describes his bringing his cats, dogs, and crickets with him when he moved from Ushigome to Nishi Okubo. The very mysteries of animal intelligence fascinated him, and, imbued as he was with ideas of pre-existence and the unity of all life, he raised them in imagination almost to an equality with man. The dog that guarded his gate at night, the dog that was everybody's and nobody's, owned nowhere.

"It stays in the house of the foreigner," said the smith's wife when the policeman asked who it belonged to. "Then the foreigner's name must be painted upon the dog." Accordingly, Hearn had his name painted on her back in big Japanese characters. But the neighbours did not think that she was sufficiently safeguarded by a single name. So the priest of Kobduera painted the name of the temple on her left side, in beautiful Chinese text; and the smith put the name of his shop on her right side; and the vegetable-seller put on her breast the ideographs for " eight hundred,"— which represent the customary abbreviation of the word *yaoya* (vegetable-seller),—any *yaoya* being supposed to sell eight hundred or more different things. Consequently she was a very curious-looking dog; but she was well protected by all that caligraphy.

His wife observed him with bewilderment as he spread out a piece of newspaper on the matting, and fetching some ants out of a mound in the garden, watched them moving about the whole afternoon. How could the little woman guess that his busy brain was weaving the fine Essay on "Ants," published under the heading of " Insect Studies " in *Kwaidan* ?

" The air—the delicious air!—is full of sweet resinous odours shed from the countless pine-boughs broken and strewn by the gale. In the neighbouring bamboo-grove I hear the flute-call of the bird that praises the Sutra of the Lotos; and the land is very still by reason of the South wind. Now the summer, long delayed, is truly with us : butterflies of queer Japanese colours are flickering about; *semi* are whizzing; wasps are humming; gnats are dancing in the sun; and the ants are busy repairing their damaged habitations. . . .

" . . . But those big black ants in my garden do not need any sympathy. They have weathered the storm in some unimaginable way, while great trees were being uprooted, and houses blown to fragments, and roads washed out of existence. Yet, before the typhoon, they took no other visible precaution than to block up the gates of their subterranean town. And the spectacle of their triumphant toil to-day impels me to attempt an essay on Ants."

After relating the whimsical story of a man, visited by a beautiful woman, who told him that she was acquainted with the language of ants, and as he had been good to those in his garden, she promised to anoint his ears, so that if he stooped down and listened carefully to the ants' talk, he would hear of something to his advantage : —

"Sometimes," says Hearn, "the fairy of science touches my ears and eyes with her wand; and then, for a little time, I am able to hear things inaudible and perceive things imperceptible."

After pages of minute description of the biology of ants, leading to a still larger significance concerning the relation of ethics to cosmic law, he thus ends his essay : —

"Apparently the highest evolution will not be permitted to creatures capable of what human moral experience has in all eras condemned.

"The greatest strength is the strength of unselfishness; and power supreme never will be accorded to cruelty or to lust. There may be no gods; but the forces that shape and dissolve all forms of being would seem to be much more exacting than gods. To prove a 'dramatic tendency' in the ways of the stars is not possible; but the cosmic process seems nevertheless to affirm the worth of every human system of ethics fundamentally opposed to human egoism."

In *Exotics and Retrospectives* Hearn has written an Essay on "Insect Musicians" that reveals his erudite

and minute care in the study of "Things Japanese."
He describes the first beginning of the custom of keeping musical insects, tracing it down from ancient
Japanese records to a certain Chuzo who lived in the
Kwansei era in 1789. From the time of this Chuzo
began the custom of breeding insect musicians, and
improving the quality of their song from generation to
generation. Every detail of how they are kept in jars,
or other earthen vessels half-filled with moistened clay
and are supplied every day with fresh food is recounted.
The essay ends: "Does not the shrilling booth of the
insect-seller at a night festival proclaim a popular and
universal comprehension of things divined in the West
only by our rarest poets;—the pleasure-pain of autumn's
beauty, the weird sweetness of the voices of the night,
the magical quickening of remembrance by echoes of
forest and field? Surely we have something to learn
from the people in whose mind the simple chant of a
cricket can awaken whole fairy swarms of tender and
delicate fancies. We may boast of being their masters
in the mechanical,—their teachers of the artificial in all
its varieties of ugliness;—but in the knowledge of the
natural,—in the feeling of the joy and beauty of earth,—
they exceed us like the Greeks of old. Yet perhaps it
will be only when our blind aggressive industrialism
has wasted and sterilised their paradise,—substituting
everywhere for beauty the utilitarian, the conventional,
the vulgar, the utterly hideous,—that we shall begin
with remorseful amazement to comprehend the charm
of that which we destroyed."

During his later days at Nishi Okubo he owned one
of these "insect musicians," a grass-lark or Kusa-
Hibari. "The creature's cage was exactly two Japanese

inches high and one inch and a half wide. He was so small that you had to look very carefully through the brown gauze sides of it in order to catch a glimpse of him. He was only a cricket about the size of an ordinary mosquito—with a pair of antennæ much longer than his own body, and so fine that they could only be distinguished against the light.

" He was worth in the market exactly twelve cents; very much more than his weight in gold. Twelve cents for such a gnat-like thing ! . . .

" By day he slept or meditated, with a slice of egg-plant, or cucumber . . . and always at sunset the infini-tesimal soul of him awaked. Then the room began to fill with a sound of delicate and indescribable sweet-ness, a thin, thin, silvery rippling and trilling, as of tiniest electric bells. As the darkness deepened the sound became sweeter, sometimes swelling until the whole house seemed to vibrate with the elfish resonance. . . .

" Now this tiny song is a song of love,—vague love of the unseen and unknown. It is quite impossible that he should ever have seen or known in this present existence of his. Not even his ancestors for many generations back could have known anything of the night-life of the fields, or the amorous value of song. They were born of eggs hatched in a jar of clay, in the shop of some insect-merchant; and they dwelt there-after only in cages. But he sings the song of his race as it was sung a myriad years ago, and as faultlessly as if he understood the exact significance of every note. Of course he did not learn the song. It is a song of organic memory,—deep, dim memory of other quin-tillions of lives, when the ghost of him shrilled at night from the dewy grasses of the hills. Then that song brought him love,—and death. He has forgotten all about death; but he remembers the love. And therefore he sings now—for the bride that will never come. . . . He cries to the dust of the past,—he calls to the silence and the gods for the return of time. . . . Human loves do very much the same thing without knowing it. They call their illusion an Ideal, and their Ideal is, after all, a mere shadowing of race-experience, a phantom of organic memory. . . ." Then he goes on in half-humorous, half-pathetic way, to tell how Hana, the unsympathetic Hana, the housemaid, when there was no more egg-plant, never thought of substituting a slice of onion or cucumber. So the fairy music stopped, and the stillness was full of reproach, and the room cold in spite of the stove. And he reproved Hana . . . "but how absurd! . . . I have made a good girl unhappy because of an insect half the size of a barley grain! . . . I have felt so much in the hush of the night, the charm of the delicate voice,—telling of one minute existence dependent upon my will and selfish pleasure, as upon the favour of a god,—telling me also that the atom of ghost in the tiny cage, and the atom of ghost within myself, were for ever but one and the same in the deeps of the vast of Being. . . . And then to think of the little creature hungering and thirsting, night after night, and day after day, while the thoughts of his guardian deity were turned to the weaving of dreams! . . . How bravely, nevertheless, he sang on to the very end,—an atrocious end, for he had eaten his own legs! . . . May the gods forgive us all,—especially Hana the housemaid!

" Yet, after all, to devour one's own legs for hunger

is not the worst that can happen to a being cursed with
the gift of song. There are human crickets who must
eat their own hearts in order to sing."

During the last few months of Hearn's life, every
gleam of eyesight, every heart-beat, all his nerve power
were directed to one subject,—the polishing of his
twenty-two lectures incorporated later under the title
Japan, An Attempt at Interpretation. This volume is,
as it were, the crystallisation and summary of his fourteen years' residence in the country, and, as one of
his most eminent critics says, "is a work which is a
classic in science, a wonder of erudition, the product
of long years of keenest observation, of marvellous
comprehension."

Though the *Romance of the Milky Way* was published later, these *Rejected Addresses*, as he whimsically
termed them, were the last product of his industrious
pen. A sudden and violent illness interrupted the work
for a time, but as soon as it was possible he was at his
desk again. "So hard a task was it," his wife tells
us, "that on one occasion he said: 'This book will
kill me, it is more than I can do to create so big a book
in so short a time.' As, at the time, he had no teaching
or lecturing at the University, he poured all his
strength into his writing at home." When it was
completed it seemed as if a load were lifted off him,
and he looked forward eagerly to the sight of the new
volume; a little before his death he said that he could
hear in imagination the sound of the typewriter in
America copying the pages for the press. The privilege,
however, of seeing the book completed was not destined
to be his.

In no book of Hearn's are impartial judgment, insight

and comprehensiveness displayed as clearly as in *Japan, an Interpretation*. It is a challenge to those who say that his views of Japan were fallacious and unreliable, and that he was only capable of giving descriptions of scenery or retailing legends and superstitions.

CHAPTER XXV

HIS DEATH

" . . . Are not we ourselves as lanterns launched upon a deeper and a dimmer sea, and ever separating farther and farther one from another as we drift to the inevitable dissolution? Soon the thought-light in each burns itself out : then the poor frames, and all that is left of their once fair colours, must melt for ever into the colourless Void. . . ."

TEN years after his arrival in Japan the lode-star of Lafcadio Hearn's life and genius rose above the Far Eastern horizon, to cast her clear and serene radiance on the shadowed path that henceforth was but a descent towards the end. We conclude that " The Lady of a Myriad Souls " had written an appreciative letter on the subject of his work, and his, dated January, 1900, was in answer to hers.

The thread was taken up where it had been dropped, the old affection and friendship reopened, unchanged, unimpaired.

Three subjects occupied Hearn's thoughts at this time to the exclusion of all others : a longing to get back to the West amongst his own people, his failing health, and anxiety for the future of his eldest boy—his Benjamin—in case of his death. Except perhaps a hint to McDonald, it is only to Mrs. Wetmore that he drew aside the veil, and showed how clearly he realised that his span of life was now but a short one. " The sound of the breakers ahead is in his ears," " the scythe is sharpening in sight." " I have had one physical warning . . . my body no longer belongs to me, as the

339

Japanese say." And again: "At my time of life, except in the case of strong men, there is a great loss of energy, the breaking up begins." With intense longing did his thoughts these days revert to the Western lands from which he had voluntarily expatriated himself. "I have been so isolated that I must acknowledge the weakness of wishing to be amongst Englishmen again . . . with all their prejudices and conventions."

The Race Problem! one of the most perplexing on earth. A man thinks he has wholly and finally given up his country, sloughed off inherited civilisation, discarded former habits and cast of thought; but, —such a stubborn thing is human nature,—sooner or later, the oft-repeated cry of the wanderer, surrounded by alien hearts, and alien faces, arises to that Power that made him what he is. "Give back the land where I was born, let me fight for what my own people fight for, let me love as they love, worship as they worship."

At the time of Kazuo's birth Hearn had expressed a hope "that he might wear sandals and kimono, and become a good little Buddhist." This was during the period of his enthusiasm for "Things Japanese." When he came to issue with the officials at Kumamoto, and later at Tokyo, a change was effected in his views, and he longed earnestly to make him an Occidental—one of his own people.

All the expansion of communion and understanding denied him in the life he had passed amongst those who viewed things from an entirely different standpoint, seemed centred on the boy. He hoped to educate him abroad, to make an Englishman of him, to put him into a profession, either in the Army or Navy, so that he might serve the country his father had forsworn. In this desire Hearn reckoned without his host. By his action in nationalising himself a Japanese, when he married Setsu Koizumi, his son is a Japanese, born in Japan under Japanese conditions, and unless he throws off all family ties and responsibilities, which, being the eldest son, are—according to communal law in Japan— considerable, he must submit to this inexorable destiny. In his father's adopted country the military or naval profession is closed to him, however, in consequence of his defective eyesight, and both would have been closed to him also in England.

Mrs. Atkinson, anxious to carry out the wishes her half-brother had expressed in his letters, with regard to the future of his eldest son, made inquiries on the subject of various people at Tokyo. The same answer was given on every side. He is a Japanese, and must conform to the dictates of the Japanese authorities. They might permit him to go away for a year or so for study, but he must serve the country his father had adopted, in some capacity, or renounce his nationality. Meantime, the boy is receiving a first-class education at the Waseda University; he is perfectly happy, and would be most reluctant to separate from his relations. As to his mother, it would break her heart if any idea of his leaving Tokyo was suggested.

In the spring of 1903, as Hearn had anticipated, he was forced out of the Imperial University, on the pretext that as a Japanese citizen he was not entitled to a foreign salary. The students, as we can see by Yone Noguchi's last book, made a strong protest in his favour, and he was offered a re-engagement, but at terms so devised that it was impossible for him to re-engage. He was also refused the money allowed to professors for a nine months' vacation after a service of six years; yet he had served seven years. On this subject Hearn was very bitter. "The long and the short of the matter is that after having worked during thirteen years for Japan, and sacrificed everything for Japan, I have been only driven out of the service and practically banished from the country. For while the politico-religious combination that has engineered this matter remains in unbroken power, I could not hold any position in any educational establishment here for even six months."

In judging the controversy between Hearn and the authorities at this juncture, it is well to remember that Japan was struggling for existence. She was heavily in debt, having been deprived by the Allied Powers of her indemnity from China. She could not afford to be soft-hearted, and her own people, students, professors, every one official, were heroically at this time renouncing emolument of any kind to help their country in her need. Hearn's health precluded the possibility of his fulfilling the duties of his engagement, and the means at the disposal of the Government did not permit of their taking into consideration the possible payment of a pension. It seems hard, perhaps, but the Japanese are a hard race, made of steel and iron, or they never could have accomplished the overwhelming task that has been set them within the last ten years. At the time when the war with Russia was raging, and Hearn got his discharge, her resources were strained to the utmost, her own people were submitting to almost incredible privations, officials who had been receiving pay that it seemed almost impossible to live upon, accepting one-half the salary they had been accustomed to, and College professors not only existing on starvation rations, but managing to pay the expenses of junior students. It must also be remembered that national sentiment had been awakened, that the Japanese were reverting to the ancient authority, and belief and foreign teaching was at a discount. All this, however, did not make it easier for Hearn; in spite of his admiration for Japanese gallantry he railed at Japanese officialism. To the listening soul of his friend beyond the ocean, thousands of miles away, he poured forth all his disillusionments, all his anxieties. To her he turned for advice and guidance, for "did she not represent to his imagination all the Sibyls? and was not her wisdom as the worth of things precious from the uttermost coasts?" He felt he must leave the Far East for a couple of years to school his little son in foreign languages. "Whether I take him to England or America, I do not yet know; but America is not very far from England. Two of the boys are all Japanese, —sturdy and not likely to cause anxiety, but the eldest," he says, "is not very strong, and I must devote the rest of my life to looking after him."

And she—his wise friend—knowing the limitations enforced by Hearn's isolation and failing health, living as she did in the midst of that awful American life of competition and struggle, enjoined prudent action and patient waiting, for after all "no one can save him but himself."

"Very true," was Hearn's answer,—and well did he know, for had not he, the half-blind journalist, worked his way unaided and alone, into the position of being one of the signal lights in the literature of the day?

"No one can save him but himself. . . . I am, or have
been, always afraid: the Future-Possible of Nightmare
immediately glooms up,—and I flee, and bury myself
in work. Absurd? . . . Kazuo is everything that a
girl might be, that a man should not be,—except as to
bodily strength. . . . I taught him to swim and make
him practice gymnastics every day; but the spirit of
him is altogether too gentle, a being entirely innocent
of evil—what chance for him in such a world as Japan?
Do you know that terribly pathetic poem of Robert
Bridges': 'Pater Filio'?"

The following are the lines to which Hearn
refers:—

"Sense with keenest edge unused,
    Yet unsteel'd by scathing fire;
Lovely feet as yet unbruised,
    On the ways of dark desire;
Sweetest hope that lookest smiling
O'er the wilderness defiling!

Why such beauty, to be blighted,
    By the swarm of foul destruction?
Why such innocence delighted,
    When sin stalks to thy seduction?
All the litanies e'er chanted,
Shall not keep thy faith undaunted.

I have pray'd the sainted Morning
    To unclasp her hands to hold thee;
From resignful Eve's adorning
    Stol'n a robe of peace to enfold thee;
With all charms of man's contriving
Arm'd thee for thy lonely striving.

Me too once unthinking Nature,
    —Whence Love's timeless mockery took me,—
Fashion'd so divine a creature,
    Yes, and like a beast forsook me.
I forgave, but tell the measure,
Of her crime in thee, my treasure."

It seems as if he were haunted by memories of his own thwarted childhood and shipwrecked youth. If possible he wished to guard and protect his Benjamin from the pitfalls that had beset his path, knowing that the same dangers might prevail in Kazuo's case as in his own, and that there might be no one to protect and guard him.

A charming piece of prose, from which I give a few extracts, was found amongst Hearn's papers after his death. The manuscript, lent to me by Mrs. Atkinson, lies by my hand as I write; it is entitled "Fear."

"An old, old sea-wall, stretching between two boundless levels, green and blue. Everything is steeped in white sun; and I am standing on the wall. Along its broad and grass-grown top a boy is running towards me,—running in sandals of wood,—the sea-breeze blowing aside the long sleeves of his robe as he runs. . . . With what sudden incommunicable pang do I watch the gracious little figure leaping in the light. . . . A delicate boy, with the blended charm of two races. . . . And how softly vivid all things under this milky radiance,—the smiling child-face with lips apart,—the twinkle of the light quick feet,—the shadows of grasses and of little stones! . . .

"But quickly as he runs, the child will come no nearer to me,—the slim brown hand will never cling to mine. For this light is the light of a Japanese sun that set long years ago. . . . Never, dearest! —never shall we meet,—not even when the stars are dead!"

By the exercise of a considerable amount of diplomacy Mrs. Wetmore succeeded at this time in inducing Jacob Gould Schurmann, President of Cornell

University, to enter into an arrangement with Hearn for a series of lectures on Japan.

As of old, she believed him capable of conquering Fate, in spite of the despotism of fact as exemplified in the loss of eyesight and broken health; she felt sure he could interest an American audience by the material he had to offer, and the scholarly way in which he knew how to utilise it.

His answer to the suggestion of the lectures is characteristic : —

" O fairy! what have you dared to say? I am quite sure that I do *not* know anything about Japanese art, or literature, or ethnology, or politics, or history. (You did not say ' politics ' or ' history ', however, and that seems to be what is wanted.) But perhaps you know *what* I know better than I myself know,—or perhaps you can give me to eat a Fairy Apple of Knowledge. At present I have no acquaintance even with the Japanese language : I cannot read a Japanese news-paper : and I have learned only enough, even of the *kana*, to write a letter home. I cannot lie—to my Fairy : therefore it is essential that I make the following declaration : —"

Then he repeats the statement made in the preface of *Japan, an Interpretation*. For these lectures prepared with so much industry and care were destined ulti-mately to go to the making of that beautiful and lucid exposition of the history and thought of a great people.

The world has to be grateful to President Schurmann for withdrawing from his contract, and cancelling the offer made to Hearn for the delivery of lectures at the University.

The excuse that illness had broken out at Cornell was hardly a sufficient one. There is little doubt that unfavourable reports of Hearn's state of health, and doubts as to the possibility of his being able to lecture in public, had drifted to Cornell, and the President, acting for the best interests of his University, did not feel justified in abiding by his proposals.

With that extraordinary mental elasticity that characterised him all his life, Hearn made the best of the situation, and set to work, polishing and repolishing his twenty-two lectures until they reached the high level of style that distinguishes *Japan, an Interpretation*. His courage was the more extraordinary as, filled with the idea that he was at last going to America, he had gone into every detail of meeting his friend. " I would go straight to your Palace of Fairy before going elsewhere," he writes to Mrs. Wetmore, " only to see you again—even for a moment—and to hear you speak in some one of the myriad voices would be such a memory for me, and you would let me ' walk about gently touching things.' . . ." Then in another letter comes a sigh of regret, and as it were farewell. " But your gifts, O Faery Queen have faded away, even as in the Song . . . and I am also fading away."

After the failure of his projected visit to America, a suggestion was made by the University of London that he should give a series of lectures there. But here was the " Ah-ness " of things. Had Hearn's health permitted he would probably have been in England in 1905, where he would have been received with honour. The Japanese had fought Russia and beaten her. People became wildly enthusiastic about Japan : the libraries were besieged with inquiries for Hearn's books,

—just at the eleventh hour, when he had become a name, he died!

All his life his dream had been to be independent, to be able to travel. Referring to a gentleman who was in Japan, he once said, " I envy him his independence. Think of being able to live where one pleases, nobody's servant,—able to choose one's own studies and friends and books."

The offer of an easy post was made to Hearn about this time as Professor of English in the Waseda University founded by Count Okuma. He closed with it at once, thus putting an end to all negotiations with the University of London.

His youngest child, Setsu-ko, was born this year, and all idea of leaving Japan was henceforth abandoned.

In his last letter to Mrs. Wetmore, dated September 1904,—the month in which he died,—he touches on the dedication he had made to her of his book, *A Japanese Miscellany*. To the last the same sympathy and understanding reigned between them. Patiently she exhorted, comforted. Her wise counsel and advice soothed his torn nerves and aching heart to the end. So this affection, untouched by the moth and rust of worldly intercourse, went down with him " into the dust of death."

Slowly but surely the years with their chequered story were drawing to an end. The sum of endeavour was complete, the secrets Death had in its keeping were there for the solving of this ardent, industrious spirit.

Many accounts have been published of Hearn's last hours, too many some of his friends in Japan think. From all of them we glean the same impression;—a calm heroic bearing towards the final mystery, a fine consideration for others, the thought of the future of his wife and children, triumphing over suffering and death.

He always rose before six. "On the morning of the 26th of September, he was smoking in his library," his wife tells us. "When I went in to say my morning greeting, 'Ohayo gozaimasu,' he seemed to be fallen in deep thought, then he said, 'It's verily strange.' I asked him what was strange, and he said, 'I dreamed an extraordinary dream last night, I made a long travel, but here I am now smoking in the library of our house at Nishi Okubo. Life and the world are strange.'

"'Was it in the Western country?' I asked again. 'Oh, no, it was neither in the Western country nor Japan, but the strangest land,' he said."

While writing Hearn had a habit of breaking off suddenly and walking up and down the library or along the verandah facing the garden. The day he died he stopped and looked into his wife's room next the library. In her *tokonoma* she had just hung up a Japanese painting representing a moonlight scene. "Oh, what a lovely picture," he exclaimed. "I wish I could go in my dreams to such a country as that." Sad to think he had passed into the country of dreams and moonlight before the next twelve hours were over!

Two or three days before his death one of the girls called O Saki, the daughter of Otokichi, of Yaidzu, found a cherry-blossom on a cherry-tree in the garden, —not much to look at,—but it was a blossom blooming out of season, in the direction of his library; she told her fellow-servant Hana, who in turn repeated it to Mrs. Koizumi.

" I could not help telling him; he came out of the library and gazed at it for some moments, ' The flower must have been thinking that Spring is here for the weather is so warm and lovely. It is strange and beautiful, but will soon die under the approaching cold.'

" You may call it superstition if you will, but I cannot help thinking that the *Kaerizaki*, or bloom, returned out of season, appeared to bid farewell to Hearn as it was his beloved tree. . . ."

In a letter written to Mrs. Atkinson, some months after Lafcadio's death, Mrs. Koizumi thus describes his last hours : " On the evening of September 26th, after supper, he conversed with us pleasantly, and as he was about going to his room, a sudden aching attacked his heart. The pain lasted only some twenty minutes. After walking to and fro, he wanted to lie down; with his hands on his breast he lay very calm in bed, but in a few minutes after, as if feeling no pain at all, with a little smile about his mouth, he ceased to be a man of this side of the world. I could not believe that he died, so sudden was his fate."

CHAPTER XXVI

HIS FUNERAL

" If these tendencies which make individuals and races belong, as they seem to do, to the life of the Cosmos, what strange possibilities are in order. Every life must have its eternal records in the Universal life,—every thought of good or ill or aspiration,—and the Buddhistic Karma would be a scientific, not a theoretical doctrine ; all about us the thoughts of the dead, and the life of countless dead worlds would be for ever acting invisibly on us."

PERHAPS of all the incongruous, paradoxical incidents connected with Lafcadio Hearn's memory, none is more incongruous or paradoxical than his funeral.

It is believed by many that Yakumo Koizumi (Lafcadio Hearn) died a Buddhist, though he himself explicitly declared that he subscribed to no religious formula, and detested all ecclesiasticism. When he faced the last great problem, as we can see by his essay entitled " Ultimate Questions " in the volume published after his death,—his thoughts soared beyond any boundary line or limitation, set by dogmatists or theologians; all fanciful ideas of Nirvana, or Metempsychosis or Ancestor Worship, were swept away, he was but an entity freed from superstitious and religious palliatives, facing the awful idea of infinite space.

Yet,—Nemesis of his own instability, revealing also how absolutely alien to his sphere of thought were the surroundings in which he had spent his latter years,— at his death his body was taken possession of by priests, who prepared it for burial, sat beside it until the obsequies were over, and conducted the burial service with every fantastic accompaniment of Buddhist ceremonial, in a Buddhist Temple!

A detailed account is given of the funeral by an American lady, Miss Margaret Emerson. She arrived in Japan imbued with an intense admiration for Hearn's writings; and made every endeavour to meet him or hear him lecture, when one morning she saw his death announced in a Yokohama paper, accompanied by a brief notice stating that the funeral procession would start from his residence, 266, Nishi Okubo, at half-past one on September 29th, and would proceed to the Jitom Kobduera Temple in Ichigaya, where the Buddhist service was to be held.

It was one of those luminous Japanese days that had so often inspired the little artist's pen. Not even the filament of a cloud veiled the pale azure of the sky. Only the solitary cone of Fuji-yama stood out, a "ghostly apparition" between land and sea. Everywhere was life, and hope, and joy; the air full of the voices and laughter of little children, flying kites or playing with their balls, amidst a flutter of shadows and flicker of sunrays, as the tawdry procession filed out under the relentless light of the afternoon sun.

He, whose idea it would have been, to slip out of life unheralded and unnoticed, was carried to his last resting-place preceded by a priest ringing a bell, men carrying poles, from which hung streamers of paper *gohei;* others bearing lanterns and others again wreaths, and huge bouquets of asters and chrysanthemums, while two boys in rickshas carried little cages containing birds that were to be released on the grave, symbols of

KAZUO (HEARN'S SON, AGED ABOUT SEVENTEEN)

the soul released from its earthly prison. Borne,—
palanquin-wise,—upon the shoulders of six men, of the
caste whose office it is to dig graves and assist at
funerals, was the coffin, containing what had been
the earthly envelope of that marvellous combination
of good and evil tendencies, the soul of Lafcadio
Hearn.

While the temple bell tolled with muffled beat, the
procession filed into the old Temple of Jitom Kobduera.
The mourners divided into two groups, Hearn's wife,
who, robed in white, had followed with her little
daughter in a ricksha, entering by the left wing of the
temple, while the male chief mourners, consisting of
Kazuo, Lafcadio's eldest son, Tanabe (one of his
former students at Matsue), and several University
Professors, went to the right.

Then followed all the elaborate ceremonial of the
Buddhist burial service. The eight Buddhist priests
dressed in magnificent vestments chanted the chant of
the Chapter of Kwannon in the Hokkekyo.

After the addresses to the soul of the dead, the chief
mourner rose and led forward Hearn's eldest son; together they knelt before the hearse, touching their
foreheads to the ground, and placed some grains of
incense upon the little brazier burning between the
candles. The wife, when they had retired, stepped forward, leading a little boy of seven, in a sailor suit with
brass buttons and white braid. She also unwrapped
some grains of incense from some tissue paper, and
placed them upon the brazier. Then after a considerable amount of bowing and chanting, the ceremony
ended and the congregation left the church.

Outside it was intimated to the assembled congregation that the body would be taken next day to the Zoshigaya Temple for the final rites of cremation in the presence of the family. Then the University students were dismissed by the Professors with a few words, and the ceremony of the day was at an end.

CHAPTER XXVII

VISIT TO JAPAN

" Every dwelling in which a thinker lives certainly acquires a sort
of soul. There are Lares and Penates more subtle than those of the
antique world ; these make the peace and rest of a home."

ON the 16th March, 1909, early in the morning, we
three ladies, Mrs. Atkinson, Miss Atkinson and myself,
left Kobe, reaching Yokohama late in the evening.
Mrs. Atkinson, who had written from Kobe to her half-
sister-in-law, announcing our arrival in Japan, expected
to find a letter from Nishi Okubo awaiting us at the
Grand Hotel. She had not made allowance for the red
tape,—the bales of red tape,—that surround social as
well as official transactions in Japan.

Before we left Kobe, Mr. Robert Young had given
us a letter of introduction to Mr. W. B. Mason, Professor Basil Hall Chamberlain's coadjutor in the editing
of Murray's *Handbook to Japan*, late of the Imperial
Department of Communications, also custodian of the
Club library at Yokohama, and a person, we were told,
to whom every one had recourse in a difficulty. He
cast sidelights on the probable reasons for delay in the
answer to Mrs. Atkinson's letter.

To begin with, Tokyo covers an area of one hundred
square miles, and though ostensibly modelled on
English lines, the Japanese postal system leaves much
to be desired, especially in dealing with English letters;
in finding fault on this score, I wonder what a London

355

postman would do with letters addressed in Japanese? Mr. Mason also reminded us that Mrs. Koizumi did not understand a word of English; she must have recourse to an interpreter before communicating with her Irish sister-in-law, but, above all, in accounting for delay, Mrs. Atkinson had addressed her letter to " Mrs. Lafcadio Hearn," a name by which no properly constituted Japanese postman would find himself justified in recognising Hearn's widow. By nationalising himself a Japanese, Hearn's identity, so far as his Occidental inheritance went, had vanished for ever. He and his wife were only known at Tokyo as Mr. and Mrs. Koizumi.

Mr. Mason, like many others whom we met, was full of anecdotes about Lafcadio, his oddities, his caprices. In days gone by he had been extremely intimate with him, but Hearn had put a sudden end to the friendship; Mr. Mason never knew exactly why, but imagined it was in consequence of his neglecting to take off his footgear and put on sandals one day before entering Hearn's house. In passing judgment on Hearn for these sudden ruptures with friends, because of their lapses from the punctilio of Japanese tradition, it is well to remember that his wife came of the ancient Izumo stock, and was educated according to Japanese rules; a dusty or muddy boot placed on her cream-white tatami was almost an indignity. Hearn deeply resented any slight shown to her, and, from the moment he married, observed all old habits and customs, and insisted on his visitors doing the same.

The expression in Japan for an unceremonious or bad-mannered person is "another than expected person"; the definition is delightfully Japanese; it explains the traditions of the race: no one ever does anything unexpected,—all is arranged by rule and order; in any other civilised country, considering the circumstances, Mrs. Atkinson would have taken a Tokaido train to Tokyo, and from the Shimbasi station gone immediately in a jinrikisha to see her sister-in-law; the two ladies would have fallen into one another's arms, and a close intimacy would have been begun. Not so in Japan.

"Patience is a virtue inculcated by life in the Far East," said Mr. Mason. "Come out with me, I will show you some of the most beautiful sights in the world, and in course of time either Mrs. Koizumi or a letter will turn up."

Anxious not to offend the little Japanese lady by any proceeding not in consonance with the social etiquette of her country, we took Mr. Mason's advice.

I had been reading *Out of the East*, and pleaded that our first pilgrimage might be to the Jizo-Do Temple, scene of Lafcadio Hearn's interview with the old Buddhist priest.

Up a hill above Yokohama we climbed, until we reached the summit, where, embosomed in fairy-like clouds of plum-tree blossom, a carpet of pink-and-white petals round its august feet, stood an ancient shrine.

From the platform in front of the great bronze bell, hanging in a pagoda-like tower, we looked out over the city of Yokohama. Again I experienced what I had felt coming up the Inland Sea, an impression, common to almost every one who visits Japan, that I was gazing on a dream world, lying outside everyday experience, a world " having a special sun and tinted atmosphere of its own," arched by a sky of magic light, the very sky of Buddha. Down the hill-side a cascade of clustering eaves and quaint curved tiled roofs, surrounded by gardens, descended to the very edge of the sapphire sea. Behind, in the distance, rose a range of dark-blue hills, and enormously above the line of them all, through the vapoury mist, gleamed one solitary snow-capped cone; we knew its familiar outline on Japanese fans and screens, in Japanese picture-books;—the sacred, the matchless mountain,—Fuji-no-yama.

There, in the stillness of the Japanese afternoon, we summoned from out the twenty years that had elapsed since Hearn's visit, a vision of the old priest, seated, brush in hand, writing one of the three hundred volumes of the history of the religions of Japan, of the interpreter Akira, and of the little Celtic dreamer seated Buddha-wise between them, while, mingled with the sound of the purring of the red cat, and the song of the *uguisu* from the plum-tree grove, we heard the murmur of their voices.

"That which we are, is the consequence of that which we have been. . . . Every act contains both merit and demerit, just as even the best painting has defects and excellence. But when the sum of good in any action exceeds the sum of evil, just as in a good painting the merits outweigh the faults, then the result is progress. And gradually by such progress will all evil be eliminated. . . . They who by self-mastery reach such conditions of temporary happiness, have gained spiritual force also, and some knowledge of truth. Their strength to conquer themselves increases more and more with every triumph, until they reach at last that world of Apparitional Birth, in which the lower forms of temptation have no existence."

Wisely had Mr. Mason counselled patience. The next afternoon, while seated at tea-time in the Hall of the Grand Hotel, we saw two figures pass through the swing door at the entrance . . . one was a Japanese lady, dressed in the national Japanese costume,—a kimono of dark iron-grey silk,—the other, a tall, slim, near-sighted youth of seventeen dressed also in kimono, wearing a peaked collegiate cloth cap and sandals on his feet. The pair hesitated at the doorway, and after questioning one of the hotel clerks, came towards us under his guidance.

Mrs. Atkinson realised at once that this was her Japanese half-sister-in-law. The nearest relations never embrace in Japan, but the two ladies saluted one another with profound bows and smiles.

Mrs. Koizumi could never have been, even according to Japanese ideas, good-looking; it was difficult to reconcile this subdued, sad-faced, Quaker-like person with Hearn's description written to Ellwood Hendrik, of the little lady whom he dressed up like a queen, and who nourished dreams of "beautiful things to be bought for the adornment of her person." But the face had a pleasing expression of gentle, sensible honesty. Had it not been for the arched eyebrows, oblique eyes and elaborate coiffure,—the usual erection worn by her country-women,—she might have been a dignified, well-mannered housekeeper in a large English establishment.

The only exception to the strict nationality of her costume was a shabby, carelessly-folded, American silk umbrella that she carried, instead of the dainty contrivance of oil paper and bamboo so generally used and so typical of Japan. There was something vaguely and indefinably suggestive, like the revival of a sensation, a shadowing of memory, blended in the associations of that umbrella; we felt certain it had been used by her "August One" in his "honourable" journeyings to and from the Imperial University.

After having placed this precious possession, with careful precision, leaning against a chair, she turned to introduce her son to his aunt. He was already bowing profoundly over Dorothy Atkinson's hand in the background.

At first the lad had given the impression of being a Japanese, but as he laughed and talked with his beautiful cousin, you recognised another race; no child of Nippon was this, the fairy folk had stolen a Celtic changeling and put him into their garb; but he was not one of them, he was an Irishman and a Hearn, bearing a striking resemblance to Carleton Atkinson, Dorothy's brother. The same gentle manner, soft voice, and near-sighted eyes, obliging the wearing of strong glasses. I remembered his father's words: "The eldest is almost of another race, with brown hair and eyes of the fairy colour, and a tendency to pronounce with a queer little Irish accent the words òf old English poems which he has to learn by heart."

Then, as the thought passed through your mind of his extraordinary likeness to his Irish relations, an impassive, Buddha-like, Japanese expression,—a mask of reserve as it were—fell like a curtain over his face, —he was Japanese again.

He spoke English slowly and haltingly; to me it was incomprehensible; his cousin, on the contrary, seemed to understand every word, as if a sort of freemasonry existed between them. There was something pathetic

CARLTON ATKINSON

in watching his earnest endeavours to make his Occidental relative understand what he wished to say.

It is a myth that Mrs. Koizumi talks English; her *Reminiscences* have been taken down and translated by interpreters; principally by the Japanese poet Yone Noguchi. If she ever knew any, it has been entirely forgotten, indeed had it not been for the intervention of Mr. Mason, who is a first-rate Japanese scholar, we should have found ourselves considerably embarrassed. One thing, however, she certainly possessed,—that most desirable thing in woman, to which her husband had been so sensitive,—a soft and musical voice.

Mrs. Atkinson had brought some gifts for the four children from England, and an old-fashioned gold locket, which had belonged to Lafcadio's father, for her sister-in-law. She tried playfully to pass the chain round Mrs. Koizumi's neck, but the little lady crossed her hands on her bosom and declined persistently to allow her to do so. Mr. Mason then told us that it was against all the rules of decorum for a Japanese woman to wear any article of jewellery.

Towards the end of her visit which lasted an interminable time,—Japanese visits usually do,—Mrs. Koizumi gave us an invitation for the following Sunday to come to dinner at 266, Nishi Okubo, and promised that her son Kazuo should come to fetch us. Needless to say, this invitation was the acme of our hopes; we accepted eagerly, and, to save Kazuo the trouble of coming to Yokohama we determined to flit the next day, Saturday, from Yokohama to Tokyo.

The Métropole, or, as Hearn dubbed it, " The Palace of Woe," was the hotel we selected. Our dinner that night was eaten in the room where Professor Foxwell, in his delightful *Reminiscences of Lafcadio Hearn*, describes him leaping from the table, darting to the window, and making for the garden, on catching sight of a young lady tourist, a friend of Professor Foxwell's, at the farther end of the room.

Next morning, as arranged, Kazuo Koizumi arrived to escort us to Nishi Okubo. That particular Sunday was the anniversary of the Festival of the Spring Equinox (*Shunki Korei-sai*). There is an Autumn and a Spring Equinox Festival when days and nights are equal. The pullulating population of Tokyo seemed to have emptied itself, like a rabbit warren into the streets. The ladies were in their best kimonos, their hair elaborately dressed, set round with pins, and the men, some of them bare-headed, Japanese fashion, in Japanese garb, others wearing bowler hats, others again dressed in ill-fitting American clothes, carrying American umbrellas. These umbrellas, I think, are one of the features that you resent most in the Occidental-ising of the Japanese man and woman. A pretty *musumé's* ivory - coloured oval face against the cream-colour background of an oiled-paper Japanese umbrella, makes a delightful picture, and nothing can be imagined more fantastically picturesque than a Tokyo street in brilliant sunshine, or under a flurry of rain when hundreds of these ineffective shelters with their quaint designs of chrysanthemum, cherry-blossom, or wisteria, are suddenly opened. Alas! in ten years' time, like many other quaint and beautiful Japanese produc-tions, these oil-paper umbrellas will have passed away into the region of faintly-remembered things.

The gentle decorous politeness of the crowd was remarkable. If any of the men had a little too much

sake on board, their tipsiness was only betrayed by
their aimlessly happy, smiling expression. Sometimes,
indeed, it could only be guessed at by the gentle sway
of a couple walking arm-in-arm down the street. In
the luke-warm air was a mingling of odours peculiar
to Japan, smells of *sake*, smells of seaweed soup, smells
of *daikon* (the strong native radish), and, dominating
all, a sweet, thick, heavy scent of incense that floated out
from the shadows behind the temple doors, while above
all was a speckless azure sky arching this fantastical
world. The city lay glorified in a joy of sunshine.

Kazuo Koizumi had told us that it was only a short
walk to the trams, and that by them we could get close
to Nishi Okubo. It seemed to us an interminable
journey as we followed the tall, slim figure over bridges,
down miles of paved streets, and at last, when we did
reach the trams, we found them full to overflowing,
not only with men and women, but with babies, babies
tumbling, rolling, laughing on the floor, on their
mothers' laps, on their mothers' backs; there was certainly no doubt of Japan having that most valuable
asset to a fighting country, male children, and that
most necessary adjunct, female children; nowhere was
there an ill-fed, ill-cared for one to be seen.

Finding the trams impossible, we induced Kazuo to
hail jinrikishas, and still on and on for miles, behind our
fleet-footed *kuruma* men, did our journey last, through
the quarter of the foreign legations, past Government
offices and military stations, beside the moat surrounding the Mikado's palace, with its grass slopes and pine-
clad fosse, down declivities and up others, through endless lanes, bordered by one-storeyed houses standing in
shrubberies behind bamboo fences. At last Kazuo

Koizumi, whose *kuruma* led the way, halted before a small gateway, surmounted by a lamp in an iron stand, stamped, as we understood afterwards, with Hearn's monogram in Japanese ideographs. Passing through, we found ourselves opposite the entrance of a lightly-built two-storey house, rather resembling a suburban bungalow in England. Directly we entered we were transported into a different era. Here no modern Japan was visible. On the threshold, waiting to receive us, was an "august residence maid," kneeling, palms extended on the floor. I glanced at the ebon head touching the matting, and wondered if it belonged to Hana, the unsympathetic Hana who had let the grass-lark die. Beside her was Setsu-ko, Hearn's youngest child, in a brilliantly-coloured kimono, while on the step above stood Professor Tanabe, who had been one of Hearn's pupils at Matsue, now an intimate friend of the Koizumi family, living near by, and acting occasionally as interpreter for Mrs. Hearn. What a picture —as an Eastern philosopher, for instance,—he would have made for Moroni or Velasquez, with the delicate grey and cream background of the Japanese tatami and paper *shoji*. He had the clear olive complexion and intellectually-spiritualised expression, result of the discipline and thought enjoined by his Far Eastern religion. He looked tall as he stood above us, the close folds of his black silk college gown descending to his feet. With all the courtesy and dignity of a Spanish Hidalgo did he receive us, holding out a slim, delicately-modelled hand, and bidding us welcome in our native tongue, in a voice harmonious and clear as one of his own temple bells. To take off our footgear in so dignified a presence, and put on the rice sandals offered us by the maid, was trying; for the little girl had raised her forehead from the matting, and, with hands on knees, with many bows had first of all surveyed us sideways like a bird, and then gently approaching with deferential liftings of the eyes and deprecating bows she took a pair of sandals from a row that stood close by, helped us to take off our boots and put on the sandals. We then remarked that she was not at all unsympathetic-looking, but a nice, chubby, rosy-faced handmaiden. We hoped devoutly we had no holes in our stockings, and after a considerable amount of awkward fumbling, got through the ordeal in time to curtsey and bow to Mrs. Koizumi, who appeared beside Professor Tanabe on the step above us, softly inviting us to " honourably deign to enter her unworthy abode."

The best rooms in a Japanese house are always to the rear, and so arranged as to overlook the garden. We followed our hostess to the *engawa* (verandah) leading to the guest-room next to what had been Hearn's study. The *fusima* or paper screens separating the two rooms were pushed back in their grooves, we passed through the opening and stood within what they called the "Buddha-room." At first I thought it was so named because of a bronze figure of Buddha, standing on a lotus flower, with hand upraised in exhortation, on the top of the bookcase, but afterwards ascertained that it was because of the *Butsudan*, or family shrine, that occupied an alcove in the corner.

Every one after death is supposed to become a Buddha; this was the Spirit Chamber where the memory of the august dead was worshipped.

At last I stood where ate, slept, thought and wrote

(for bedroom and sitting-room are identical in Japan) the author of *Kokoro, Japan, an Interpretation*, and so many other wonderful books, and I felt as I looked at that room of Lafcadio Hearn's that the dead were more alive than the quick. The walls,—or rather the paper panels and wood laths that did duty for walls,—were haunted with memories.

I pictured the odd little figure—dressed in the kimono given him by Otani embroidered in characters of letters or poems,—" Surely just the kind of texture which a man of letters ought to wear! "—with the prominent eyes, intellectual brow, and sensitive mouth, squatting " in the ancient, patient manner " on his *zabuton*,—smoking his *kiseru*, or standing at the high desk, his nose close to the paper, covering sheets and sheets with his delicate handwriting, every now and then turning over the leaves of the quarto, calf-bound, American edition of *Webster's Dictionary* that stood on a stand next his desk.

There was an atmosphere of daintiness, of refined clean manners, of a sense of beauty and purity in the room; with its stillness, almost eerie stillness, offering an arresting contrast to the multitudinous rush and clamour of the city outside,—it gave an impression of restfulness, of calm, almost of regeneration, with its cool, colourless, stainless matting and delicate grey walls, lit by the clear light of the Japanese day that fell beneath the verandah through the window panels that, like the *fusima*, ran in grooves on the garden side of the room. I understood from Mrs. Koizumi that when Hearn had added on the study and guest-room to the existing house, glass had been substituted for paper in these window panels. He, who had so devoutly hoped

years before that glass would never replace paper in
the window panels of Japanese houses! Not only that,
but an American stove with a stove pipe, had occupied
the corner where now stands the *Butsudan*, contaminat-
ing that wonderful Japanese atmosphere he had raved
about, that " translucent, crystalline atmosphere " un-
sullied by the faintest breath of coal smoke. These
hardy folk told us that they were always catching coughs
and colds, when they had the stove and glass windows,
so they took both out, and put back the paper *shoji*
and the charcoal brazier.

It was illuminating indeed to see many Western
innovations against which Hearn had railed in his
earlier days in Japan, in various parts of his study.
The *andon*—tallow-candle—stuck in a paper shade
—national means of lighting a room—had apparently
been discarded, and a Queen's reading lamp stood in
all its electro-plated hideousness on a little table in the
corner. On another was an electric bell with india-
rubber tube.

Japanese rooms are never encumbered by ornament,
a single *kakemono*, or piece of fine lacquer or china
appearing for a few days, and then making room for
something else; but here, the Oriental and Occidental
thought and life—that Hearn blended so deftly in his
work—joined hands. Round the room at the height
of about four feet from the floor, bookcases were placed,
filled with books, English most of them,—De Quincey,
Herbert Spencer, Barrie, were a few of the names I
caught a glimpse of; against the laths separating the
household shrine from the shelves near the *Butsudan*
rested volumes of Browning and Kipling.

I wondered where the many things that Hearn must

have collected, the old prints, and bronzes, and enamelled ware, he so often alluded to, had been put away. Above all, where was the photograph of the "Lady of a Myriad Souls," and the one of Mitchell McDonald that he mentioned as hanging on the ceiling?

It is customary in Tokyo, we were told afterwards, to warehouse in a depository or "go-down" (a name derived from the Malay "godong" given to the fire-proof storehouses in the open ports of the Far East) all valuable and artistic objects; the idyllic innocence of Tokyo is a thing of the past; thieving is rife; it is well also to protect them from fire, earthquakes and floods.

Above the bookcases all was thoroughly Japanese in character; the ceiling mostly composed of unpainted wood laths, traversing a delicate grey ground.

On the wall opposite the guest-room hung a *kake-mono* or scroll-picture representing a river running quickly between rocks. "The water runs clear from the heights," was the translation given to us of the Japanese ideographs in the corner,—by Professor Tanabe. It had been a present from Kazuo to his father.

Two of the younger children now appeared, the third boy Iwayo, we heard, was away, visiting some of the ships in the harbour; the two we saw were Idaho, the second son, and Setsu-ko the little girl.

Presently, I don't quite know how, it was intimated that the dinner-hour had arrived, and I must confess that the announcement was a welcome one. Owing to our wanderings in the Tokyo streets, and the lateness of the hour, our "honourable insides" were beginning to clamour for sustenance of some sort.

Japanese dinners have been described so often that
it is unnecessary to go into all the details of the one
of which we partook at Nishi Okubo that Sunday afternoon. It was served in the guest-room next Hearn's
study, and lasted well over an hour. To me it was
exasperating beyond measure. My impression is that
the Japanese delight in discomfort. They own a
country in which any one could be happy. A climate
very much like our own, with a dash of warmth and
more sunshine than we can boast, a climate where anything grows and flourishes and an atmosphere clear as
crystal; instead of enjoying it and expanding to the
delightful circumstances surrounding them they set to
work to make themselves uncomfortable in what seemed
to me such an irritating and futile way. That any sane
people should eat a succession of horrible concoctions
made up of raw fish, lotus roots, bamboo shoots, and
sweets that tasted of Pears' soap, whisked into a lather,
with a little sugar added as an afterthought, eaten
Japanese fashion, was worse than the judgment passed
on Nebuchadnezzar, and with the beasts of the field
Nebuchadnezzar, at least, had no appearances to keep
up, whereas we had to respond to a courtesy that was
agonising in the exquisiteness of its delicacy.

The very dainty manner in which it was all served,
in small porcelain dishes, on lacquer trays, with little
paper napkins, the size of postage stamps tied with gold
cord, seemed to emphasise the utter inadequacy of the
food. The use of chop-sticks, too, was not one of the
least of our trials, especially as we were told that if we
broke one of the spilikins it was an omen of death.

I really must say that I sympathised with the youth of
modern Japan when I heard that most of them sat on

chairs at their meals and now use knives and forks like ordinary people. Mrs. Koizumi, indeed, told us a story of one of Hearn's Tokyo pupils, who, on making a call on the professor, found him seated orthodox Japanese fashion with his feet under him. The visitor, accepting the cushion and pipe offered him, could not refuse to follow suit. Soon, however, he found his position intolerable. Hearn smiled. " All the new young men of Japan are growing into the Western style," he said, " I do not blame you, please stretch your legs and be comfortable."

After dinner we returned again to the study. A wintry sunlight fell athwart the garden, a regular Japanese garden; to the left was a bamboo-grove, the lanceolated leaves whispering in the winds. On the right, at the foot of two or three steps that led to a higher bank, was a stone lantern such as you see in temple grounds. On the top of the bank a cryptomeria threw a dark shadow, and a plum-tree near it was a mass of snowy white bloom.

But what arrested our attention was a small flower-bed close to the cedarn pillars of the verandah. It was bordered with evergreens, and within we could see some daffodils, blue hyacinths and primroses; round about was a border of evergreens. Mrs. Koizumi told us that the bed was called the " English garden," and that Hearn had bought the bulbs and plants and made the gardener plant them. Somehow that little flower-bed, in that far-away country, so alien to his own, seemed to me to express most of the pathos of Lafcadio Hearn's life.

Here, " overseas, alone," he had put in those " English posies," daffodils, and primroses, and hyacinths, with a longing in his heart to smell once more the peat-laden atmosphere of his Irish home, to see the daisy-strewn meadows of Tramore, and the long sunlit slopes of Lough Corrib.

> " Far and far our homes are set round the Seven Seas,
> Woe for us if we forget, we that hold by these,
> Unto each his mother beach, bloom and bird and land—
> Masters of the Seven Seas, Oh! love and understand ! "

CHAPTER XXVIII

SECOND VISIT TO NISHI OKUBO

" Evil winds from the West are blowing over Horai; and the magical atmosphere, alas! is shrinking away before them. It lingers now in patches only, and bands,—like those long bright bands of cloud that trail across the landscapes of Japanese painters. Under these shreds of the elfish vapour you still can find Horai—but not elsewhere. . . . Remember that Horai is also called Shinkiro, which signifies Mirage,—the Vision of the Intangible. And the Vision is fading,—never again to appear save in pictures and poems and dreams. . . ."

BEFORE we took our departure Mrs. Koizumi,—through the medium of Professor Tanabe,—asked us again to honour her " contemptible abode " on Friday the 26th, the day of the month on which the " August One " had died, when therefore, according to Japanese custom, the incense sticks and the lamp were lighted before the *Butsudan* and a repast laid out in honour of the dead.

That day also, she told us, Kazuo would conduct us to the Zoshigaya Cemetery where we might see his father's grave, and place flowers in the flower cups before the tombstone. The invitation was gladly accepted, and with numerous bows on both sides (we were gradually learning how to spend five minutes over each hand-shake) we made our return journey to the Métropole Hotel.

The four subsequent days were spent by my friends sight-seeing; they went to Nikko, an expedition which took three days, and the feasibility was discussed of obtaining a permit from the British Legation to visit one of the Mikado's palaces. But I felt no desire to see the abode of a Europeanised Mikado, who dressed in broadcloth, sat on a chair like any other uninteresting Occidental monarch and submitted to the dictates of a Constitution framed on the pattern of the Prussian Diet. No sight-seeing, indeed, had any significance for me, unless it was connected with memories of a half-blind, eccentric genius, not looked upon as of any account except by a small circle of literary enthusiasts.

The sphere which has been allotted to us for our short span, grants us in its daily and yearly revolutions few sensations so delightful as encountering social conditions, material manifestations, totally different to anything hitherto experienced or imagined. The impressions of those enchanted weeks in Japan, however, would have lost half their charm, had they not been illumined and interpreted by so sympathetic an expositor as the author of *Glimpses of Unfamiliar Japan*. To me, reading his books, full of admiration for his genius, the ancient parts of the city, the immemorial temples, the gardens still untouched by European cultivation, became permeated with spiritual and romantic meaning. A Shirabyoshi lurked behind every screen in the Yoshiwara quarter; the ululation of the dogs as I heard them across the district of Tsukiji at night, seemed a howl in which all the primitive cries of their ancestors were concentrated; every cat was a Tama seeking her dead kittens, while the songs sung by the children as they played in the streets gained a new meaning from Hearn's translations. I even wandered in the ancient parts of the city to see if I could find a Japanese maiden slipping the eye of the needle over the point of the thread, instead of putting the thread through the eye of the needle; and there, seated on *zabutons* in a little shop, as large,—or rather as small,—as life, I caught them in the act. How they laughed, those two little *musumés*, when they saw me watching them so intently. I felt as I passed along that I had acquired another proof of the " surprising *otherness* of things " to insert amongst my notes on this extraordinary land of Nippon.

I fear I also violated every rule of etiquette by visiting Japanese houses in Tokyo without appointment, where I was told people lived who had known Hearn and could give me information concerning him.

Professor Ume, of the Imperial University, was one. In her *Reminiscences* Mrs. Hearn says that an hour or two before he died Hearn had told her to have recourse to Professor Ume in any difficulty, and I thought he might by chance throw some light on Hearn's last hours, and any dispositions of property he might have made on behalf of his widow and children.

A very exquisite house was the Professor's, with its grey panels and cedar-wood battens, its cream-coloured mats, its embroidered screens, and azaleas in amber-crackled pots. For half-an-hour I waited lying on a *zabuton* (I had not yet learnt to kneel Japanese fashion), the intense silence only broken by the gentle pushing backwards and forwards, at intervals, of the screen that separated the two rooms, and the entrance of a little maid bringing tiny cups of green tea with profuse curtseys and bows. When the gentleman of the house did appear, he behaved in a manner so profoundly obsequious that I, despite a slight feeling of irritation at the time I had been kept waiting, and the vileness of the tea of which I had been partaking, grovelled in self-abasement. The moment I attempted, however, to touch upon the subject of Hearn, it was as if a drawer with a secret spring had been shut. The Japanese are too courteous to change a subject abruptly; they slip round it with a dexterity that is surprising. When I endeavoured to ascertain what communication Hearn had held with him, and if he had named executors and left a will,—Koizumi San was fond of smoking and sometimes honoured his contemptible abode to smoke a pipe,—further than that he knew nothing. The same experience met me at the Imperial University (Teikoko Daigaku), where I was audacious enough to penetrate into the sanctum where the heads of the college congregated. Needless to say I was there received also with studied civility, but an impenetrable reserve that was distinctly awe-inspiring. A slim youth was summoned and told to conduct me into the University garden, to see the lake, said to be Hearn's favourite haunt between lecture hours. There was no undue haste exhibited, but you felt that the endeavour to obtain information about the former English Professor at the University was not viewed with any sort of favour by his colleagues.

In the hotel were tourists of various nationalities, half of whom spent their time laughing at the "odd little Japs," the rest were divided between Murray and Baedeker, and went conscientiously the round of the temples mentioned in their classic pages. Two American girls were provided with Hearn's books, and had made up their minds to go off on an extended expedition, visiting Matsue and the fishing villages along the northern coast.

A week of cloudless weather reigned over the land, and in company with these American ladies I went to various places of interest, clambering up flights of steps, along avenues leading to ancient shrines, under the dim shadow of centenarian trees; puzzling over the incomprehensible lettering on moss-grown tombstones and *sotobas*, gazing at sculptures of Buddha in meditation, Buddha with uplifted hand, Buddha asleep in the heavenly calm of Nirvana. But all these smaller Buddhas sank into insignificance before the great Buddha of Enoshima, the celebrated Dai Batsu. Somehow as I stood before this colossal image of calm, backed by the cloudless Eastern sky, a memory was recalled of the granite image that crouches on the edge of the Sahara Desert. The barbaric Egyptian had invested his conception with talons, and surrounded it with sinister legends; but the same strange sense of infinity broods over both. Solemn, impenetrable, amidst the upheavals and decay of dynasties and people, the Sphinx sits patiently gazing into futurity. Here, on this Japanese coast, tidal waves overwhelm towns, earthquakes and fire destroy temples, but this bronze Buddha, throned on his lotus, contemplates the changes and chances passing around him, an immutable smile on his chiselled lips. Hitherto I had looked upon the people of this ancient Nippon as utterly alien in thought and point of view, but here, along roads thousands of miles apart, from out the centuries of time, Oriental and Occidental met and forgathered. No one knows if a master mind directed the hands of the artificers that hewed out the great Sphinx, or brazed the sheets of bronze to shape the mighty image of the Dai Batsu; rather do they seem the endeavour of a people to incarnate the idea that Eternity presents to man the vagueness and vastness of something beyond and above themselves. The humanity of centuries will be driven as the sand of the desert about the granite base of the Sahara's Sphinx, nations will break as the waves of the sea round the lotus-pedestal of the Kamakura Buddha, while, deep and still as the heavens themselves, both remain to tell mankind the eternal truth : ambition and success, exultation and despair, joy and grief will pass away as a storm passes across the heavens, bringing at last the only solution futurity offers for the tumult and suffering of human life—infinite calm, infinite rest.

" Deep, still, and luminous as the ether " . . . was the impression made on Hearn by this embodiment of the Buddhist faith, with its peace profound and supreme self-effacement. Is it to be wondered at that henceforth he attempted to reconcile the great Oriental religion which it represented, with every scientific principle and philosophical doctrine to which he had hitherto subscribed?

It was bitterly cold on the afternoon of Friday the 26th; even the shelter of the house at Nishi Okubo with its *shoji* was comforting after our long jinrikisha ride in a biting wintry wind. We had come prepared to find a certain amount of sadness and solemnity reigning among our hosts, it being the month-day commemorative of the August One's death. But we were greeted with the same laughter, bows, genuflections by the maid and little Setsu-ko as on our previous visit, while on the upper step of the *genkan* (entrance-room) with extended hands and smiling welcome, stood the slim figure of Tanabe. At first, when Mrs. Hearn, talking cheerily and gaily, led us to the alcove occupied by the family shrine, we thought for a moment that she was moved by a feeling of amusement at the eccentric little genius to whom she had been married. Then we recalled various incidents of our travels in the country, and Hearn's essay on the Japanese smile: "To present always the most agreeable face possible, is a rule of life . . . even though the heart is breaking, it is a social duty to smile bravely." Taught by centuries of awful discipline, the habit that urges people to hide their own grief, so as to spare the feelings of others, struck us, when we mastered its signification, as having a far more moving and pathetic effect than the broken tones and ready tears of Occidental widows when referring to the departed.

The doors of the *Butsudan* were set wide open, and on the *kamidan*, or shelf in front of the commemorative tablet, stood a lighted lamp and burning incense rods. Tiny lacquered bowls containing a miniature feast of his favourite food, and vases of artificial sprays of iris were placed side by side. In front of Hearn's photograph stood a pen in a bronze stand. This pen, we understood from Tanabe, was one of three that had been given to him by Mitchell McDonald. The one in the shrine was Kazuo's, presented to him in memory of his father, another was given to Mrs. Atkinson by her half-sister-in-law that Friday afternoon, the third had been buried with the writer of *Japan*, beneath his tombstone in the Zoshigaya Cemetery.

As we stood in the study opposite the *Butsudan* the ghostly charm, the emotional poetry, of this vague and

mysterious soul-lore that regarded the dead as forming part of the domestic life, conscious still of children
and kindred, needing the consoling efficacy of their
affection, crept into our hearts with a soothing sense
of satisfaction and comfort.

Yone Noguchi, in an account he gives of a visit to
266, Nishi Okubo, describes the spiritual influence of
Hearn permeating the house as though he were still
living. None of the children ever go to bed without
saying, "Good-night, happy dreams, Papa San," to his
bas-relief that hangs in the study.

Morning and evening Mrs. Koizumi, a daughter of
the ancient caste, subscribing to Shinto beliefs, holds
communion with the august spirit. Now she murmured a prayer with folded hands, and then turned
with that gentle courtesy of her countrywomen, and
made a motion to us to occupy the three chairs placed
in a row in the middle of the room. Kneeling down
in front of us, she opened a cupboard under the shrine,
pulled out a drawer wherein lay photographs, pictures
and manuscripts that had belonged to her husband, a
photograph of Page Baker and his daughter Constance,
and one of "friend Krehbiel with the grey Teutonic
eyes and curly hair"; portraits also of Mrs. Atkinson
and her children, one representing her eldest girl and
boy in panniers on either side of the donkey that had
created so much amusement in the establishment,—a
donkey being an unknown animal in Japan,—when it
arrived at Kumamoto. Another represented the Atkinson barouche, with its pair of horses, coachman and
groom. The Mikado's State equipage was the only
conveyance, these simple people told us, they had ever
seen to equal its splendour.

It was very cold, and we frigid Occidentals sat close
to the apology for a fire, three little coals of smoulder-
ing charcoal that lay in the brazier. One of the ends
of my fur stole fell into the ashes; I did not perceive it
for a moment or two, until the smell of the smoulder-
ing fur attracted the attention of the others. Profound
silence descended upon the company as they watched
me extinguish it with a certain amount of difficulty.
I am certain they thought it an omen of some sort—
everything amongst the old-world Japanese is looked
upon as a good or bad omen.

Setsu-ko cuddled up to her aunt, either because she
was cold, or because her mother,—for politeness' sake,
I imagine,—told her that Mrs. Atkinson was her father's
sister, and that she was to look upon her with the same
respect as upon her father. Kazuo, Iwayo, and Idaho,
Hearn's three boys, were there, all of them fine specimens of Eurasians. The remembrance recurred to me
as I looked at them of Herbert Spencer's dictum on
the subject of Anglo-Japanese marriages. What would
Hearn have said if he had known that the "greatest
thinker on earth" had committed himself to the statement, in an interview with the Japanese Ambassador in
1898, of the extreme inadvisability of marriages between Englishmen and Japanese, declaring that the
children of mixed parentage are inferior, both in mental
endowments and health. This statement, we may say,
like many others made by the "greatest thinker on
earth," is flatly contradicted by fact. There are thousands of instances in the Far East of the fine race
produced by the mixture of Occidental and Japanese,
especially indeed in the Koizumi children, who are
unusually healthy and intelligent.

What a singular picture this family of Lafcadio Hearn made in kimonos and sandals, with their dark complexions, Irish eyes and Irish smile—for on each of them fate has bestowed a gift from the land of their father's birth—with the background of bookcases full of English books, the Buddhist shrine and Japanese *kakemonos* and ideographs.

Some of the bitterest disillusionments of Hearn's life would most likely have been caused by his own children, had he lived to see them grow up. The ship of his eldest son's life that he spent his latter days "freighting and supplying for its voyage" would most likely have gone down on the sunk rock of alien blood and a different "race-ghost."

I doubt Miss Setsu-ko adapting herself to her father's ideal of unassertive femininity, or contenting herself with being merely a household chattel, subservient to mother and father-in-law, her knowledge of the world circumscribed by Kanbara's *Greater Knowledge for Women*. Was it my imagination, or did I see a slightly impatient, indulgent acceptance on Kazuo's part of the little rites before the *Butsudan*, as if he looked upon them from the height of his modern education as a maternal weakness?

"The Japanese child is as close to you as the European child," says Hearn, "perhaps closer and sweeter, because infinitely more natural, and naturally refined. Cultivate his mind, and the more it is cultivated the further you push him from you. Then the race difference shows itself. As the Oriental thinks naturally to the left, where we think to the right, the more you cultivate him the more strongly will he think in the opposite direction from you. Finis: sweetness, sympathy.

After the decoction, colour of pale whisky, that under the name of " tea," accompanied by tiny sponge-cakes (Kasutera)—his Papa San's favourite cake, Kazuo told us—had been handed round and partaken of, jinrikishas were called, for our expedition to the Zoshigaya Cemetery. As we stood on the verandah before starting, a wintry ray of sunlight fell across the garden, and a breeze rustled through the bamboo-grove, stirring the daffodils and hyacinths in the flower-bed beneath. It was the last sunlight we saw that afternoon! Over the dusty Tokyo Parade-ground, where little men, in ill-fitting khaki uniforms, were going through various evolutions on horses about the size of Welsh ponies,—along by rice swamps, through narrow lanes, bordered by evil-smelling, sluggish streams of water (the Japanese may be clean inside their houses, outside, the streets of Tokyo are insanitary to an unspeakable extent), we prosecuted our journey, while a cold wind whistled round us, and inky-black clouds heaped themselves on the horizon. When at last we reached the cemetery it seemed to have but little charm to recommend it. Nothing " was beautiful with a beauty of exceeding and startling queerness "; on the contrary, rather distressingly European, with straight gravelled paths and formal plots, enclosed by a box edging and a little wicket gate. I am under the impression that it was a portion of the Japanese cemetery allotted by Government for the burial of " foreigners "; as no information was volunteered upon the subject, however, we did not like to ask. Walking along the gravel path, behind Kazuo's kimonoed figure, we at last reached the tomb, distinguished by an upright granite slab, the same shape as Hearn's Ihai in the Buddhist shrine, slightly rounded at the top. A thick-set circle of evergreens transplanted from the Nishi Okubo garden by Mrs. Koizumi's orders, sheltered it behind. On one of the stones in front of the slab was an oval cavity filled with water; two smaller round holes for burning incense flanked the larger one. On either side were bamboo cups in which flowers were placed. On the slab was the inscription—

"Shogaku In-den Jo-ge Hachi-un Ko ji,"—"Believing Man Similar to Undefiled Flowers Blooming like Eight Rising Clouds, who dwells in Mansion of Right Enlightenment."

The light was fading and the air felt bitterly cold as we stood beside the grave; the dark clouds that had lain in ambush, as it were, in the background, came driven across the sky by gusts of wind, swaying the thicket of evergreens, and the tall maple and plane-trees beyond the cemetery boundary. Snowflakes began to fall, and, with the suddenness characterising all atmospheric changes in this unstable land, a thin coating covered the evergreens in a few seconds, and lay on the plum-blossom in the bamboo holders, placed on the stone platform in front of the tombstone. The "Snow Woman" (or Yuki-Onna), of whom Hearn wrote his strange legend, seemed to touch our hearts with her cold hand, as we turned and walked away, saddened by the thought of our kinsman, Lafcadio Hearn, whose name was on so many English-speaking lips at the moment, buried,—an alien amongst aliens,—in a Buddhist grave, under a Japanese name, thousands of miles away from his own land, his own people.

CONCLUSION

LAFCADIO HEARN's was a personality and genius which people will always judge from the extreme point of view in either direction. Most ordinary common-sense folk, with whom he came in contact, looked upon him as an odd, irritable, prejudiced little man, distinctly irreligious, and rather immoral; but the elect few, admitted to his intimacy, recognised the tender heart, luminous brain, gentlemanly breeding, and human morality that lay hidden behind the disguise of Japanese kimono and obi, or beneath the flannel shirt, reefer coat, and extraordinary headgear of his New Orleans days. As to his genius, the English public, who consistently ignored it until a few years ago, are now inclined to blow his trumpet too lustily. He has recently been placed by critics amongst the greatest English letter-writers; declared to be " a supreme prose-poet," " one of those whose influence will last through the ages "; while Miss Bisland, his American biographer, has no hesitation in locating him amongst the greater fixed stars in the literary firmament.

If you cherish a deep sympathy for a man's intellect and character, the worst service you can render him is to veil his failings and qualities behind a mist of eulogy. Lafcadio Hearn, with his shy, sensitive nature, would have shuddered at the " plangent phrases and

384

canorous orismology " that have been bestowed upon him by his friends. Sometimes the idea may have vaguely come to him, " like the scent of a perfume, or the smell of a spring wind," that one day he might write something great; but, on the whole, his estimate of his own mental powers was a humble one—" not that he was modest in literary matters," he says, on the contrary satanically proud, but like an honest carpenter who knows his trade, he could recognise bad workmanship, and tell his customer : " That isn't going to cost you much, because the work is bad. See, this is backed with cheap wood underneath—it looks all right, only because you don't know how we patch up things."

Although in our day Hearn's work has an original and significant appeal, will it have the same for the generations following us in the century on which we have entered? Each period brings in its train many literary interests and fashions, which the next rejects; but for Lafcadio Hearn's work there is no authentic equivalent, no substitute.

He had the extraordinary advantage of seeing a phase of civilisation of absorbing interest, and found himself well-equipped to interpret it. Evanescent in itself, he gave it stability and form, and, what is more, discerned the outward demonstration of a deep-lying essential ideal—the ideal that has influenced mankind so often through the centuries : oblivion of self, the curbing of natural appetites as a means to more elevated happiness and well-being than mere pleasure and self-indulgence. All this phase in Japanese life he has recounted in exquisite and finished prose, and for this alone will be prized for many a day by cultured readers and thinkers.

Besides his Japanese work, his delightful letters have achieved a unique place in the literary world, because of the variety of subject, and because of that great incentive to literary interest and sympathy—the eternal answering of intellect to intellect, of feeling to feeling, of enthusiasm to enthusiasm. But when you declare him—as Miss Bisland does in the Preface to the last *Volume of Letters*—great as Jean Jacques Rousseau, it is well to remember what each accomplished. The author of the *Contrat Social* gave a new gospel to Europe, and initiated a social and political upheaval, the influence of which has lasted to our own day. Hearn was incapable of initiating any important movement, he never entered into the storm-swept heart of the world, outside his own mental horizon. He could interpret moods and methods of belief and thought, and pour forth a lyrical outburst on the subject of a national hymn, but his deductions from significant artistic movements in the history of Occidental civilisation, were neither broad nor unbiassed. A thing was so because he so viewed it at the moment, if his view varied it was not so, and he was equally firmly convinced the new aspect in which it appeared to him was right. If you disagreed with him, or attempted to argue it out with him, he would grow impatient, and throw up the game. He was quite incapable, indeed, of taking any view of a question but his own, and he never was of the same opinion two days together. Unmindful of the spaces of thought that lay between one method of sentiment and another, he swooped to conclusions without having really endeavoured to inform himself of details before discussing them.

As to his feelings on the political development of

Japan, so entirely conservative were his prejudices, and so intense his dislike of the modernisation of the ancient civilisation, that he found satisfaction in the insulting remarks cast at him as he passed through the streets of Kobe, and in the relinquishing of the instruction of English literature in their colleges. He declared his horror of the ironclads that Japan was adding to her navy, a fishing-boat with tatami sails, or a sampan rowed by men in blue cotton jerkins, was to him a far more impressive sight than the "Splendid Monster" that he saw at Mionoseki. Worthy of all praise, he stated, were the laws in the Chinese sacred books, that "he who says anything new shall be put to death," and "he who invents inventions shall be killed!"

Hearn's literary judgments were as capricious and biassed as his political ones. A mental nomad, he pitched his tent in whatever camping-ground he found by the roadside, folding it and moving on again whenever the fancy prompted him. Gautier, Flaubert, Tennyson, Percival Lowell, Edwin Arnold, Du Maurier, were some that abode with him for a season.

It is doubtful if he had any discernment for ancient art, until late in his artistic career. His New Orleans Hellenism was the Hellenism of the banks of the Seine, in 1870, rather than the Hellenism of Greece. He dedicated the translation of Gautier's tales "To the Lovers of the Loveliness of the Antique World," whereas nothing was less antique than Gautier's Parisian classicism, with its ornate upholstery and sensuous interpretation of Greek fable. The very fact of Hearn's comparison between the art of Praxiteles and Phidias, and the grotesque whimsicality of Japanese imaginings, shows that he had not grasped the dignity and breadth of Greek culture. He confesses that it was only when he was turning grey, that he really understood the horror and the beauty, the reality and the depth, of Greek legend; of Medusa, who freezes hearts and souls into stone, the "Sirens singing with white bones bleaching under their women's breasts, and Orpheus, who sought Hell for a shadow and lost it."

Hearn was a Latin, and follower of the Romantic in contradistinction to the Realistic School. "Have you ever attempted to mount sóme old tower stairway, spiring up through darkness, and in the heart of that darkness found yourself at the cobwebbed edge of nothing? The emotional worth of such experience—from a literary point of view—is proved by the force of the sensations aroused, and by the vividness with which they are remembered." This prelude to one of his ghostly Japanese legends, with its *frisson*, its suggestion of awe, its mystery, its strangeness, breathes the very essence of Romanticism.

Literary brother to Loti and Rénan on his Celtic-Breton side, with their sense of style and the rhythm of the phrase, Hearn had all the Celtic longing for something beyond the elements of everyday life, gazing with longing, like the man in Meredith's poem, at the mist-veiled hills on the other side of the valley, losing his illusions, and sighing to return when he had attained to the reality of the vision, and found the slopes as stony, and the paths as rugged, as in the region he had quitted. At New Orleans the Celtic spirit of vague unrest led him to long for the tropics, or the Spanish Main; in the West Indies, he regretted the "northern domain of inspiration and achievement," and towards the end of his stay in Japan, suffered from nostalgia and the sense of exile from the land of his birth. In spite of his acknowledgment, however, of the greatness of the West, and the appreciation of it, born of life in an alien land, he returned to the memory of his Japanese home—the simple love and courtesy of Old Japan and the charm of the fairy world seized his soul again, as a child might catch a butterfly.

Combined with Celtic melancholy and dreaminess, he had also inherited, without doubt, some unhealthiness of mind. To all intents and purposes, he was at times a madman, and at others certainly very near the border-land of insanity. " Mason is always sane," he says, " whereas, for the greater part of my existence, I have been insane." It was this strange, unforeseen element in his nature that accounts for so much that is other-wise inexplicable. Impossible is it to say how much of the very strength of his work did not proceed from nervous susceptibility. If it made him subject to moods of unreasonable suspicion and self-tormenting dejection, it also gave him power to see visions and retain memories.

His excitable mental attitude towards one of the ordinary events of a literary man's career, the cor-rections of a printer's reader, " that awful man, without wrath and wholly without pity, like the angels! " . . . The yells of anguish in bed at night, when he thought of the blunders in the proofs he had returned, dis-closes a piteous state of highly-wrought nerves. Hearn's strangely uncontrolled nature is certainly a striking exemplification of the statement that concentra-tion on daily mental work is the best antidote to insanity. During the period, towards the end of his life at Tokyo, when most subject to attacks of coma and mental hysteria, he wrote his sanest book, a model of lucid historical narrative. " Art! Art! Bitter deception! " cries Flaubert. " Phantom that flows with light, only to lead one on to ruin." For Lafcadio Hearn, Art was the one reality, the anchor that kept him from drifting to mental wreckage; out of his very industry and determination grew a certain healthy habit of thought and life.

It has been said that Hearn had no creative ability. With regard to his capability of writing a complex work of fiction, this is perhaps true, he had forfeited his birthright to produce a *Pêcheur d'Islande;* but on most of his Japanese work his individuality is unmistakably impressed. He had a wonderful memory and was an omnivorous reader. To Chamberlain he acknowledged, that observations made to him, and ideas expressed, were apt to reappear again in work of his own, having, after the lapse of a certain amount of time, become so much a part of his thought, that he found it " difficult to establish the boundary line between meum and tuum." We can see the verification of this statement by phrases and epithets, inspired by other writers, scattered through his pages. " The Twilight of the Gods " is an echo of " The Burden of Nineveh." The sub-title, " Hand and Soul," of *Gleanings in Buddha Fields*, was taken from Rossetti's prose romance. Keats's sonnet on the Colour Blue, probably prompted his essay on Azure Psychology. Yet, in spite of small borrowings here and there, how inviolate he keeps his own characteristics and intimate method of thought ! Percival Lowell's *Soul of the Far East* had enormously impressed him, even in America before he went to Japan;

but there is not a sentence akin to Lowell in *Glimpses of Unfamiliar Japan*. He knew Kipling's writings from end to end, yet Kipling, in his letters to the *Pioneer* on Japan, afterwards published in a volume entitled *From Sea to Sea*, is insensibly more influenced by Hearn than Hearn was ever influenced by Kipling.

As to his knowledge of Japan having been gleaned from industriously exploited Japanese sources, he himself would have been the first to admit the truth of this statement. Nishida Sentaro, Otani, Amenomori, all contributed experiences, and by this means he came into possession of accurate and living sources of inspiration, that acquired a deeper significance as they passed through his imaginative brain. He endeavoured, as he says, to interpret the East to the West, on the emotional rather than on the material side. By the perception of his genius he enables us to see how the Japanese took natural manifestations and wove them into religious creeds, coarse and uncouth, perhaps, at times, but proving the vitality of the hearts of the primitive folk surrounding him. He recognised that the people, the man in the rain coat, the peasant who tills the rice-fields and feeds the silk-worms, and weaves the silk, are those that have laid the foundations of the wonderful empire. The moralising of a decrepit old Buddhist priest, the talk of a peasant at the plough, the diary of a woman in indigent circumstances, with her patient resignation and acceptance of her cheerless lot, are told with pathetic simplicity and realism.

Querulously he complained that people would not take him seriously, that they treated him as a fabulist. Inaccurate he may have been in some of the conclusions he drew from superficial manifestations, and his out-

bursts of enthusiasm or dislike may be too pronounced
to please the matter-of-fact man who knows not what
enthusiasm means. " It is only in the hand of the
artist," some one has said, "that Truth becomes impressive." You can hardly take up a newspaper now-
a-days without finding a quotation from Hearn on the
subject of Japan. His rhythmic phrases seem to fall on
men's ears like bars of melodious music, his picturesque
manner of relating prosaic incidents turns them into
poetic episodes, convincing the most practical-minded
that in dealing with a country like Japan, interpretation
does not solely consist in describing the thing you see,
but in the imaginative power that looks beyond and
visualises what is invisible to ordinary folk. What a
personal quality and profound significance, for instance,
is to be found in his reverie in Hakata, the town of the
Girdle Weavers, as he stands in front of the enormous
bronze head of Buddha, and sees the pile of thousands
of metal mirrors, contributed by Japanese women, to
make a colossal seated figure of the god; hundreds had
been already used to cast the head, thousands would be
needed to mould the figure—an unpractical and extrava-
gant sacrifice of beautiful things, but to Hearn far more
was manifest than merely the gift of bronze mirrors.
Into the depths of a mirror the soul of its owner is
supposed to enter. Countless legends relate that it
feels all her joys and pains, a weird sympathy with her
every emotion; then in his fanciful, whimsical way he
conjures up shadowy ideas about the remnants of souls,
the smiles, the incidents of home-life imaged on their
surface. Turning the face of some of the mirrors, and
looking into their depths, he imagines the possibility
of catching some of these memories in the very act of
hiding away. " Thus," he ends, " the display in front

of the Buddha statue becomes far more than what it seems. We human beings are like mirrors, reflecting something of the universe, and the signification of ourselves in that universe. . . . The imagery of the faith of the Ancient East is, that all forms must blend at last with that Infinite Being, whose smile is Eternal Rest." Thus subtly does he interpret the dim, far-reaching vision, and pathetic imaginings of a susceptible people.

As to Hearn's veering round in his opinion of the Japanese, which has by some been called insincere and double-faced, because while he was drawing a salary from the Japanese Government, and adapting himself to Japanese social conditions, he was damning the Japanese and expressing his hatred of those surrounding him, the only answer to be given to those who blame him is to tell them to visit Japan, to reside in the primitive portions of the country, with its ancient shrines, quaint villages, courteous ways, and afterwards go to Tokyo or one of the open ports, see the modern Japanese man in bowler hat and American clothes,—then and then only will they be able to understand what an artist, such as Hearn, must have suffered in watching the transformation being effected. On the subject of Old Japan he never changed his opinion, which was, perhaps, from certain points of view over-enthusiastic. This very enthusiasm, however, enabled him to accumulate impressions which, if he had been indifferent, would not have stamped themselves on his imagination. Hearn's genius was essentially subjective, the outer aspect of his work was the outcome of an inward vision. We should never have had this inward vision so clearly revealed, if it had not been, as it were, mirrored in a heart full of sympathy and appreciation. You must strike an average between his admiration and dislike of the kingdom of his adoption, as you must strike an average in his expressions of literary and political opinion.

In consequence of Hearn's railings against Fate, the world has come to the conclusion that his was a particularly ill-starred life. But the tragedy really lay in the temperament of the man himself. Circumstances were by no means adverse to the development of his genius. The most salient misfortune that befell him, the loss of his inheritance, saved him, most likely, from artistic sterility. With his impressionable nature, an atmosphere of wealth and luxury might have paralysed his mental activity. It was certainly a lucky star that led him to New Orleans, and later to the West Indies; and what a supreme piece of good fortune was the chance that came to him of spending the last fourteen years of his life in Japan, before the ancient civilisation had been swept away. It was pitiful, people say, to think of Hearn's poverty in the end, but when you see his Tokyo house, with its speckless cleanliness, its peace, its calm, you will no longer regret that his means did not enable him to leave it. Japan was the country made for him, and not the least benign ordinance that Fate imposed upon him was his inability to accept the invitation, given to him during the last years of his life, by University College, London. We can see him amidst the mist and fog in the hurry and bustle of the great city, the ugliness of its daily life and social arrangements: he would have quarrelled with his friends, with the University professors, with his landlady, ending his life, most likely, in a London lodging, instead of sinking to rest surrounded by the devotion and care of those that loved him.

An intrepid soldier in the ranks of Literature was Lafcadio Hearn. His work was not merely literary material turned out of his brain, completed by his industrious hand; to him it was more serious than life. He is, indeed, one of the most extraordinary examples of the strange and persistent power of genius, " ever advancing," as he himself expresses it, " by seeking to attain ideals beyond his reach, by the Divine Temptation of the Impossible! " Well did he realise that the more appreciation for perfection a man cherishes, the more instinct for Art, the smaller will be his success with the general public. But never was his determination to do his best actuated by any hope of pecuniary gain. From the earliest years of his literary career, his delight in composition was the pure delight of intellectual activity, rather than delight in the result, a pleasure, not in the work but in the working. According to him, nothing was less important than worldly prosperity, to write for money was an impossibility, and Fame, a most damnable, infernal, unmitigated misery and humbug.

To enjoy moments of delight in the perception of beauty " in this short day of frost and sun," is the only thing, says Walter Pater, that matters, and " the only success in life."

Judged from this point of view, Hearn's was certainly a successful life. To the pursuit of the beautiful his days and years were devoted.

> " One minute's work to thee denied
> Stands all Eternity's offence "—

he quotes from Kipling.

This it is that gives his career a certain dignity and unity, despite the errors and blunders defacing it at various periods. Man of strange contradictions as he was, there was always one subject on which he never was at issue either with himself or destiny.

Like those pilgrims, whom he describes, toiling beside him up the ascent of Fuji-no-yama, towards the sacred peak to salute the dawn, so through hours of suffering and toil, under sunshine and under the stars, turning neither to the right hand nor the left, scorning luxury and ease, Lafcadio Hearn pursued his path, keeping his gaze steadily fixed on one object, his thoughts fixed on one aim.

In one of those eloquent outpourings, when his pen was touched with a spark of divine fire, he gives expression to the pervasive influence of the spirit of beauty, " the Eternal Haunter," and the shock of ecstasy, when for a moment she reveals herself to her worshipper. Indescribable is her haunting smile, and inexpressible the pain that it awakens . . . her witchery was made in the endless ebb and flow of the tides of life and time, in the hopes and desires of youth, through the myriad generations that have arisen and passed away.

What a lesson does Hearn teach to the sons of Art in these days of cheap publication and hurried work. His record of stoical endeavour and invincible patience ought to be printed in letters of gold, and hung on the study wall of all seeking to enter the noble career. His re-writing of pages, some of them fifty times, the manner in which he put his work aside and waited, groping for something he knew was to be found, but the exact shape of which he did not know. Like the sculptor who felt that the figure was already in the marble, the art was to hew it out.

As the years went by, the elusive vision ceased to

consist merely of the beauty of line and form, and took the higher beauty of immortal and eternal things. Emotions that did not set flowing a current of sensuous desire and passion, but appealed to those impulses that stir man's higher life, made him realise that there are enthusiasms and beliefs "which it were beautiful to die for."

INDEX

Akira, 195, 197, 358
Alma Tadema, 75
Amenomori Nobushige, 194, 212, 269, 302, 303
American Criticism, An, 170
Ancestor Worship, Hearn's views on, 168, 169, 174
Ancestral Tablet, The, 287
"Ants," Essay on, 332
Arnold, Matthew, 77
Arnoux, Leopold, 180
Asama-Yama, 169
Atkinson, Mrs., 16, 27, 248, 341, 345, 355; letters to, 46–65, 74, 86, 87, 106, 121, 135, 233, 253, 287; visits Japan, 355, et seq.
Atkinson, Mr. Buckley, 231
  „ Carleton, 16, 66
  „ Dorothy, 355, 360
Avatars, 17

Baker, Constance, 379
Baker, Page M., 127, 131, 269, 276
Ball, Sir F., 289
Bangor, 41
Baudelaire, 81
Beale, Mr. James, 291, 292
Behrens, Mrs., 322
Berry, Rev. H. F., 59
Bisland, Miss Elizabeth, 132, 133, 149, 157, 177, 303; marriage of, 216, 232, 233, 234; letters to, 184, 207; joint-editor of Cosmopolitan, 154
Borrow, George, 311

Boston, 296
Brenane, Mrs. Justin, 14, 27, 28, 30, 36, 38, 41, 46
Bridges, Robert, quoted, 344
British Museum, image of Buddha in, 75
Bronner, Milton, 79
Brown, Mr., 231
Brownings, The, 77, 367
Buddha of Enoshima, 376, 377
Buddhism, 58, 166, 169
Butcher, Miss, 30

Calidas, 171
Chamberlain, Basil Hall, 134, 191, 232; letters to, 139, 196, 205, 220
Chinese Ghosts, 131
Chita, 51, 52
Cholera at Kobe, 275
Cincinnati, 71, 83, et seq.
  „ Brotherhood, 136
Civilisation, attack on, 283
Cockerill, Colonel John, 93
Collins, Wilkie, 78
Commercial, The, Hearn joins, 105
Concerning Lafcadio Hearn (G. M. Gould), 88
Conventual Orders, 14
Corbishly, Monsignor, 57, 59, 61
Corfu, 19–22
Correagh, 14, 20
Crawford, Mrs., 32, 36
Crescent City, The, 114
Crosby, Lieutenant, 162
Cullinane, Mr. and Mrs., 71, 82

"Dad," *see* Watkin
Dai Batsu of Enoshima, 376
,,   ,,   of Kamakura, 166
Dancing Girl, The, 222
Darwin, Charles, 77, 78, 164, 165
Daunt, Mr. Achilles, 62, 65, 69,
Delaney, Catherine, 71, 75
"Dengue Fever," 121
De Quincey, 328
Dragon Flies, 323
Dream of a Summer's Day, 39
Dublin, 17, 23, *et seq.*
Du Maurier, 82
Dust, Hearn's Essay on, 67

Elwood, Frank, 41
,,   Mrs., 39
,,   Robert, 39, 41
Emerson, Miss Margaret, 352
Enquirer, The, Hearn on staff of, 93–8
"Eternal Feminine," Article on, 319
Exotics and Retrospectives, 320, 321, 333

Fantastics, 149
First Principles, Spencer's, 166
Flaubert, Gustave, 59
Foley, Althea, 100, 102, 207
Ford Castle, 15
Formosa, 229
Forrest, General, funeral of, 109
Foxwell, Professor, 144, 316
Franco-Prussian War, 80
Froude, James, 179
Fuji, First sight of, 188
Fuji-no-Yama, 169, 352
Fujisaki, Captain, 324

Garden Folk Lore, 217
Gautier, Théophile, 80
Ghostly Japan, 322
Gleanings in Buddha Fields, 310, 318
Glimpses of Unfamiliar Japan, 190, 199, 304, 373

Gould, Dr. George Milbury, 88, 174, 184
Greek Culture, 388
Gulf Winds, 51

Hall, H. H., 320
Halstead, Mr., 107
Hamamura, Cemetery of, 22
Hana, 336
Harper's Weekly, 161, 162
Harrison, Frederic, 168
Hawkins, Armand, 125
Hearn, Lafcadio, birth, 13, 22 ;
Hibernian ancestors, 14 ; English origin, 14 ; the interpreter
of Buddhism, 17 ; maternal
lineage, 17, 18 ; Hellenic associations of birthplace, 22 ;
memories of Malta, 23 ; reminiscences of childhood, 33 ;
separation of his parents, 35 ;
adopted by Mrs. Brenane, 36 ;
his defective eyesight, 44, 62,
65 ; relations with Mr. Molyneux, 46 ; views of ideal
beauty, 53 ; at Tramore, 54 ; at
school at Ushaw 56 ; literary
tastes at school, 60 ; unattractive appearance, 66 ; in London, 70, *et seq.* ; literary vocation, 73 ; Paris, 80 ; Cincinnati, 82 ; his shyness, 84 ;
reaches the depths, 86 ; servant in boarding-house, 87 ;
secretaryship, 93 ; on staff of
Enquirer, 93 ; ascends Cincinnati church spire, 95 ; his translations, 96 ; and Althea Foley,
100 ; and Marie Levaux, 105 ;
joins staff of *The Commercial*,
105 ; at Memphis, 107 ; destitution, 114 ; fever, 121 ; *Times Democrat*, 126 ; method of argument, 134 ; intellectual isolation, 134 ; intolerance of amateur art, 137 ; characteristics,
142 ; visits West Indies, 155 ;
letters, 158 ; arrangement with

Harper, 161; marriage, 158, 206–214; political opinions, 167; visits Mr. Watkins, 173; the Krehbiels, 174; musical sense, 176; arrives in Yokohama, 186; terminates contract with Harper, 190; Professor Chamberlain, 191; philosophical opinions and character, 194; appointment in Matsue, 195; Japanese estimate of, 203; passion for work, 212; family, 229; naturalisation, 252; symptoms of physical failure, 276; devotion to family, 295; emotional trances, 326; love of animals, 331; death, 339, *et seq.*; his religion, 351; funeral, 351; children, 381; personality, 384; biassed deductions, 386; literary judgments, 387; his romanticism, 388; quotations from, 392; his opinion of Japanese, 393; estimate of his work, 395

Hearn, Charles Bush, 16, 19, 20, 23, 29, 30, 36, 37, 231

Hearn, Mrs. Charles, 17, 23, 25, 27, 28, 35, 36

Hearn, Mrs., 175; *Reminiscences of*, 313

Hearn, Rev. Daniel, 14, 30, 79, 231

Hearn, Leopold Kazuo, 250
  ,, Rev. Thomas, 14
  ,, Miss, 16
  ,, Miss Lillah, 231, 232
  ,, Richard, 23, *et seq.*, 175
  ,, Susan, 24, *et seq.*
  ,, family in Waterford, 14

Hearn's Life and Letters (Wetmore), 298

Henderson, Mr. Edmund, 93, 95

Hendrik, Ellwood, 148, 299; letters to, 180, 205, 296

Heron, Francis, 16
  ,, Sir Hugh de, 15

Hijo, 217
Hirn, Professor, letter to, 85
Holmes, Elizabeth, 18
Hugo, Victor, 80
Huxley, Professor, 78, 165

Ichigaya, 352
Idolatry, 54
Imperial University, Japanese, 374
In Ghostly Japan, 170
"Insect Studies," 332
"Intuition," 90
Ionian Islands, 17
Izumo, 298

Japan, discipline of official life in, 71; spirit of, 262; old Japan, 393
Japan, an attempt at Interpretation, 337
Japanese character, analysis of, 203
Japanese constitution promulgated, 184
Japanese day, A, 236
  ,, funeral, A, 353
Japanese Miscellany, *A*, 322
Japanese regimen, 264
  ,, school classes, 230
  ,, training of children, 242
Jefferies, Richard, 327
Jitom Kobduera Temple, 352
Jiu-jitsu, 230
Jizo-Do Temple, 357

Kentucky, 91
Keogh, Miss Agnes, 68
Kinegawa, 267
Kingsley, Charles, 315
Kinjuro, 217, 219
Kipling, Rudyard, 267, 307, 367, 391
Kitinagasa Dori, 277
Kobduera, Temple of, 297
Kobe, 195, 221
Kobe Chronicle, 195, 280

Koizumi, Mrs. Setsu, 15, 42, 79, 324, 341, 349, 356, *et seq.*, 379; *Reminiscence* of, 146; letter of, 350

Koizumi, Idaho, 368

„ Iwayo, 368

„ Kazuo, 16, 248, 315, 340, 353, 361, *et seq.*, 382

Koizumi, Setsu-ko, 348, 364, 368, 380

Kokoro, 84, 131, 283, 285, 302

Krehbiel, Henry, 18, 41, 93, 98, 99, 125, 134, 136, 178

Kumamoto, 27, 83, 221, 228, 229

" Kusa-Hibari " (grass-lark), 334

Kusimoki Marahige, 273

Kwaidan, 39

Kyoto, 286

Kyushu, 229

"Lady of a Myriad Souls" (Miss Bisland), 136, 147–160

Lamb, Charles, 328

Levaux, Marie, 105

Literary College, Tokyo, 15

Loti, Pierre, 45, 103

Lough Corrib, 40, 266

Louisiana, 112

Lowell, Percival, 391

Luck of Roaring Camp (Bret Harte), 97

Malta, 17, 23

Martinique, 180

Mason, Mr. W. B., 145, 168, 325, 355, 357

Matas, Dr. Rudolf, 123, 177

Matsue, 167, 195, 199–205

McDermott, Mr., 92

McDonald, Capt. Mitchell, 129, 150, 194, 303, 308, 313, 322, 325, 339, 368, 378

Memphis, 107–112

"Midwinter, Ozias," 78, 108, 119

Mifflin, Houghton & Co., 239

Millet, François, 81

Mionoseki, ironclads at, 387

Moje, 271

Molyneux, Henry and Mrs., 14, 38, 43, 46, 68, 88

Montreal, 186, 187

"Moon Desire," 328

Morris, William, 77

"Mountain of Skulls," 171

My First Romance, 85

My Guardian Angel, 45

Mythen, Kate, 43, 52, 53

Nagasaki, 243, 265

New Orleans, 78, 105, 113–122; yellow fever at, 121; Exposition at, 161

New York, 155

Nightmare Touch, 44

Nishi Okubo, 296, 306, 324, *et seq.*

Nishida Sentaro, 194, 208, 212, 301, 391

Okuma, Count, 348

Osaka, 271

O Saki, 349

Otani, 366

Otokichi, 317, 349

Out of the East, 265, 276, 357

Papellier, Dr., 277, 285, 306

Pater, Walter, 77, 395

Philadelphia, 155, 296

Pre-Raphaelites, aims of, 77

Principles of Ethics (Spencer) cited, 164

Rachel, picture of, 90–92

"Raven, The," 92

Redhill, 46, 61

Romance of the Milky Way, A, 337

Rossetti, D. G., 77

Rousseau, Jean Jacques, 386

Ruskin, 77, 327

Sackville, Lionel, Duke of Dorset, 14

" St. Ronite," 61
Santa Maura, 13, 22
Schurmann, J. G., 345, 346
Seaton, Viscount, 19
" Serenade, A," 171
Setsu-ko (Koizumi), 348, 364
Shadowings, 322
Shinto worship, 58, 169, 194
Shirabyoshi or Dancing Girl, 222
Shunki Korei-sai, 362
Spencer, Herbert, cited, 78, 164–8, 195, 367, 380
Steinmetz, General, 140
Stevenson, R. L., 43, 82, 328
Stray Leaves, 130, 149
Suruga, 50
Sylvestre Bonnard, 59

Takata, 40
Tanabe, Professor, 353, 364, *et seq.*, 372
Tennyson, 77
Thomson, Francis, 56
" Toko, The," 234
Tokyo, 85, 295, *et seq.*, 355
"Torn Letters," 153
Toyama, Professor, 288
Tramore, 14, 35, 43, 46, 49–50, 55
Treves, Sir Frederick, 179
Trilby, 82
Tunison, Mr. Joseph, 36, 62, 79, 99, 177
Two Years in the French West Indies, 130, 177
Tyndall, 78

"Ujo," 217
Ume, Professor, 374

Ushaw, 43, 44, 52, 56–67
Ushigome, 311–333

Vickers, Thomas, 93
" Voodoo Queen, The," 105

Waseda University, 341, 348
Waterford, 50
Watkin, Henry (" Dad "), 60, 83, 8₁, 89, 93, 110, 120, 134, 174, 188, 268, 293
Watkin, Miss Effie, 293
Weatherall, Mrs., quoted, 32, 33, 253
Welton, Charles, 185
West Indies, Hearn in, 173, *et seq.*
Westmeath, 14, 21
Wetmore, Mrs. (Miss Bisland, *q.v.*), 310, 320, 339, 345, 348
Wexford, 52
Whistler, James, 77, 82
Wiseman, Cardinal, at Ushaw, 56
Worthington, Mr., 128
Wrennal, Father William, 62

Yaidzu, 50, 317, 328
" Yakumo," 253
Yashiki Garden, 295
Yokohama, 306, 355
Yone Noguchi, 212, 298, 341, 361, 379
Young, Mr. Robert, 168, 280, 355
Young, Mrs., 280, 355
" Yuko," 266
Yvetot, 80

Zoshigaya, 315